book   598

274.9

Healing the Heart of Croatia

Joseph Kerrigan and William Novick, M.D.

To Father Terence

Thanks for Your Support

Wm. M. Novick

Paulist Press
New York/Mahwah, N.J.

598

The Publisher gratefully acknowledges use of the following materials: "Love's as Warm as Tears" from *Poems* by C. S. Lewis, copyright © 1964 by the executors of the estate of C. S. Lewis and renewed 1992 by C. S. Lewis Ptd Ltd and Walter Hooper, reprinted by permission of Harcourt Brace & Company.

Jacket design by Sandra Bertoia

Interior design by Joseph E. Petta

Library of Congress Cataloging-in-Publication Data

Kerrigan, Joseph, 1960–
    Healing the heart of Croatia / by Joseph Kerrigan and William Novick.
      p.   cm.
    ISBN 0-8091-0501-2 (alk. paper)
    1. Family–Christian life–Croatia. 2. Yugoslav War, 1991–Croatia. 3. Yugoslav War, 1991–Destruction and pillage–Croatia. 4. Yugoslav War, 1991–Children–Croatia. 5. Yugoslav War, 1991–Medical care–Croatia. 6. Yugoslav War, 1991–Personal narrative, American. 7. Heart–Biblical teaching. 8. Coronary heart disease–Alternative treatment. 9. Spiritual healing–Biblical teaching. 10. Kerrigan, Joseph, 1960–   . 11. Novick, William J. I. Novick, William J. II. Title.
BX2351.K47   1998
274.972′0829–dc21   98–8518
                                                                                           CIP

Published by Paulist Press
997 Macarthur Boulevard
Mahwah, New Jersey 07430

www.paulistpress.com

Printed and bound in the
United States of America

Contents

J.K.

For the people of the
Church of the Holy Spirit, Memphis, Tennessee,
whose missionary spirit
knew no boundaries

W.N.

To my children,
Alessandra, Celena, and Bryant,
who shared their father
for the benefit of all the children
the foundation has touched

Preface

Along the beach of the Adriatic Sea near the Croatian town of Ploce the late afternoon sun throws a deep golden hue onto a pair of faces already tinged with health. Zvonimir Rak and Marija Culjak are two three-year-olds who alternate among holding hands, fighting, and running away from each other on the rocky Dalmatian beach, several meters ahead of their parents. When photographs of this outing were developed, it looks as if little Zvonimir and Marija were the only two people in a picture-postcard world framed by shore, sea, sun, and sky.

But to arrive, in October 1995, at such a seemingly secluded snapshot in paradise, the Croatian children had first to chart arduous paths through serious congenital heart defects and lifesaving operations in Memphis, Tennessee. Their rebirth coincided with Croatia's own rebirth as an independent republic in the violent aftermath of the breakup of the former Yugoslavia.

The stories of Zvonimir and Marija and the other children featured in the following pages is the real heart of Croatia. Both medically and spiritually the hearts of these children and their families were tested in extraordinary ways, as the country's heart was simultaneously tried. The heart is the great symbol of the inner self, the soul, the core of our being, and so to probe it in any fashion is to explore the center of the human person and the energy we give to life. The heart is where our virtues and vices find their source; it is the place where we love or hate. It is where our freedom, emotions, and consciousness all meet, where we say yes or no to those most basic realities: life, love, and, of course, God.

"God is in our heart!" declared Andjela Bencun, a resident of the Adriatic city of Zadar, to her mother in the midst of an animated discussion about prayer. For those present, her forthright proclamation carried added force in the knowledge that it was coming from a ten-year-old girl with Down's syndrome who was facing what would be successful heart surgery the next day in Memphis.

As a pediatric heart surgeon and a Roman Catholic priest, we believe that the stories of these children, from both our medical and spiritual perspectives, provide a unique prism for viewing the life and people of embattled Croatia in the 1990s. We write from Memphis, Tennessee, in the mid-South of the United States, which may seem an unlikely source of commentary on the Balkans, given the distance and the dearth of Eastern European migration to this part of the country. However, the South shares with the Balkans an enduring and intimate connection to the land, religion, and history (especially regarding the Civil War). Memphis, in particular, where Dr. Martin Luther King Jr. was assassinated and where racial issues still divide, may be the American city that most closely approximates the former Yugoslavia in terms of our nation's own unfinished business with civil strife.

An electrocardiogram needs twelve wires to analyze the heart fully. Jesus of Nazareth commissioned twelve apostles to blanket the globe with the gospel. We have chosen twelve children who span a wide range of heart defects, geography, and socioeconomic backgrounds to tell the story of *Healing the Heart of Croatia*. Our hope is that, through these children and the lives they touched, you will discover the truth behind the words of the Croatian poet A. G. Matoš: "As long as there are hearts to love, there will be Croatia, too." If we are successful, *Healing the Heart of Croatia* will find its way to speak to your heart as well.

Foreword—
Franjo Cardinal Kuharic, Archbishop Emeritus of Zagreb, Croatia

In the reader's hands is a book entitled *Healing the Heart of Croatia*. The authors are a Catholic priest, Fr. Joe Kerrigan, and a heart surgeon, Dr. William Novick.

Surgery on children with heart defects gave rise to this book. It holds a message about an undertaking started by the scriptures in order to help a fellow man in his trouble, without repayment.

Fr. Joe Kerrigan started a charitable activity in America to acquire the means so that children in Croatia, whose lives could be extended only by heart surgery, could be operated on free of cost. Dr. William Novick organized a team that travels to Croatia from time to time and performs the needed surgery. Ivan Malcic, a Croatian doctor, also participated.

Love is ingenious, and these benefactions are inspired by love that is efficient. That is how the words of the scriptures come true: "Amen, I say to you, whatever you did for one of these least brothers of mine, you did for me" (Mt 25:40). A person with a good heart always finds a way to do good. That is why a priest and a doctor have united to do good by granting surgery to sick children. They come from America to Zagreb and by performing successful surgery bring joy to the parents. To the children who were operated on, they bring the delight of a healthy life. The motif of love toward a fellow man makes the act dear to God and to the people.

As the archbishop of Zagreb, in the name of all who received, I thank the benefactors and I ask the Lord to overwhelm them with his gifts. In this self-ish world, unselfishness is of a great value. Our experiences with the war we have gone through have shown us that these acts are the foundation of peace.

Introduction
"With all your heart"
–Luke 10:27

"Love Your Neighbor with All Your Heart"

Conflict in the former Yugoslavia began in 1991 after nearly a decade of economic decline and nationalist resurgence in the country. The rise of Slobodan Milosevic to power, along with his call for a greater Serbia, quickened the demise of Yugoslavia, which had been held together by strongman Josip Broz-Tito from World War II until his death in 1980. The violence began in earnest in the summer of 1991, when the republics of Slovenia and Croatia declared their independence from Yugoslavia. Seeing the republics' action as a secession, the Yugoslav People's Army (JNA) launched an abortive ten-day invasion of Slovenia. The Slovenes successfully overturned the army's efforts to bring them back into the state. Next, ethnic Serbs began the war in Croatia with the backing of the JNA.

Croatia is known to Americans primarily through the exploits of its athletes, basketball players Toni Kukoc, Dino Radja, and the late Drazen Petrovic, or the tennis stars Iva Majoli and Goran Ivanisevic, who frequently make their way onto American sports pages. A bit smaller in land mass than West Virginia, this country of over four million people boasts an impressive variety of rich beauty, ranging from the many attractive towns along the Adriatic Sea to the lush forests and mountain areas inland.

In its early days as a republic, however, Croatia had little opportunity to celebrate its newfound independence, as it was deeply engaged in defending itself from attack. Among the more unfortunate events of the war was the complete leveling of the town of Vukovar and the sustained shelling of Dubrovnik, the historic Adriatic city. By the time a cease-fire was reached in Croatia in January 1992, an estimated seven thousand people were killed, with over twenty-five thousand wounded. One-third of the country was taken by the Serbs before nearly all of it was reclaimed in Croatian military offensives in 1995. More than a hundred thousand refugees were forced to relocate from homes that were wantonly robbed and burned. Cultural and religious monuments were especially targeted for destruction. Nearly five hundred churches were damaged.

The war moved to Bosnia-Herzegovina in the spring of that year, where it picked up steam. By the time a peace agreement was finally signed in Dayton, Ohio, in November 1995, hundreds of thousands of people had died. In Bosnia the estimates on war damage were significantly higher than in Croatia. Non-quantifiable aspects of the hostilities, such as the level of torture and degree of hatred involved, also seemed more hideous in Bosnia. Everywhere, it seemed, neighbor hated neighbor. They stood in fear and mistrust of one another.

There was a scholar of the law who stood up to test him [Jesus] and said, "Teacher, what must I do to inherit eternal life?" Jesus said to him, "What is written in the law? How do you read it?" He said in reply, "You shall love the Lord, your God, with all your heart, with all your being, with all your strength, and with all your mind, and your neighbor as yourself." He replied to him, "You have answered correctly; do this and you will live."

But because the man wished to justify himself, he said to Jesus, "And who is my neighbor?" Jesus replied, "A man fell victim to robbers as he went down from Jerusalem to Jericho. They stripped and beat him and went off leaving him half-dead. A priest happened to be going down that road, but when he saw him, he passed by on the opposite side. Likewise a Levite came to the place, and when he saw him, he passed by on the opposite side. But a Samaritan traveler who came upon him was moved with compassion at the sight. He approached the victim, poured oil and wine over his wounds and bandaged them. Then he lifted him up on his own animal, took him to an inn and cared for him. The next day he took out two silver coins and gave them to the innkeeper with the instruction, 'Take care of him. If you spend more than what I have given you, I shall repay you on the way back.' Which of these three, in your opinion, was neighbor to the robbers' victim?" He answered, "The one who treated him with mercy." Jesus said to him, "Go and do likewise." (Lk 10:25–37)

A mirror of Jesus' own method of ministry, the challenging yet uplifting parable of the Good Samaritan condenses major gospel teachings on suffering, compassion, and the predominance of love over legalism. It presents a glimpse of God's justice and sets a demanding standard for the Christian's relationship with those in need. "Neighbor" is defined more broadly than physical proximity. In the story the true neighbor is the one who acts decisively in response to another's pain, no matter if the neighbor is a despised foreigner: a Samaritan. To the Jewish hearer of Jesus' time, reference to the virtuous role played by the Samaritan might have been doubly surprising, given the fierce rancor that existed between the Jews and the Samaritans, a mixed race of Israelites and Assyrians. The parable reverses the socioreligious stereotypes of the Jewish culture, lauding the Samaritan's behavior while casting that of the priest and Levite in an unfavorable light. Scripture scholar G. V. Jones writes, "The parable is not a pleasant tale about 'The Traveler Who Did His Good Deed,' but a damning indictment of social, racial and religious superiority."

The perceptive Christian can observe the story of the Good Samaritan playing itself out continuously in the world. Around and around the parable goes, like a carousel, in worldwide versions as well as in personal and local renditions that revisit our lives again and again. In one scenario a person may be the neglectful priest or the Levite; in the next episode he or she may be the victim; in yet another set of circumstances that same person may embody the responsiveness of the Samaritan. One of the strengths of the parable is that it leaves no room for complacency. Today's hero can be tomorrow's villain.

The story of the Good Samaritan is not a fable of who's good or who's bad as much as it is a story of who is trapped by his or her own ideas, and

who sees reality. The priest and the Levite each had religious and cultural conceptions that justified their failure to assist the robbery victim.
Only the Samaritan was free to see the man for who he was—a person in
need. Unfortunately, we often try to grow and establish ourselves in life
by isolating ourselves, by drawing lines around who we are and who we
are not, defining an "us" and a "them." The fact is, these lines aren't
very helpful if they keep us from helping people in need, or if they
strengthen our prejudices.

If the parable of the Good Samaritan is not a clear enough moral
directive to live beyond narrow outlooks and simple formulas, the war
in the former Yugoslavia provides a tragic alternative version of the
gospel parable. In the collapse of Yugoslavia no "Samaritan" arrives to
save the day, and the victims are not left half-dead but are brutally tor-
tured and killed in large numbers. The dubious roles of the priest and
Levite are played by an unresponsive international community. In this
regard the infamous story of Kitty Genovese may make a better analogy
of modern-day apathy and passivity. Genovese, a New York City cocktail
waitress, was gruesomely murdered in front of her apartment building
in Kew Gardens, Queens, New York, in 1964. It was reported that thirty-
eight people in the complex had watched the attack, which took place
over a half-hour period and involved numerous stabbings. Not one person notified the police.

"It's too complicated to understand."
"We don't want another Vietnam."
"It's not in the American interest."
"It's not as bad as you think."
"This is a war over ancient hatreds and religions. There's nothing we
can do."

In words frighteningly similar to the self-serving rationalizations of the
priest and Levite, political leaders from western Europe, the United
States, and the United Nations defended their inaction. As the toll of dead
and injured in Croatia and Bosnia-Herzegovina mounted, and as revela-
tions of torture and ethnic genocide surfaced, this question could be
posed: Has the world's conscience become so jaded that the only thing on

which to take a stand is to have no stand; the only principle for which to fight is to have no principles; the only responsibility is to take no responsibility for our brothers and sisters? If the story of the Good Samaritan had been heeded with greater integrity, we would have seen another way, with the possibility that we, at times, could escape the original envy and anger that led Cain to kill Abel and then evade responsibility by asking, "Am I my brother's keeper?" Surveying the carnage of the former Yugoslavia and the evil of years of unchecked ethnic genocide, can we say that the world has progressed much from the attitudes of Cain, of the priest and the Levite, or of Chamberlain toward Hitler?

Of course, defining who our neighbor is doesn't automatically produce love; in fact, in the story of the former Yugoslavia it is possible that proximity produced hatred. Only love can produce neighbors. Neighborhood can grow only among those who dare to love their neighbor in this fashion.

Love arises from the human heart. It is no coincidence that the story of the Good Samaritan is prefaced by a restatement of the command to love God "with all your heart, with all your being, with all your strength, and with all your mind, and your neighbor as yourself." The Good Samaritan is good because he is able to love with all his heart; he saw the victim and "was moved with compassion." Because of the disposition of his heart, the Samaritan stopped beside the man and did not "pass by on the other side." Moreover, the Samaritan was unsparing in his pursuit of the victim's well-being; once the immediate crisis was handled, he saw to it, through the innkeeper, that the man would have adequate means to regain his bearings.

"With all your heart"—from either a medical or spiritual standpoint the optimal functioning of the human heart is nothing short of awesome. The heart, a four-chambered pumping muscle, is the center of the body's cardiovascular system, which delivers oxygen and nutrients throughout the body and allows all the various functions of the body to proceed. Over two thousand gallons of oxygen-rich blood course through the heart each day. The heart is the only organ in our body that performs an active function on a continuous basis, day and night, beating over four thousand times per hour, whether we care about it or not. Heart surgeon Dr. Willis Potts once noted, "The heart is a very tough organ, a marvelous mechanism, that mostly, without repairs, will give valiant service to its owner for up to 100 years." After fifty years the heart has already generated enough energy to lift a battleship out of the water.

Human beings use oxygen as fuel to generate energy for all activity in human life—breathing, walking, talking, and everything else. Oxygen is carried in the blood, and the heart pumps the blood. The heart is actually two pumps welded together. The pump on the right side pushes blood solely to the lungs, where the blood receives a new supply of oxygen. The pump on the left side pushes this newly oxygenated blood to the rest of the body, where it serves as fuel for all activity.

In light of some of the defects described in the following pages, it may also be helpful to envision the heart a little more technically, in terms of the four chambers of the heart, which are structured to supply the body with oxygen. The chambers are a right and left ventricle and a right and left atrium. The ventricles and the atria are separated from each other by a muscular wall or *septum*, a ventricular septum for the ventricles and an atrial septum for the atria.

With this in mind, circulation through the heart works as follows: Bluish blood returning to the heart from the hands or feet or any other part of the body goes through the right atrium, where it passes through a valve and into the right ventricle. The right ventricle, in turn, pumps the blood out of the pulmonary artery and into the lungs, where it is supplied with oxygen that turns the blood bright red. From the lungs the blood returns to the heart through the left atrium, where it is next sent to the left ventricle, through the aorta, and back out into the body. As long as the heart and the vessels carrying blood to and from the heart are formed properly, the heart works well.

The simplest of organs, about the size of an adult fist, the heart's sole function is to pump. It doesn't have to worry about cleaning the blood or making sure that all the minerals in the blood are at the proper level. It doesn't have to worry about changing the amount of acid in the blood or about how much oxygen is present in the blood. It only has to pump, and yet by virtue of the heart's pumping, oxygen and other nutrients are delivered throughout the body.

The metaphor of the heart is as vital to the spiritual life as the heart is to biological life. For example, in the ancient Greek world the heart, or *kardia*, was the site where the soul lived. In Hinduism the heart is the place of enduring wisdom, the pathway for the reversal of passions from the earthly to the spiritual. In the Qur'an, the infallible word of God in the Muslim tradition, we read, "God has inscribed the faith in their very hearts, and strengthened them with a spirit of his own" (58:24).

In the Judeo-Christian tradition, from the time of the prophetic writings of the Hebrew scriptures, the heart is the chosen seat of God's activity and direction within the human person. As the prophet Jeremiah records, "I shall put my law within them and write it on their hearts" (Jer 31:33). In the book of Sirach, found in the Catholic Bible, God "plumbs the depths and penetrates the heart" (Sir 42:18). In praying for his people David asks that God will "direct their hearts toward you" (1 Chr 29:18), reflecting the belief that the heart is the center for the understanding of divine things.

Jesus' maxim, "For where your treasure is, there also will your heart be" (Mt 6:21; Lk 12:34), captures the importance of the heart in the spiritual journey of the gospels. In both citations Jesus' words conclude a lesson on how dependence on God is more crucial to the believer than material things. Seek the kingdom, store up treasures in heaven, he says, rather than engage in anxiety about acquiring food, clothing, and belongings. Your heart will be the ultimate measure of your spiritual richness. In Jesus' Sermon on the Mount (Mt 5–7), "the clean of heart" are promised that they will see God.

In the scriptures that record the life of the Christian community subsequent to the ministry of Jesus, the heart remains the center of God's action. "The love of God has been poured out into our hearts through the holy Spirit that has been given to us," the apostle Paul writes in his letter to the Romans (5:5). "The community of believers was of one heart and mind, and no one claimed that any of his possessions was his own, but they had everything in common" (Acts 4:32)—in the Acts of the Apostles, the heart is named as a symbol of the unity of the ideal Christian community. Several times, as in the letter to the Hebrews, Christians are exhorted not to "lose heart" (Heb 12:5).

The *Catechism of the Catholic Church* states, "The heart is the dwelling-place where I am, where I live; according to the Semitic or biblical expression, the heart is the place 'to which I withdraw.' The heart is our hidden center, beyond the grasp of our reason and of others; only the Spirit of God can fathom the human heart and know it fully. The heart is the place of decision, deeper than our psychic drives. It is the place of truth, where we choose life or death. It is the place of encounter, because as image of God we live in relation: it is the place of covenant" (#2563).

From a Christian perspective, Jesus of Nazareth is the epitome of one whose life is given wholeheartedly over to God. Jesus demonstrated this in many astounding and exemplary ways: in the closeness he developed in prayer with Abba, his Father; in the life he led of physical insecurity and few possessions; in the unique connection to "neighbor" he made, which manifested itself in his choice of disciples; in his emphasis on building community; and in his healing and forgiving of others. The late Jesuit theologian Teilhard de Chardin wrote, "The great secret, the great mystery is this: there is a heart of the world (a fact we can arrive at through reflection), and this heart is the heart of Christ."

Many Christian mystics have explored the symbol of the heart in their attempts to express adequately the presence of God in their lives. In the final stanza of his poem "The Living Flame of Love" the sixteenth-century Spanish mystic St. John of the Cross writes:

How gently and lovingly
You wake in my heart,
Where in secret You dwell alone;
And in your sweet breathing,
Filled with good and glory,
How tenderly You swell my heart with love!

Unhappily, the functioning of the physical and spiritual heart is usually not fully appreciated until something has gone awry. In all its simplicity one small problem with the biological heart's functioning can cause a catastrophe. If the oxygen the heart requires is reduced, or if the blood supply to the heart is constricted, then the performance of the heart is lessened, which in turn can cause a cascade of events that can lead to life-threatening problems. The suffering borne by people who live with something less than "all" their heart—whether babies born with congenital heart disease or adults with arteriosclerotic disease or congestive heart failure—is known by over sixty million Americans today, according to estimates from the National Center for Health Statistics.

In utilizing the symbol of the heart to describe the facets of evil in humanity, the Bible is no less profound than in its expressiveness of the heart as a symbol for good. Here is a sampling of scripture passages that identify spiritual pathologies associated with the heart:

Duplicity: "Softer than butter is their speech, but war is in their heart." (Ps 55:22)

Hard-heartedness: "His heart is hard as stone." (Jb 41:16)

Sloth: "Gross is the heart of this people." (Mt 13:15)

Hypocrisy: "This people draws near with words only and honors me with their lips alone, though their hearts are far from me." (Is 29:13, quoted later by Jesus in Mt 15:8)

Evil: "Why has Satan filled your heart?" (Acts 5:3)

"A Mission of Love from the Heart"

Before they came together in their mission for the children of Croatia, Dr. William Novick and Father Joe Kerrigan had been doing their best, as a pediatric heart surgeon and a Catholic priest, to enable people to live with all their heart.

Novick was born in 1954 in Gadsden, Alabama, in the north-central part of the state, because there was no hospital in Pell City, the town where his parents lived. As a child, due to his father's ownership of a variety of small businesses, which ranged from a dry-cleaning operation to an orange grove to a lobster boat fleet, young Novick moved about frequently, with stops in Fort Pierce, Florida, along with Anniston and Montgomery, Alabama, before returning to Florida for middle and high school, which he split between Fort Lauderdale and Pensacola.

During his senior year in Pensacola, Novick met his first serious girl-friend, whose father happened to be a cardiologist. "That was when I first became fascinated with the workings of the heart," he recalled. "The girl's brother was a cardiologist in training at Emory University, and so the family was heavily involved in medicine and I got interested in it."

Senior year ended, as did Novick's romance with the cardiologist's daughter, although his fascination with the heart endured. At the same time the strapping teenager with sandy brown hair and a focused gaze that would serve him well later as a surgeon, was forming an interest in snorkeling and scuba diving and was hoping to pursue a career in marine biology. In his first semester at Troy State University he made a trip to the coastal city of Mobile, Alabama. While diving there, he ruptured both eardrums. As a result of the mishap, Novick would no longer be able to dive deeper than thirty feet without suffering pain, and his career plan was ended.

Novick turned to chemistry, which evolved into an interest in biochemistry. When he was accepted into the graduate program at the University of Alabama, Novick's earlier interest in the heart reemerged, and he opted for studies in cardiac biochemistry.

About six months into the program Novick was approached by the biochemist for whom he was working at the university and invited to consider going into medicine. "He said to me, 'You like the heart, you like your research, go into cardiology,'" Novick explained. The mentor felt that the M.D. Ph.D.s were going to have the best opportunity for funding from the National Institutes of Health, and that research work that had clinical application was going to come to the forefront in the future.

Novick considered the suggestion and decided to follow it, but as a cardiac surgeon and not a cardiologist. Novick reasoned that, as a cardiologist, he would only be able to determine what somebody needed but not be able to provide the actual help. "I would have been completely frustrated with that," he said. At the time there were no cardiac interventions available, such as the balloon angioplasties that are commonplace today.

Early in medical school Novick narrowed his vocational choice even further by deciding to become a pediatric heart surgeon. He was influenced by one of his instructors, Dr. John Kirklin, a pioneer in congenital heart surgery. Novick felt that "children's hearts are far more interesting anatomically and physiologically than adults' hearts."

In choosing pediatric heart surgery Novick selected a field that reaches all the way back to the first three weeks of a woman's pregnancy. About eighteen days from conception the first formation of the heart can be detected as a primitive tubelike structure. A few days later that structure begins to beat, and circulation starts. The heart then goes through a series of contortions and folds upon itself several times. During the course of the maturation it becomes a four-chamber, two-artery, multiple-vein device that will sustain life on a continuous basis. From the forty-fifth day after conception the heart has the appearance that it will have for the rest of its life.

When the heart first forms in the womb, the body is only three times bigger than the heart. The ratio increases to 200:1 by adulthood. During that time the heart muscles gain in strength and build fiber to help offset the shift in ratio.

Children's hearts are unique in several ways. For one thing, they are highly dependent on heart rate. The heart of a child has to beat very fast in order to move the necessary blood and oxygen through the body. Under stress, fever, or other sickness, the pediatric heart cannot increase the output by squeezing harder but only by squeezing more frequently. New parents who look at their children carefully when they are sick or feverish notice the soaring heart rate and become alarmed, unaware that it is a normal response for a child.

The second distinctive feature of a child's heart is that up until approximately five years of age the child has the unique ability to continue to build muscle fibers. As they go through their normal sedentary lives, very few people continue to build muscle fibers. Certainly competitive athletes have profoundly healthy cardiovascular fitness, but this is the result of a conscious effort to make the heart more efficient.

As a high-school baseball player Fr. Kerrigan may have been building an efficient cardiovascular system, but a batting average below .200 in his senior year thwarted all dreams the New Jersey native had of a career in professional baseball. "I was obsessed with the game in every way, but by my senior year it was clear that I wasn't going any further," he admitted. However, like Novick's fortunate meeting with his first girlfriend's father, the cardiologist, Kerrigan's high-school years were also marked by an encounter that would prove significant for his ultimate vocational decision.

The eldest of six brothers and sisters, Kerrigan attended St. Joseph's High School in Metuchen, New Jersey, administered by the Brothers of the Sacred Heart (an interesting name in light of Kerrigan's later work with congenital-heart-disease patients). "To me, the brothers there were the model for how the religious life could be appealing. They were normal, in the sense that they were aware of current events, sports, politics, culture. They swore at times, they sweated, they wore normal clothes. And yet they were still religious. You could tell they were driven by God and not by the world."

Until he reached his high-school years, growing up in a predominantly Catholic environment in Iselin, a central New Jersey town about twenty-five miles from Manhattan, Kerrigan assumed that "thinking about being a priest or nun was in the back of any Catholic boy's or girl's mind as they were going through school." But he saw two unattractive extremes in the large number of priests he encountered at St. Cecilia's Church in Iselin, a parish which at one time had an incredible fourteen Masses each weekend. "There was the pastor, an older monsignor, who never seemed to leave the property and never seemed to be out of character as anything other than 'the monsignor.' The street in front of the church was finally named after him. That seemed too boring a life. And then there was this steady procession of priests from Ireland or India or Poland or the Philippines, and I just couldn't see myself taking that risk of going to another country. But I couldn't get rid of the idea of becoming a priest, either."

As Novick perceived a difference between cardiology and cardiac surgery, so Kerrigan found a distinction between becoming a brother and a priest. "The Sacred Heart Brothers lit a spark, but I never really considered becoming one myself because they weren't priests. They couldn't preach, and to me, at that time, preaching was the name of the game."

As a student at Fordham University in the Bronx, Kerrigan commuted from Iselin but attended St. Cecilia's on occasion. One Sunday he spotted a "Missionaries to North America" poster at the back of the church. It was an advertisement for the Paulist Fathers, a missionary order of priests that works in North American cities. "The concept of being a missionary and still working in my own culture interested me a great deal.

When I attended the Paulist church in midtown Manhattan and heard some tremendous preaching there, I was hooked. They covered that middle ground of the priesthood, between the stay-at-home pastor and the itinerant missionary, that I hadn't found before. I didn't even know a single Paulist, but I wanted to become one."

After receiving a master's degree in divinity from the Catholic University of America and completing a year of internship at a downtown parish in Toronto, Kerrigan was ordained a Catholic priest in New York City in 1990, at the age of twenty-nine. He did not specialize in child or youth ministry in his first years of service, although he was no stranger to the significance of the childlike qualities invoked in the gospels. Jesus' own birth and infancy are given extensive coverage in the gospels, and in his ministry, Jesus speaks of the child as a model of discipleship. "Let the children come to me; do not prevent them, for the kingdom of God belongs to such as these. Amen, I say to you, whoever does not accept the kingdom of God like a child will not enter it" (Mk 10:14–15). Some translations read, "Unless you acquire the heart of a child, you will not enter the kingdom." For Jesus, the kingdom is child's play, not in the sense of ease but of simplicity. The kingdom is to be welcomed and received, and children, who are by nature recipients, without physical power or status, dependent upon others for the necessities of life, are excellent examples of the receptivity needed for the kingdom. Throughout his ministry Jesus received life as a child of the kingdom. He went from family to Pharisees, disciples to strangers, crowds to solitude, criticism to praise, and happily received all. Ultimately, he welcomed even suffering and death, only to arise victorious as the Savior.

Jesus preached a good news of salvation that was not complicated. In praising the Father in Luke's gospel Jesus states, "Although you have hidden these things from the wise and the learned you have revealed them to the childlike" (Lk 10:21).

Children are also involved in Jesus' manifestation of the kingdom through some of his mighty deeds. A boy's five barley loaves and two fish are the source for the miracle of the multiplication of loaves (Jn 6:1–15). A twelve-year-old girl, the only daughter of Jairus, a synagogue official, is brought back from death in a dramatic healing by Jesus (Lk

8:40–56). A boy was one of several demoniacs Jesus healed in the gospels (Mt 17:14–21).

Kerrigan would utilize these themes in the course of his day-to-day ministry, but his primary interest was in encouraging individual believers and parish communities to live their faith to the fullest. He promoted Catholic evangelization—the process of having the gospel permeate the life of the community as much as possible. "Evangelization really means non-complacency, attacking the status quo and apathy in a church," he said. Projects beyond the routine of Masses, funerals, and weddings became his bailiwick, as he crafted outreach programs for fallen-away Catholics and special events to revitalize the life of a parish.

"Despite the concern for running its institutions, maintaining the infrastructure, and all the rest of the visible priorities, the church really has only one honest purpose for its existence, and that is to evangelize: to energize and transform the world," he emphasized. "A church that is not vigorous in taking risks to make a difference in a believer's life and in the life of the world is truly like a person's heart that is not beating properly."

A non-evangelizing church may be able to camouflage itself better than someone with a heart problem, however. Congenital heart disease, in particular, bestows a cruelly apparent fate on a child's heart. Nearly 1 percent of the world's children are born with congenital heart disease,[1] and at least half of those children need open-heart surgery to survive to adulthood. During the period from eighteen to forty-five days after conception, something happens to some babies maturing in the womb—a chromosomal abnormality, an environmental cause—and the heartbeat is affected. Worldwide, only one-third of children with congenital heart disease are properly diagnosed. This is due to several interrelated factors: (1) it is estimated that 35 percent die during the first year, most in the first week.[2] A high percentage are children whose heart problem is only one of many medical problems they confront; (2) of the survivors, almost one-third go undetected, since physicians who are trained to recognize the symptoms of such diseases are very unevenly distributed among the world's population, as are specialists who could treat the illness; (3) a small portion of the children have no symptoms, and the condition is not discovered until later in life.

In undeveloped countries issues of basic survival often override other concerns. This is true in Haiti, for example, where 106 out of every 1,000 infants die, while in the United States there are fewer than 9 infant deaths per 1,000.

No two cases are exactly alike, but the typical symptoms of congenital heart disease include weakness, slow or halted development, exhaustion upon exertion, and difficulties in feeding.

In 1990, during Novick's cardiac surgery residency at the University of Alabama at Birmingham, he helped treat a twelve-year-old Nigerian girl for a complicated heart condition that, in the surgeon's words, "would have been corrected in the United States at age two." Because of the delay, the girl was "doomed to die." Novick assisted in providing an operation that could only buy her some more time; the procedure would not correct her defect, and it would not save her life. "I explained all that to her mother, and their profound gratitude for what was only a palliative operation stimulated a thought process in me about how many children like this there might be in the world. It made me realize how fortunate we are in this country and how unfortunate other people are. When I began private practice, one of the commitments I made was that if there were any children in Third World or even industrialized countries who didn't have the money for surgery, I would operate on them for free, if they could travel to where I was located.

"Imagine that you live in a country that's divided by war, and has been for the last five years or so, and that the part of the country in which you live has been overrun once or twice by that war, and that you're separated routinely from your family. Your child is born—a beautiful baby boy or girl—and the pediatrician doesn't see the baby because it looks healthy. You come home, but four days later your baby is breathing quite heavily, and you bring your child back to the hospital. Now the pediatrician sees the baby and announces to you that not only is the child breathing fast because it is ill but the baby also has a major cardiac malformation that cannot be corrected in your country. So here you are, in a country where hospitals are rare, advanced medical care is even more rare, and the ability to deal

with a child born with a serious cardiac malformation is low. That is a very
scary situation, but it happens daily all around the world. I want to do all I
can to correct this scenario in many families' lives.

"It's really an obsession; I feel as though I have to do this," said
Novick, in words that remind one of the apostle Paul's commitment to
itinerant preaching (1 Cor 9:16). "I've learned to be a lot more appreciative of my life, and I feel that I owe society—the society that has allowed
me to attain this position—a certain amount of free surgical care, good
will, and selflessness."

In his private practice in Orlando, Novick worked with seven other cardiac surgeons and operated in four different hospitals in the city. In his
first year he completed three hundred cases. He began to establish con-
tacts for patients from Jamaica and Nicaragua, and he made a trip to
Colombia to perform surgery. Even though her ailment could not be corrected, that ill-fated Nigerian girl—whose name Novick cannot recall—was
the inspiration behind what was now evolving into the steady and successful care of other children born with congenital heart disease all over
the world.

In the spring of 1992 Novick received a call from Dr. Josef Vacek, a
pediatrician and native Croatian who lived in Orlando. "The secretary
told me that there was a physician on the line with a heavy Eastern European accent who said he wanted to speak to me," the surgeon recounted.
"He proceeded to tell me the story of children with congenital heart disease in Croatia."

The strife caused by the dissolution of the former Yugoslavia resulted in
not only hundreds of thousands of direct victims of the fighting but also
innumerable indirect victims as well. Croatian children born with congenital heart disease were one such group of victims. Prior to the war, the two
hundred to three hundred children born with heart defects in Croatia each
year were sent to institutes either in Belgrade, Serbia, or Ljubljana, Slovenia. Now, with the republics ripped from the confederation, Croatia was
left to appeal to the wider international community for help. Bordered by
Hungary to the north, the Adriatic Sea to the south and west, and the former Yugoslav republics of Slovenia, Serbia, and Bosnia-Herzegovina, the
country was surrounded with less-than-congenial neighbors. During the

war it is estimated that only thirty to fifty of the two hundred to three hundred new cases received adequate treatment. With no surgeons specializing in pediatric heart surgery, the Croatians made do with their adult heart surgeons.

Dr. Vacek read about the work Novick had performed for children in Latin America, and he wanted to know whether something could be done for Croatian children. Novick agreed to treat children referred to him by Vacek. In September 1992 Novick operated on the first of three children brought from Croatia to Orlando for surgery. After the third surgery Novick called Vacek with a proposal for *him.* "These Croatian moms have been telling me that there are countless others who need this surgery. I would be interested in putting a surgical team together and going over there to operate, if the Croatians would feed us, put us up in a hotel, and get us to and from the hospital."

Three days after Novick's proposal Vacek called back with word from Croatian officials: "They would very much like you to do this. When can you go?"

Novick assembled a team and made his first trip to Zagreb in April 1993, when he operated on fourteen children at Rebro University Hospital. He met Dr. Ivan Malcic, a pediatric cardiologist whose leadership and organization of surgical care on the Croatian side of the ocean would prove vital to the success of the program. Soon after, Malcic founded a charitable organization, Big Hearts for Little Hearts, to mobilize support for children with congenital heart disease.

Novick returned in August of that year to treat twenty-seven more children. The next month he moved from Orlando to Memphis, taking the position of assistant professor of surgery at the University of Tennessee–Memphis and also reaching an agreement with the pediatric hospital in Memphis, LeBonheur Children's Medical Center, to bring international children to the downtown facility for surgery at reduced cost.

Memphis, which means "established and beautiful," was named after the ancient Egyptian city along the Nile River. Set on the Mississippi River in the southwest corner of Tennessee, modern-day Memphis is the largest city in the state, with over 600,000 residents and about a million people residing in the metropolitan area. Originally populated by the Chickasaw Indians, today African-Americans constitute the majority in the city. Memphis is known for such disparate celebrities as Elvis Presley, who began his recording career there; Danny Thomas, the founder of the pioneering and world-renowned St. Jude Children's Research Hospital; W. C. Handy, who made Beale Street into the birthplace of the blues; B. B. King, who popularized the blues throughout the world; Dr. Martin Luther King Jr., who was assassinated in Memphis in 1968; and of course, "Old Man River," the Mississippi River, the distinguishing geographic feature of an otherwise flat terrain.

Because of its location near the center of the country and the abundance of cotton and lumber in the region, the city has been an important transportation and distribution hub for many decades. The world's largest overnight package courier, Federal Express, was established in Memphis in the early 1970s and retains its headquarters in the city.

"I like this town, I really do," said Novick, who feels Memphis is a bigger version of the small southern towns he lived in as a youth. "It's a beautiful city, very green with all the trees. To me, Memphis culturally is the 'Old South,' it's not the 'New South,' like Nashville or Atlanta. The mentality here is, 'Let's not change things too much,' which is kind of ironic since Memphis is the home of St. Jude's and Federal Express."

In the 1990s, perhaps as a result of its resistance to change, the city found itself with a local economy that lagged behind the rest of the nation and a crime rate higher than the national average. Memphis scored especially high in auto theft, burglary, rape, and homicide.

Another part of the "Old South" label is the persistence of racial tension in Memphis. With few exceptions a drive through the city reveals a marked division between white and black neighborhoods, and the underlying tension is the subtext to many conversations about the city.

Earlier in its history, especially in the 1870s, Memphis suffered a series of devastating yellow fever epidemics, in which thousands died and thousands more fled. Upon Memphis's rebirth the city became a leading medical center in the mid-South with the establishment and growth of religiously affiliated hospitals such as Baptist Memorial Hospital, Methodist Hospital, and St. Joseph Hospital. Though not aligned with a particular denomination, St. Jude Children's Research Hospital was inspired by entertainer Danny Thomas's devotion to the hospital's namesake.

LeBonheur Children's Medical Center was founded in 1952 and has grown to a facility of 225 beds with a medical staff of nearly 500 people, treating more than 100,000 children annually throughout the region on an in-patient or out-patient basis.

Soon after settling into Memphis and LeBonheur, Novick crossed the Atlantic a third time in January 1994, when he performed operations on eighteen children. In the spring of 1994 Novick began bringing Croatian children to Memphis. He was poised to launch a non-profit foundation, the International Children's Heart Foundation, to facilitate the care of children with congenital heart disease. Novick's overall strategy was not unlike that expressed in the old missionary adage, "Go where you are needed but not wanted, and stay until you are wanted but not needed." Novick hoped that relationships with countries like Croatia; the surgical team trips to those countries; care of selected patients flown to Memphis; donation of medical supplies, and diagnostic and life-support equipment; and training fellowships for doctors and nurses would, after several years, raise the level of heart care to the point where his services would no longer be needed.

At that time, shortly after Easter 1994, Kerrigan entered the scene and experienced his own resurrection. On the same Labor Day weekend in 1993 that Novick moved to Memphis, Kerrigan left the Paulists and began laboring as a diocesan priest. He was assigned to the Church of the Holy Spirit, a twelve-hundred-family parish that lies about fifteen miles east of downtown in suburban Memphis. Originally sent to Memphis as a Paulist, Kerrigan decided to remain in the city because of the keen sense of social justice present in the Catholic community. (When the Diocese of Memphis was founded in 1971, its first bishop, Carroll T. Dozier, christened it informally, "The Good Samaritan along the banks of the Mississippi.") Kerrigan also saw abundant opportunities for evangelization in a part of the United States where the Catholic population was less than 5 percent. With Novick and the Croatians, however, the priest's most ambitious evangelization adventure was about to fall into his lap.

The odds are not terribly promising that a pediatric heart surgeon and a priest will meet in the course of their professional duties, even if they are working with the same patient. But this book is not about odds and percentages as much as it is about the ways of the Spirit of God, who charts an inexorable course through human lives.

In April 1994 Mario Miklosic, the second child to travel to Memphis from Croatia for Novick's surgical care, sat in his intensive-care bed the day after surgery. Kerrigan was visiting a patient in the neighboring bed, a four-year-old boy named Blake Haines, who was recovering from successful surgery for a malignant brain tumor. John and Nancy Dominis, parishioners of Holy Spirit, recognized their priest, introduced themselves to him, and asked if he could visit Mario. John Dominis, a native of Zadar, Croatia, was translating for Mario and his mother, Vesna. Through Mario and the Dominis family, Kerrigan met Novick, who happened to be looking for the priest because he had heard from Cathy McCown, an intensive-care unit nurse, that Kerrigan wrote a weekly evangelization column in the Catholic newspaper *Common Sense*. Novick thought the priest might be interested in writing about the outreach to Croatian children. There would be much, much more to write about.

Kerrigan volunteered not only to write a column but to look after the spiritual needs of the incoming Croatian children and to enlist the support of his parish to provide host families. The collaboration and friendship between the priest and the surgeon were forged. It was the first time either man dealt with someone in the other's profession, and they had to overcome some initial misconceptions.

"Bill was the first surgeon I ever really met," said Kerrigan. "Because my mother and two sisters are nurses, I have a profound respect for the medical community. But I always felt that surgeons were in another class altogether, either through their talents or egos or both, so I never felt I would have much to say to one. But when I met Bill for the first time in his surgical scrubs in the intensive-care unit, with his height and all the confidence he exudes, and heard him say that he'd been looking for *me*, as if we were long-lost friends, and when he then invited me back to his office for a chat, those assumptions I had about surgeons never even had time to register in my mind."

Besides the Southern Baptist faith of his parents, Novick as a youth had encountered the Russian Orthodox Church, Roman Catholicism, Judaism, and Hinduism—all present within his circle of family and friends. For one reason or another he found them all wanting and nominally retained his Baptist affiliation. As a surgeon he would again experience a range of religious traditions in the form of the hospital chaplains and other ministers who worked with his patients. "I saw pastoral care as a superficial religious experience, with the exception of pastors who were very familiar with their patients," said Novick of ministerial work. "Joe has a different place in his heart for these children, their moms, and the situation."

By October 1997, 39 children had been brought to Memphis for surgical care, and eight trips had been made to Zagreb, where an additional 141 children were treated (from both Croatia and Bosnia-Herzegovina), making a total of 180 children served from the two countries. As the following pages will document, some of the first surgical procedures of this kind in the history of Croatia were performed by Novick and his team. And, as the next chapters will also indicate, it became clear that it was more involved than just operating on children's hearts.

Enormous obstacles and enormous openings emerged, and the entire program could be viewed as a study in good and evil. The effects of the war were an ongoing menace and prevented children from getting timely care. The machinations within the Croatian Ministry of Health slowed the speed with which children could be brought to America. Although never proven, there was plenty of talk by parents about Croatian doctors whose care for children depended on how much money could be slipped under the table. There were longstanding prejudices to challenge, such as the Croatians' perception that patients with mental handicaps did not warrant the expense of corrective surgery. And there were emergencies to handle, such as the time a Memphis host-mother abandoned a Croatian mother and child at the hospital on the day of pre-operative testing, because she didn't have time for them.

But the moments of grace more than compensated for the setbacks. The mobilization of Kerrigan's affluent, suburban parish for the work of international pediatric heart care was astounding. Two young women from the Church of the Holy Spirit decided to go into nursing after hosting Croatian children. The return of several Croatian mothers to church attendance as a result of their experience with their sick children was equally uplifting. One Croatian doctor decided to become a Catholic after seeing the faith in her American counterparts. And, of course, the actual physical healings of the children were more than gratifying.

"This demonstrates the inexhaustible quality of human solidarity and goodness, despite all the disappointments we have experienced in this war," was how Malcic, the founder of Big Hearts for Little Hearts, summarized the effort.

In the stories of children born in Croatia with congenital heart disease the parable of the Good Samaritan thus takes on a different twist. These children, along with their families, are clearly the victims, like the man who was attacked by robbers in the parable. But just as clearly, these children and their families are also the heroes. In their inner strength and depth of spirit they shine as brilliant testimonies to the sacredness of human life. The Serbian instigators of the war could be cast as the "robbers" of the parable, and although it is not as easy to make a clear association with the priest and the Levite, there is no shortage of candidates: the bureaucrats in the Croatian health ministry, the doctors who impede the treatment of the children, and the international community, to the degree that the war was lengthened by its inaction. The many Memphis families who hosted the children and their parents gave added dimension to the role of the innkeeper, who was instructed to "take care" of the injured man.

As for the Good Samaritan, we are reluctant to claim that role for two reasons. For one, our flaws are well-known to us and to others. Novick has been described as someone who smokes, drinks, and eats more like a heart patient than a heart doctor. Kerrigan's antics at Mass have included walking on the altar rail, throwing a football into the congregation, and flicking water into the faces of his altar servers. The Good Samaritan is known only for being good, while we know there is much that is weak and sinful in us.

Also, to take the part of the Good Samaritan implies that the role is filled and the story is complete, when, in fact, even in pediatric heart care in Croatia the drama is very much open and ongoing. In the classic line of St. Augustine, "Our hearts are restless until they rest in you." That restlessness takes the shape of victims who still lie along the road, awaiting urgent assistance. Owing to human nature and the strength of nationalism, Croatians are still helped to a great extent only by their own: Croatian-Americans, Croatian-Canadians, Croatian-Australians. The casting call still goes out for the true foreigner, or Samaritan. Perhaps others can find in these pages an invitation to become involved.

If *Healing the Heart of Croatia* offers new and helpful insight into the parable of the Good Samaritan, so be it. Our wish is that if it does, it is because the portrayal of the victims—these children—is amplified so we can see them and their families as the real heroes. If the Good Samaritan is anyone, he or she is the one who allows the victims to express their greatness. For that Samaritan, the reward is unlimited. As the Qur'an states, "Whoever killed a human being...shall be deemed as though he had killed all mankind; and whoever saved a human life shall be deemed as though he had saved all mankind" (5:32).

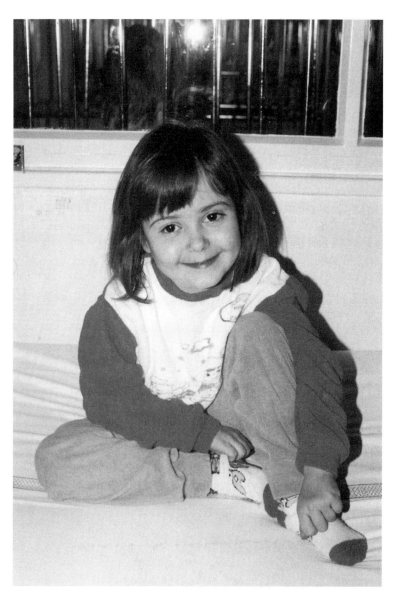

Karmen Košcak

1
Karmen Koščak

"The heart has reasons that reason knows not"
—Blaise Pascal

Somewhere between the elephants and the bears, Karmen Koščak (pronounced Kosh-chak) had had enough. She drifted away from the five adults and children who were strolling unhurriedly with her, enjoying the Memphis Zoo on a delightfully breezy, cool, and sun-filled March morning, found a spot along a curb to sit down, buried her head in her hands, and began to weep quietly.

Who could blame Karmen? After surviving a fourth open-heart operation in the four short years of her life and dealing with the rigorous rehabilitative regimen that followed, Karmen was more than entitled to throw a brief pity party for herself at the zoo.

After a few minutes of weeping, Karmen—with the help of a little cajoling by her mother, Radmilla—bounced back to her feet and soon began trying her best to win the attention of some monkeys behind a glass wall. A tiny brunette with large, mournful brown eyes, Karmen wore a bright pink sweatshirt emblazoned with an image of Princess Jasmine, the Arabian heroine from the Disney movie *Aladdin*.

Karmen was born in Koprivnica (Koh-preev-knee-tsah) with a very complicated heart defect, "one of the most unusual I have ever seen," according to Novick, as he began to recite the litany of her problems. "Her heart was placed on the right-hand side of her body instead of the left, with the heart also pointing right instead of left. She had transposition of the great arteries, a condition where the heart chambers are abnormally connected to the arteries. In addition, Karmen's left pumping chamber was smaller than normal, and she had a complete atrioventricular canal, which means there was a big hole between the pumping chambers on the bottom and the top of her heart. Instead of two valves on top, there was only one. Karmen had a constriction of her pulmonary arteries, which made her appear very blue when she was born. Her condition was very, very rare."

At birth, Karmen's prognosis was every bit as ominous as the condition was rare. The physician from the girl's hometown said she had no future. Other physicians who were consulted believed a good outcome was unlikely and did not recommend surgery. As if this was not enough, Karmen had the added misfortune of entering the world at the low point in Croatia's war with the Serbs.

That Karmen was born with her heart on the wrong side was the least of her medical problems. (Novick commented: "You just have to prepare yourself before you go into the operating room, remembering that the operation will be conducted on the other side of the body and forcing yourself to think in a mirror image.") That she was born on the wrong side of the line between war and peace, on the wrong side of the divide between the "haves" and the "have nots," was a much more imposing predicament. With Croatia in a panic in Karmen's first few days of life—President Franjo Tudjman went on national television to encourage the nation not to lose heart—the plight of an infant born with heart disease in a tiny village near the Hungarian border was not a top priority.

After the dire diagnosis of Karmen's heart condition at birth, her first hopeful breakthrough came when the case was referred to pediatric cardiologist Dr. Ivan Malcic at Rebro University Hospital in Zagreb. Malcic had been organizing the care of Croatian children with heart disease along with Novick, and he was also a topnotch diagnostician. Moreover, Malcic appreciated the spiritual aspects of healing as deeply as the medical.

"I believe more and more that the physician can help carry the cross with the patient in the sense of making the situation easier," the youthful-looking doctor said in a deliberate, unruffled tone. "For me, this is Veronica or Simon helping Jesus along the way, and Jesus' way is, after all, our way. All of us are invited to help in this way."

Out of all his recorded healings—healings that continue to offer solace and comfort to millions of Christians to this day—there is no evidence that Jesus of Nazareth ever helped anyone with a heart attack or congestive heart failure. To our knowledge, he treated no children with congenital heart defects. He never performed cardiopulmonary resuscitation. Today his healing techniques would not get him anywhere near heart patients' beds even as a visitor, much less as a physician. In healing a deaf man he "put his finger into the man's ears and, spitting, touched his tongue" (Mk 7:33); in the cure of a blind man, Jesus smeared clay and his saliva into a blind person's eyes (Jn 9:6); elsewhere in the gospels people "sought to touch him because power came forth from him and healed them all" (Lk 6:19). Jesus was not a medical healer in the way we know today. He also was not a spiritual healer as we think of one; he didn't pray for healing, and he rarely laid on hands in the fashion of television evangelists or ministers from the more charismatic Christian traditions. Perhaps he did not treat certain kinds of afflictions or heal in the manner to which we are accustomed in order to leave room for incredible healing stories like that of Karmen Koščak.

Ivan Malcic was born in 1952 and has been a physician for twenty years. In the normal course of his practice he estimates that he sees the deaths of two patients per week from congenital heart disease. His workload in cardiology has increased, because other physicians do not want to risk cancer by working with X rays, an indication of the lack in fundamental areas of Croatia's healthcare system. And yet, Malcic's clinical specialty is a new, rare, and puzzling complication of advanced surgical techniques—protein-losing enteropathy, a syndrome where poor heart function affects the patient's ability to retain protein, a building block for much of the body's functioning. It is believed that some of the more complicated heart procedures change the flow of blood into the liver, and for a small percentage of patients, this change in blood flow triggers protein-losing enteropathy. Half of all patients who develop this syndrome die within one year.

Each morning Malcic prepares for the life-and-death consequences of his job by praying during his lengthy drive from the Zagreb suburb of Velika Gorica to the cardiology clinic in the eastern part of Zagreb. He also spends a few minutes reflecting on a passage from the New Testament before seeing his first patient.

As a youngster Malcic felt called to be either a doctor or a priest. He reasoned, "Life is very short, and it is necessary in this life to do some good. In every area of life it is possible to do good, but as a priest or as a physician it is possible to be a victim for the good, to be the victim for others." His parents reminded him that because of the active persecution of priests in communist Yugoslavia, his "victimhood" might come sooner and more dramatically than he would like. Malcic decided to become a doctor.

He became a pediatrician "because a lot of education is necessary to help the people," adding that his duties sometimes include telling mothers how to breastfeed or how to stop diarrhea in a child. On a deeper level Malcic is motivated by the pursuit of "the understanding of life, the ultimate origin of life." When the Memphis surgical team arrives in Zagreb, Malcic converses with Kerrigan about theology almost as frequently as he meets with Novick about patients. Besides his work in cardiology, Malcic also specializes in rheumatology, the science of connective tissue, a field where "all is clear, all is not clear; all is possible, all is impossible."

Rheumatology takes its nomenclature from *rheuma*, the Greek work for pain, and it is evident that Malcic is willing to take on some of that pain himself in his profession. Malcic's sense of service for others, that desire for "victimhood," remains an important motivation. "If the physician can explain the situation well and have a good rapport with the children and their parents, then this profession enables me to be a physician and a priest at the same time. This is the reason that I am happy in my profession, in spite of the difficulties and frustrations."

For Malcic, these difficulties and frustrations are manifold, although they cannot be easily read from his even temperament. "It is a very difficult job, because it is not always successful—very often the children die," he began softly. "It is not easy to be with parents who have a high hope and then the child dies. This is why this job is depressing and frustrating. This is compounded by congenital heart diseases that we can help in theory, but we cannot help with our particular surgeons and intensive-care teams. This is the more difficult situation. The diagnosis is good, because we know pediatric cardiology and we know what we need to do, but every week I see children who die because of the difficulty in arranging surgery outside Croatia. For me, this is especially difficult, because the parents come to me with the question, 'Why is my child dead? You are here and my child is dead. We did not expect this situation.'

"Eight years ago, I had an eleven-year-old boy who was very sick and could die at any moment. But the child looked very good to the parents. I sent him to Ljubljana for an operation, and the child died on the table during the procedure. The father called me, and he was very aggressive; he calls me every year on the birthday of the child. 'You are guilty of the death of my child. I will kill you! You think you are good man, but you have killed my child,' he tells me. I don't know what to do but to pray for this man.

"When the family believes in God, and the child lives one year or one day, the people can say, yes, this is the life of my child, because every day of life for my child is a present from God. Then, it is easy. For God, twenty years or one year or one hundred years are the same, and when people really believe in God, they understand. They are thankful for all we can do for this child. Other people, who expect only success in life, cannot understand that pain has value, that suffering is important to improve the person. Mostly, these families go home without a 'thank you' or contact in the future."

Malcic was well aware of Karmen's unique difficulties. "Karmen came to me as a small, blue baby after her birth," he began. "As a newborn she was a child without hope. All of the physicians said there was no good outcome possible for this baby; we didn't believe Karmen had a chance. And yet I catheterized this child because I believe in palliative procedures. And after the first palliation I was sure that this child had a future."

Palliation in medical parlance is a bridge built to buy time between the "here" of the patient's immediate problem and a "there" of total correction; palliative surgery makes an initial step toward healing, while allowing the body to adjust and prepare for the next operation. When a patient's condition is too severe for total correction, palliation is also performed simply to extend his or her life. In the cold efficiency of the communist system in countries like the former Yugoslavia, palliation as an extension of a patient's life was frowned upon as a poor outlay of limited resources.

From Malcic's Christian perspective, though, palliation always has merit, because for him, there is always an additional factor besides the medical. "The children and their parents are not just bodies; they have souls," he stated. "It is not possible to speak only about physical changes in the heart when I am with the patients and the families. This is only one aspect of medicine. The other aspect is the personal or spiritual."

"I liked Karmen because, even as a newborn, she was a very, very good fighter," said Malcic. "In this situation we performed a palliative operation, and we performed it successfully." A pathway was made in the pulmonary artery to provide adequate blood flow to her lungs, and after a quick recovery, the infant was taken home to Koprivnica.

Before Karmen's birth, Radmilla and Zvonko Koščak enjoyed a life that was uncomplicated and relaxed. The diminutive duo—Radmilla stands about 4′11″ and Zvonko 5′3″—forged modest careers as a kindergarten teacher and a furniture-maker while raising their healthy first child, Denis, who was born six years before Karmen. "Our economic situation was such that we couldn't buy anything that was not absolutely needed," said Radmilla, who, despite a warm and open countenance, spoke as sparingly as she spent money, rarely giving more than one-sentence responses in conversation.

Koprivnica, a charming town of about sixty thousand residents, is located only a few miles from the Drava River, the country's northern border with Hungary. The town is home to Podravka, the largest food producer in Croatia, as well as to an art colony trained in the Hlebine or "naive" style of oil painting. Hlebine painting emerged from Croatia in the early part of the century; the peasant-artist Ivan Generalic was perhaps its most famous practitioner. The works, generally painted backward on glass, from foreground to background, are characterized by simple, colorful depictions of everyday (usually rural) life that embody a certain fairy-tale quality. Despite the simplicity, the peasant characters are invariably portrayed with a beguiling awareness.

Zvonko Koščak painted casually in the Koprivnica circle but was without work during the war. He traveled to Germany to seek employment but returned in the last weeks of Radmilla's pregnancy. The family spent a great deal of time in the basement before Karmen's birth, anxious about JNA shelling, which never materialized. Even without the bombing, "we lived through all the stress and fear," said Radmilla.

A bomb did fall, however, with Karmen's birth and diagnosis. "It was very, very hard. We were shocked, because no one in our family ever had such a thing," the girl's mother reflected. "We did have hope and faith that Karmen would be okay. Faith and hope are very important in the life of every person, but we knew we would now have to live out our faith and hope in a very personal way."

As Novick began to take his first referrals for Croatian children in Orlando in the fall of 1992, Karmen was edging toward her first birthday. Not long after, she began to turn blue and her development appeared to lag. It was time to begin considering the little girl's next operation. Her case was handed to Novick during a trip to Zagreb in 1993. "When a case like Karmen's is presented, with all the complexity of her anatomy, you break it down into its component parts," the surgeon said. "Taking a conservative approach, the decision was made for Karmen to undergo the operation in two stages." Children with defects of this magnitude require operations that involve intricate diverting of blood flow and/or the creation of new pathways for the blood, and these corrections often cannot be accomplished in a single procedure.

The complexity of Karmen's operation also required that it be performed in the United States; Croatia's intensive-care doctors and nurses simply do not have enough experience treating such patients. In fact, it was only in April 1993—about the time when Karmen's need for surgery began to resurface—that the first operation of this kind was performed in Croatia's history (more than twenty years after the procedure became commonplace in the United States). Ironically, the successful recipient of

Novick's handiwork was a ten-year-old boy from Koprivnica, Zoran Ernecic, but his anatomy was not as complex as Karmen's.

The trip to America created additional considerations, as the notion of a humanitarian foundation was still nascent in Novick's mind. The day-to-day details of treating international children with heart disease was as organized as the scraps of paper in Novick's pockets or on his desk. There were no standard answers to the questions: Who will pay for the Croatian children? How will they be housed in America?

Fortunately, the Podravka Food Company of Koprivnica, learning of Karmen's plight, paid the bulk of the twenty thousand dollar hospital charge for the operation. A visual arts association in Koprivnica collected Hlebine works of art on Karmen's behalf; these were sold in Croatia and the United States to raise funds. At least two dozen artists were involved in the project.

In the spring of 1994, when Karmen was ready to venture to America, Novick was still fairly new to Memphis, having moved from Orlando only six months before. There were few people he could rely on to host a patient from a foreign country for several weeks. Fortunately, one of his cardiovascular nurses from Orlando, Elizabeth Jameson, had just moved to Memphis with her brother and sister-in-law, David and Kim Jameson.

Kim Jameson's acceptance of the invitation to host Karmen and her mother was not a complete leap into the unknown. The floral and interior designer had a daughter, Jessica, who was the same age as Karmen. That made it easier for Kim to relate to Radmilla. "I kept putting myself in Radmilla's place and tried to make her more comfortable," she said. Half Lebanese, Kim could also recall when her relatives fled from Beirut to America during the civil war in Lebanon. "That was a significant experience in my life, to know that I had family who had to leave their country because of war," she said, acknowledging that it sensitized her to events in the former Yugoslavia.

Still, there was much about her mission that was overwhelming. "I felt so helpless with Karmen's physical state. I knew there was not much I could do except pray. She was Jessica's age, and although they were about the same height, she was much more frail and she was blue. You just knew that she was sick. She was strong-willed, though, even as a baby; you could see it in her eyes. Then there was Radmilla, who was by herself, didn't know the language, and had to await the outcome of her child's surgery."

Kim sensed a strongly internalized faith in Radmilla that she could not express until she hosted another Croatian child, Nikola Koš, a couple of months after Karmen. "I noticed that her mother, Marija, kept looking across the street at something," she said. "It turned out that she was looking at how the windows in the house across the street formed a cross, and she was praying to it." Kim saw that these two mothers, in the midst of their adversity, found their inner focus—literally, in Marija Kos's case—in their faith.

For Kim, Karmen's circumstances "sure make you appreciate what you have," but she was not the only one with a sense of appreciation. The Koščaks were grateful for plenty themselves.

"Radmilla brought me a glass painting from the Hlebine school that Zvonko painted for me," said Novick. "Zvonko painted this for me as a gift, not knowing whether his child would die in the operating room. Through the years the parents have exhibited an absolutely unwavering faith in God to take care of their child. Even after the later operation, in June 1995, when Karmen was ill with pneumonia in the intensive-care unit, I could tell that Radmilla and Zvonko believed that she was going to be fine. It wasn't a clinging, straw-grasping belief but a rock-solid faith. Sometimes parents have a false sense of security about their child, but not the Koščaks."

True to her parents' faith, Karmen came through the surgery smoothly and her entire post-operative course went without a hitch. In their first collaborative media effort Kerrigan interviewed a satisfied Novick for the Catholic weekly *Common Sense* at Karmen's bedside in the intensive-care unit. "She had a combination of defects that are not even described in the routine books," Novick reported at the time. "Without the surgery, she would have died within a few years." Kerrigan, beginning his crash course in pediatric cardiovascular surgery, was amazed that the little girl was doing so well with all the tubes and monitors attached to her; the specifics of her condition were still well beyond his comprehension.

Mother and daughter were soon back in Croatia under Dr. Malcic's care.

"It is normal for a doctor to have a favorite patient, and I had a big interest in saving this child," he revealed. "I developed a good relationship with the family. They were very poor but very cultured and very interesting."

For Radmilla, one of the highlights after Karmen's return from surgery in Memphis was her entry into preschool. "She did not stand apart from her classmates. She was evolving physically and intellectually like the others in the group. She felt and looked good—only a little tired— and she loves her brother and father."

The good news proved to be short-lived. In January 1995 Malcic called Novick to report that Karmen was becoming blue again. The cardiologist repeated a cardiac catheterization to determine the exact problem. He found a leak in the conduit that Novick had constructed in Memphis, and he asked if the surgeon would complete the correction.

As it turned out, Karmen's need for surgery coincided with the June 1995 arrival of Novick, Kerrigan, and the rest of the International Children's Heart Foundation team at Rebro University Hospital in Zagreb for two weeks of operations. Rebro, from the Croatian word for rib, was founded during the Second World War and is the leading hospital in the country. Karmen's total correction was performed uneventfully, but in the postoperative period she contracted pneumonia and remained in the hospital for a month. Novick explained the lengthy stay: "Medical care in Croatia for children with congenital heart defects is extremely difficult; the physicians tend to keep them in the hospital longer after operations than we do. They also tend to bring them into the hospital for postoperative evaluations and actually keep them in the hospital for a day or two, which is unheard of in the United States. Out-patient management and adjustment of medicines are still rare in Croatia for children with congenital heart disease."

During the June trip, in a weekend visit to Koprivnica, the foundation was presented with the first twelve paintings by the local community of artists. The whole city seemed to rally around Karmen, who, in all her photogenic beauty, presented Dr. Novick and others with roses during the ceremony. "It was an extremely emotional ceremony," said Novick. "I was shocked and moved to tears several times during the day." An additional fifty paintings were promised, and they were delivered for sale in an art auction later that year in Memphis.

The festivities in Koprivnica could have been viewed as the closing ceremonies to Karmen's four-year medical Olympics. After three operations and the resulting complications over that span, a guardedly happy ending for Karmen seemed to be reached. The girl's original defect was corrected as well as possible with current medical knowledge and skill. Although the nature of her disease was such that her longevity would likely be significantly shorter than that of those born with healthy hearts, the cloud of upcoming operations finally had lifted. Karmen could bask in the sunshine of childhood.

Not quite. Early in 1996 Malcic again called Novick. "He said that Karmen was back in the hospital again. She had been readmitted for fluid in her abdominal cavity and swelling in the legs," Novick remembered. "She had developed protein-losing enteropathy, a terrible complication." Ironically, this complication was Malcic's specialty.

For reasons still not entirely known, a small percentage of children who receive the type of operation that Karmen did—a procedure called the Fontan operation—experience protein-losing enteropathy. "These children lose protein from their intestines and they swell up everywhere," said Novick. In one case the bloating was so severe in a young girl referred to Novick that when the surgeon made an incision on her sternum, he first drew water from the patient's skin instead of blood.

Since the Fontan operation is relatively new—about twenty years old—so is the complication. "Physicians are not sure what to do," said Malcic. "Diagnosis is not easy, because there are no established criteria. Children lose protein, but we don't know which level of proteins the children need in order to make a diagnosis." Worse yet, statistics have indicated that more than half of patients who have the syndrome die within one year, and for those who need an operation to try to correct the problem, the mortality rate rises to 70 percent. "Besides protein, they lose calcium and immunoglobulins—they lose what is important for life," said Malcic in explaining the high death rate.

To Novick, it seemed strange that Karmen developed this syndrome so quickly after her last operation. He asked his friend Malcic to perform a repeat cardiac catheterization. The procedure showed "a big area of scar tissue at the site of our last operation in Croatia," said Novick. Such scarring is an occasional and unpredictable postoperative event. Novick felt he could solve the protein problem by surgically removing the obstruction. Malcic was worried about the mortality rate for protein-losing enteropathy children who had repeated operations. Novick kept prodding Malcic, "Pack Karmen up and send her over here, and we will repair that area again. I think we can get her through this." He based his optimism on some scientific information. "A number of people who have developed protein-losing enteropathy have developed it because of a structural problem or an arrhythmia that has subsequently led to bad cardiac function. Well, Karmen still had excellent heart function. Although we were flying in the face of the odds, she was in a better situation than the odds indicated."

In February 1996 Karmen and Radmilla were back in Memphis for the girl's second operation in the city and fourth overall. Having formed the International Children's Heart Foundation since Karmen's last visit to Memphis, funding from several sources was now in place for her surgery. Kim Jameson was not able to host the Koscaks this time around, however. In the intervening two years she had given birth to a second child, Joseph, and had had her own bout with a heart problem. When Kim was six months pregnant with Joseph, she was found to have a liter and a half of fluid around her heart. Before the fluid was drained, she had difficulty breathing and was told by doctors that at any point her heart could have just stopped, although the doctors were not able to find the cause of the buildup. Now perfectly healthy, Kim attended to Karmen and Radmilla on their second trip as much as her new responsibilities permitted.

Prompted by an appeal that Kerrigan had made at Mass at the Church of the Holy Spirit in the summer of 1994, Vicki Merchant and her fiancé, Mike Buckley, decided to volunteer for the host family program of the International Children's Heart Foundation. Nearly two years later they were assigned Karmen and Radmilla Koscak. "We wanted to do something to begin our marriage that would help our church and have an impact on someone else," said Vicki.

Vicki, in particular, knew what it was to like to have someone open doors for her. In January 1991 her first husband, Scott, a pilot for Federal Express, was diagnosed with stomach cancer. This was a crushing blow for the pair, who had been married for nine years after they met in college and flew together as pilots for the Marine Corps. Just three months later, Scott died. Vicki was alone with two-year-old Elizabeth and four months pregnant with her second daughter, Alexandra.

During Scott's illness Vicki experienced the support of many friends and churchgoers, which helped in her decision to host Karmen. "For so many months so many people did things for me; I felt it was time to do something for someone else," she said. "I weighed the possibility that Karmen might not do well, but I finally felt that you don't wait to help someone else."

When a bloated Karmen arrived, "she was a little butterball with total body edema," according to Novick. Kim Jameson observed that Karmen was now bigger than her own daughter Jessica. She also saw an impish and self-aware side of the girl that she had not noticed on her first visit to Memphis. "Karmen was a veteran of surgery now, so she knew what was coming and what to do. It seemed that she had Radmilla wrapped around her finger, because the mother was hovering over her much more than before." Vicki Buckley was impressed by how serious Karmen seemed. "You could see it on her face; so much pain for such a short life."

Karmen had her operation on February 29, leap-year day. As Vicki and most host mothers learn, surgery day is an exceedingly tense time. "The hours in surgery seemed like an eternity," she said. Actually, the operation went smoothly and normally. Over the next several days Karmen lost her excess weight. She went home in late March.

More than any medical highlights, Karmen's second Memphis visit was characterized by episodes like the crying incident at the zoo described at the beginning of this chapter. The pain and suffering involved with the chest incision, the insertion of tubes and IVs, and the constant monitoring by medical personnel who didn't speak her language were finally taking their toll on the little girl, and Karmen began to balk. Novick commented: "Karmen is a very bright child. She knows how to manipulate the feelings of the crowd. When it is beneficial for Karmen to be happy and gay, she is. When it is beneficial for Karmen to be sickly and ill, she is."

Following her discharge from the hospital, Karmen refused to do anything but languish on the couch all day at the Buckleys, watching Disney movies instead of walking and doing breathing exercises. Novick gave Kerrigan a portable pulse oxymeter to check Karmen's oxygen saturation level—an indication of her heart's ability to oxygenate the blood. "It was really more of a psychological ploy," said Kerrigan. "Just the mention of the word *bolnica* [hospital] would send her into a crying fit, so I would say, 'OK, if you don't want to go to the hospital again, you have to have good numbers on this machine, you have to walk and eat normally.'"

When Karmen returned to Croatia before Easter, she impressed Malcic during her postoperative checkup. She had no symptoms: no swelling, no extra fluids in her body. There was another celebration in Koprivnica when the Memphis surgery team returned in April 1996. "She looked great when she met us, walking in the streets, dancing, playing, having a great time," recalled Novick.

Kerrigan returned to Croatia in May for a vacation, and he was surprised to run into Karmen as a patient at Rebro. The suspicion was that the protein-losing enteropathy had returned. Malcic ran some tests but couldn't find anything wrong. He put her on diuretics and steroids to reduce the chances of any fluid buildup, and she responded well.

At last report, in the spring of 1997, five-year-old Karmen was going to Croatia's equivalent of kindergarten. "She is a pure joy, enjoying life," said Radmilla. "She knows what she wants and she is interested in participating in everything. I hope she will continue to be healthy and can continue going to school, playing with her friends, and enjoying life."

At the same time, the first years of Karmen's life have taught all who know her to be cautious and concerned. "Every day I love Karmen more and more, and when she is ill I am totally gripped with fear. I am always close to my rosary beads for Karmen and for all sick children now," Radmilla continued. "Karmen is also her father's great love, and he can't paint when she is in the hospital because she is the center of his life."

Ivan Malcic reported, "She must eat a lot of protein and not a lot of fat, and she is very good about this. She gets some steroids because some theorists have spoken of the good effect of steroids on this condition. Altogether, Karmen is a very sick child, but despite that, she feels normal, and to her parents she is normal. Only for me she is not normal. I hope the complication will not develop much."

"Karmen has a bad anatomical situation," Novick summarized. "We know that the Fontan operation, although it does enable children to look pink again and provides them with adequate oxygenation, is unfortunately not completely curative."

Easter—the Christian commemoration of Christ's rising from the dead—came in April 1996, and the Košcaks sent Novick a bright, colorful card. In English, Radmilla wrote, "Karmen is home. She is good. We are happy—Mother Radmilla, Family Košcak, and Karmen." When opened, the card made a sound like a chirping bird, which Novick, who is deaf to high pitches, could not hear. (Kerrigan cites this when he teasingly hypothesizes that Novick's deafness is symbolic of a deeper inability to hear the thanks from his patients' families.) However, the surgeon did perceive the appreciation that came with the card. "I'm always overwhelmed with the degree of their gratitude," he said.

The Koprivnica community has continued to be one of the most significant supporters of children born with congenital heart disease. The Podravka Food Company has supported the International Children's Heart Foundation surgical teams with lavish dinners and financial help in covering hotel bills during their surgical missions in Zagreb. Workers of Podravka appealed for help for a couple of the other children to come to Memphis. The art colony continues to donate its work on behalf of the children.

Malcic turned philosophical when discussing the meaning of his work with Karmen. "During the treatment of this child I gained a lot of experience in medicine and otherwise. The most difficult problem in medicine today is people who think we can totally understand nature. We have to understand that we cannot understand. When we realize that we cannot know the origin and outcome of all life, then we can be good physicians. A physician who thinks he or she can change the relationship between God and life is dangerous.

"The equilibrium in the body is unbelievable, and damage to one element can be dangerous to life. To me, that is the big secret. I cannot understand people who think they can change this. As a physician I know I can *help* but not *change* nature. I can try to correct damage but not the origin of life. Different physicians think they change the origins of life in genetics and so on. But my medical opinion is: help, do not change.

"One theory of congenital heart disease is that the defects come from outside influences, especially during the first twelve weeks of intrauterine life. But investigations cannot answer this question. We only know of some ailments and viruses that we can say have 100 percent influence on the development of organ systems. But the incidence of congenital heart disease is the same throughout the world, independent of these influences. This is very interesting. Why? Who can answer this question?"

Malcic had cause to pose these questions when his son, Hrvoje, was born with a heart defect in 1982, after the cardiologist had already chosen to specialize in the disease. Malcic and his wife, Slavka, have three children, Ana, Hrvoje, and Iva, born in three-year intervals, beginning with Ana in 1979. The boy's defect of the ventricular septum was minor and resolved itself spontaneously. Again, the doctor posed a question: "Who can say why? I can only say that I was very happy. The human heart is not only a pump. It is a very complicated system of nerves, vessels, pressures, and relationships with the lungs and circulation, lymph, and so on. There is contact between the heart and the central nervous system. The heart can influence every organ system."

The heart can also express itself in many ways. In a special way the hands choreograph the heart. Hands speak eloquently and deeply when they are thrown up in despair, lifted in exultation, joined in love. Little wonder, then, that to punctuate the reality of his resurrection, the risen Christ says to the apostle Thomas, "'Bring your hand and put it into my side, and do not be unbelieving, but believe.' Thomas answered, and said to him, 'My Lord and my God!'" (Jn 20:27–28). If Karmen Koščak has not yet been told this gospel story, she can probably relate to *Aladdin*, where twice the movie's namesake reaches out to Princess Jasmine with an outstretched hand and asks, "Do you trust me?" before the pair embark on death-defying escapes. Outstretched, Aladdin's hand challenges Jasmine, but when she grasps it, the hand represents trust.

Along a street in Koprivnica, after Karmen's last surgery, a contingent of local dignitaries and the Memphis-based surgery team make their way from one building to another. Karmen, with her four operations behind her, breaks forth from the other Koščaks at the back of the pack, running and shouting "Doctor No-veek, Doctor No-veek" in a high-pitched tone, catching up with the surgeon and grabbing his hand from behind. When their hands join, the gap between healed and healer suddenly coalesces, if only temporarily.

In March 1996 Karmen Koščak and her mother, Radmilla, pose in front of the Memphis Zoo shortly after the girl's fourth open-heart operation.

Ivan Pozaric

2
Ivan Pozaric

"The star...stopped over the place
where the child was"
—Matthew 2:9

The Christian feast of the Epiphany, commemorated shortly after
Christmas each year, recalls the divine manifestation already present in
the infant Jesus, who as a newborn was able to draw people to himself
from afar. In the gospel passage proclaimed on the feast, Matthew
2:1–12, significant forces are set in motion by the birth of this baby: a
star charts a purposeful path; wise men from the East pursue the child to
pay homage; and the reigning king, Herod, also seeks the infant Jesus,
but with the intent of killing him.

If a star didn't actually stop over the place where two-year-old Ivan
Pozaric was, many hearts, minds, and lives certainly hovered very closely
over this Croatian boy from Krapina, a small town near the Slovenian
border, from his arrival in Memphis for heart surgery in August 1994
until his untimely death in Zagreb in January 1995. With more than a
little help from his extraordinary and gallant mother, Zdravka, Ivan was
able to draw Memphians to himself and to the circumstances of Croatia
unlike any other heart patient from his homeland.

Fifty or so of those whose lives Ivan had touched, along with a local television crew, gathered in the Catholic Church of the Holy Spirit in Memphis on January 8, 1995, the feast of the Epiphany. The Matthean text about the star was proclaimed. The altar was still arrayed in its Christmas finery, brilliant poinsettias and a ceramic nativity scene filling most of the space. The congregation had not assembled for the Epiphany, however, but for a memorial service for Ivan, who had died in Zagreb three days before. A poster-size portrait of the young Croatian served as a reminder of why everyone was there. Many in the assembly had not even known Ivan as he was pictured in the photo: an intent, peaceful-looking boy with brown hair neatly combed to the side. The seemingly healthy, chubby-faced and rosy-cheeked Ivan was nattily attired in denim, his mother's hands seen along the edge of the photograph gently steadying him.

"We're here to celebrate a life," began Kerrigan in his sermon that night, "to celebrate a life that, despite suffering and helplessness, was still able to draw people not only to him but out of themselves. How many people went out of their way to help Ivan—the elderly woman who gave Zdravka the contents of her recently deceased sister's wallet comes to mind; the anonymous financial gifts; the thousand dollars for airfare that a handful of churchgoers came up with in less than twenty-four hours in order to fly Ivan's dad, Dejan, to Memphis at an especially critical juncture; the extra time the nurses spent checking on Ivan even when he wasn't their patient; and on and on and on. This tells us that no matter how deep and sustained the suffering, suffering does not need to carry the day. No matter the darkness that covers the earth, no matter how thick the clouds, adversity need not obscure the star that always shines for us to follow."

Krapina, Croatia, does not strike a visitor as a place of clouds and darkness. The town of about twenty-five thousand residents is located approximately forty miles north of Zagreb, roughly halfway between Zagreb and Maribor, Slovenia, in the heart of a region called the Hrvatsko Zagorje, the Croatian Hinterland. A group of hot springs and a Catholic pilgrimage site honoring the Virgin Mary (Marija Bistrica) are among the region's key tourist attractions. The eye-catching variety of baroque churches, medieval castles, unpeopled hills, and fertile farmland in Hrvatsko

Zagorje hearken to an earlier, simpler era. One of Krapina's unique features goes way, way back, in fact: a life-sized sculpture of Krapina Man, a pre-Neanderthal human whose fossilized remains were discovered in a Krapina park, is displayed in the park along with sculptures of animals of that era.

Besides Krapina Man, the Croatian Hinterland is also the birthplace for two prime examples of another sort: the political autocrat. Both Josip Broz-Tito and Franjo Tudjman, government leaders who played significant roles in Croatian history in the twentieth century, hail from the region.

In the spring of 1991 Zdravka's romance with her high school sweetheart, Dejan Pozaric, was blooming. Meanwhile, the curtain was falling on the country and the Communist Party, which Tito had held together for over forty years until his death in 1980, giving way to runaway nationalism, championed in its Croatian form by Tudjman, who would soon be elected president of the new republic. "Brotherhood and unity," Tito's motto to hold Yugoslavia—and nationalism—at bay was now replaced by restrictive slogans like Tudjman's "Croatia is for Croats."

With the onset of the political turmoil and military hostilities initiated by the Serbs in 1991, the tranquil, pastoral life in places like Krapina was soon overshadowed. "We were all attacked," said Dejan, a tall, square-jawed, dark-featured young man in his mid-twenties, who made a striking contrast to the tall, blond, blue-eyed Zdravka. "And so we were all caught up in what was going on." Dejan was drafted and had to quit his factory job to train and await the call to fight on the front line, which thankfully never came. His battle was closer to home, for his son's life.

Ivan was conceived around the time that Slovenia and Croatia declared their independence and were reborn as new republics in June 1991. "Maybe all the tension influenced Ivan's health," Dejan speculated nearly a year after his son's death. Zdravka and Dejan married in December 1991. When they did, Zdravka, whose first name contains health (*zdrav*), took on a last name of fire (*pozar*), a combination that would prove prophetic for Ivan, whose health was threatened numerous times following surgery in Memphis by fever and "scalded skin syndrome," a complication that simulates the effects of burns. Even though United Nations mediator Cyrus Vance negotiated a cease-fire and fourteen thousand UN peacekeeping troops were sent to Croatia, the "war" was just starting for the newlyweds when Ivan was born February 28, 1992.

At birth Ivan was diagnosed with a condition known as transposition of the great vessels, an abnormal relationship between the cardiac chambers and the great arteries. Some exchange between these chambers and arteries must exist to sustain life. Normally, the blue blood from the veins comes back into a filling chamber on the right side of the heart, gets pushed into the pumping chamber, and then into the pulmonary arteries and lungs. In the lungs oxygen turns the blue blood red and the red blood comes back into the left filling chamber, gets pushed into the left pumping chamber, and into the aorta, the body's main artery. Transposition is a situation in which the blue blood comes back, but the arteries are reversed. Thus the blue blood never goes to the lungs but goes back out to the body without receiving oxygen. The red blood comes in from the lungs and goes back out to the lungs to get re-oxygenated again. The blue blood and red blood travel in parallel circuits. The only way the blood can mix is if there's an abnormal connection, a hole between the two filling chambers, a hole between the two pumping chambers, or a vessel that connects the pulmonary artery and the aorta. In the human body's effort for life, such abnormalities compensate for the primary defect.

"A nurse noticed from the first day of Ivan's life that there was a problem with his heart. He started turning blue, and when we went to Zagreb they told us that he had no chance to live," said Dejan.

"I saw that the blood was not mixed enough to sustain life," said Ivan's cardiologist, Branco Marinovic, "so we sent him to Ljubljana in the hope that surgery there would improve his condition."

The palliative procedure in Ljubljana, where his atrial septum was removed, bought some time and a sense of normality to the young parents. For the next two years, Zdravka and Dejan threw their energy into raising their young son.

Zdravka, Dejan, and Ivan lived with Dejan's grandmother in a comfortable two-story home that belonged to Dejan's parents, who were living in Switzerland. The house's foundation, which was set a bit below street level, along with its dark wooden interior paneling combined to give a somber subterranean feeling to the home.

Ivan was a precocious child, who had mastered the tricycle and had learned to operate a television by the time he was two. "His imagination was great," said Dejan. "He knew how to play if he was alone; he liked to sort things out according to size, and he liked to space things evenly." Ironically, the child who found his balance on a tricycle at age two and was beginning to make some harmony out of his universe was progressively thwarted by the functioning of the one organ that should have been the most faithful and harmonious in his body—his heart.

"I first saw him on a list of patients when he was around two years old, and it was a little late to do a Senning operation by routine standards; his anatomy was not straightforward," recalled Novick about his endorsement for Ivan to come to Memphis for corrective surgery. As it turned out, there would be nothing routine or straightforward about the boy's medical course. "He had a few very large blood vessels from his aorta to his pulmonary arteries that were open, and his pulmonary pressures were high. There was at least a 10 percent chance that his next operation would not succeed, because of his age and high pulmonary artery pressure."

In 1959 Ake Senning had perfected one of two operations to switch the way the blue blood and the red blood get routed as they return to the heart. The atrial septum is cut so that there is only one big atrium, and the patient's own atrial tissue is used to create pathways to switch the blood flow. The blue blood is "downshifted," as Novick terms it, to the ventricle connected to the pulmonary arteries. The red blood is "upshifted," so that it goes to the ventricle connected to the aorta. "The operation, technically speaking, is not difficult, and the children usually do quite well," said Novick.

Debbie and Marty Petrusek, parishioners at the Church of the Holy Spirit, responded to an appeal made by Kerrigan for volunteers to house international mothers and their children with congenital heart disease. The genial and outgoing natives of New Orleans were ideal candidates to be a host family, having raised three children of their own in a welcoming, sociable home. Debbie's job as an instructor in Holy Spirit's Mothers' Day Out program gave her added skill in handling the special needs of the child.

In principle, the hosting arrangement for patients in the International Children's Heart Foundation works like this: A Memphis family, Novick, host-family coordinator Elizabeth Jameson, and a translator greet the patient and his or her parent at the airport. The patient spends a quiet first day or so in Memphis getting adjusted to the time change and new surroundings before visiting LeBonheur for a day of pre-operative testing. Surgery is usually scheduled for the next day. At a minimum the host families provide housing, food, and transportation, and they monitor, as much as possible, the health of both child and parent. Within these first few days an emotional attachment invariably begins, and the hosts find themselves showing their guests around town, inviting friends and family to visit, and making the new arrivals the focus of their lives. The Petruseks were no exception.

"When I first came home and asked what they thought about hosting a family, everyone sort of shrugged and said, 'Do what you want to do,' but after one day with Ivan, everyone was hooked," said Debbie. "He was the kind of child who could get into your heart, and he did, with all of us."

The day of surgery is an intense and emotionally draining experience for the hosts, who stay with the parent in the waiting room until the child can be visited in the intensive-care unit, usually in the late afternoon following the operation. Subject to the course of the recovery period, a child can move from the ICU to a regular patient floor within two days of the surgery, and at LeBonheur a parent can stay overnight in the room with the child. After several days in the hospital the patient may be discharged and will return—depending on complications—to the host family for several days before a final checkup at the hospital clears the patient for returning home.

With all this in mind, the Petruseks welcomed Ivan and Zdravka to Memphis on August 10, 1994, five days after Ivan's paternal grandfather had died of cancer. "He was a regular kid with big, bright, happy eyes, and all the kids in the neighborhood came to play with him," said Debbie. "He was full of the desire for energy but would suddenly tire out, so he would play for a short spurt, rest for a while, and try again," added Marty. "There was an impish quality about him."

Debbie's first impression of Zdravka was that she was mature beyond her twenty-five years. "I was surprised to find out how young she was—she didn't seem intimidated by the situation at all." The language barrier was tremendous, but they survived by making frenzied use of a yellow, palm-sized Croatian-English dictionary. "Where's the yellow book?" was heard often.

Even when language was not a barrier and she was with people who had befriended her, Zdravka was reticent in talking about herself or in engaging in small talk. Like a person who politely refuses to have her photograph taken, Zdravka would always respond with a friendly, "Ništa" ("Nothing"), when asked by Kerrigan to offer some commentary.

All the meaning Zdravka intended to communicate could be discerned without words, however. Her compelling, vulnerable face, especially her blue eyes, revealed a fiercely determined faithfulness to her son and to God. Over the next four months emotions and tears swept across her face like the weather, but her faithfulness ruled. No matter that the health and life of her only child was slowly receding; Zdravka's steadfastness never flagged.

Ivan spent four full days with the Petruseks before surgery, and with his mom experienced American food, shopping malls, and parks, as well as late-summer Memphis heat and humidity. On Sunday, August 14, the day before his scheduled surgery, Ivan went with his mother and the Petruseks to the Church of the Holy Spirit. At the Sunday Mass, Kerrigan met them and anointed Ivan with the sacrament of the sick. "He was a very active two-year-old who couldn't stay still long enough for me to anoint him at Mass," he recalled.

Finally surgery day arrived, and the emotional hours of anxiety-filled waiting were followed by a sudden, terse verdict. "What I remember is that Dr. Novick came down to the ICU waiting room, talked to Zdravka, and stated that everything went fine," said Debbie, who was keeping vigil with Zdravka through the surgery. "It was about four or four-thirty in the afternoon before we saw Ivan in the ICU. We stayed for a short time, went downstairs for a bite to eat, and then returned to his bedside. When we returned, he was coming out of the anesthesia. He knew his mom and called her. He was thirsty and wanted a drink, which because of the tubes they couldn't give him yet."

"I went to see one of my patients whom I was taking care of in the ICU, and the first person I saw was Zdravka's son, Ivan. It was just after surgery. He was asking for water and he looked rather stable," reported Dr. Azra Sehic, a nephrologist and a native of Sarajevo who moved to Memphis in 1988 with her husband and two sons. "His nurse told me that his mother was in the waiting room. I told Ivan not to be afraid and that the nurse would give him some water soon; I think she put some moisture to his lips. I went to the waiting room to introduce myself to Zdravka and spent some time with her."

With the initial good news about Ivan accompanied by the pleasant surprise of meeting a physician who spoke Zdravka's language, the first hours after surgery could not have been brighter. However, it would be the last unclouded day in Ivan's life. His thirst, taken as a hopeful indicator of Ivan's reentry into the world of human interaction, was more akin to Jesus' plea, "I thirst," from the cross (Jn 19:28)—a sign of failing life. "The next morning we got there after eight o'clock, and he was different—restless," Debbie stated. "They had him intubated [back on the breathing machine] again the next day; it was such a disappointment because he had been taken off the previous evening. Zdravka and I were still hopeful, but it was downhill from then on."

Novick commented: "Ivan did quite well immediately after the operation. He was off the respirator at 10 P.M. on the night of his operation and appeared quite well the morning after surgery. We kept him in the ICU because he started breathing a little fast. But one day turned into two, and into three; his breathing did not improve. By the fourth day he was extremely lethargic, with very labored breathing. We put him back on the respirator, and when he woke up from his lethargy, he had severe choreoathetosis [a movement disorder]. It was the beginning of a profoundly disturbing course for him."

Dr. Elizabeth Christ was an intensive-care fellow who would become great friends with Zdravka. A tall, attractive, intense brunette from southern Louisiana, she bore a faint resemblance to Zdravka despite the geographic and ethnic differences. She first encountered the mother and son from Krapina when she wrote the admission memorandum for Ivan's entry into ICU, and she had these recollections of the immediate postoperative days: "He did all right after coming back from surgery. He was sitting up and talking, but then had breathing problems that we couldn't figure out. Indicative of his respiratory condition was the fact that he was being given 50 percent oxygen, while normal is 21 percent oxygen. He had to be put back on the respirator a couple of times; that's when we suspected that he had a paralyzed diaphragm. Then one day, for some reason that is still unclear, he just didn't wake up—he just lay there with the movement disorder. After that there was hope that maybe if we just kept him on the respirator for a couple of weeks maybe his diaphragms would come back—it was really strange for both of his diaphragms to be affected. His whole course was a mystery: why the movement disorder; why the paralysis of both diaphragms; why, for a while, he had no respiratory effort when he wasn't on the ventilator; why one thing after another."

Some things can be explained statistically—3 percent of all cyanotic children, such as Ivan, who have begun to form alternative blood-flow structures develop choreoathetosis following surgery. The disorder is twofold: *choreo* is a fast-jerking movement of the shoulders and hips, while *athetosis* is characterized by slow, writhing, snakelike movements.

Choreoathetosis is thought to be related to hypothermia during cardiopulmonary bypass (CPB). The effects on the patient of new technology to support circulation and breathing during complex surgery are still mysterious. This is especially true for children, whose physiology is different. Adult surgery involving CPB is usually less complex than children's surgery, so less drastic measures are called for during the bypass period. For example, unlike adults, whose body temperature is usually not lowered beyond 25 °C, pediatric CPB patients are exposed to temperatures in the 15 °–20 °C range to sustain the extensive surgery.

Whenever the body is significantly cooled, the normal process of sending blood to all organs and tissue beds is upset; the body reacts by making new priorities. The brain, the most sensitive of these organs, is the most prone to adverse reactions. Apparently, when an inadequate blood supply goes to a portion of the brain, the result is a movement disorder in a fraction of patients. For Ivan, the choreoathetosis was a painful irony; the once precociously intelligent boy with a sick heart was now a brain-damaged boy with a healed heart.

So, although Ivan's newly mended heart was beating healthily, the child was now fighting a new and more lethal war for survival on two fronts—neurological, with the movement disorder, and pulmonary, with the suspected paralyzed diaphragm. He struggled mightily just to keep breathing. After three weeks of oxygen support and continued episodes of respiratory arrest, a tracheostomy was performed to facilitate long-term ventilator assistance.

The choreoathetosis, however, set in motion a staggering series of new complications. Two incidents of tracheal bleeding, when Ivan's flailing arm knocked the tube from his trachea, were the first events directly attributable to the movement problem. Each time he was rushed to the operating room, and each time his mother was told that he might not make it.

As late summer moved into autumn, Ivan was weaned to a point where he depended very little on the ventilator. He was moved to a step-down care unit but never quite made it completely off the breathing machine. He developed infections, such as pneumonia and scalded-skin syndrome, attributable to the combination of prolonged stays in intensive care and multiple drugs. Scalded-skin syndrome, an especially nasty infection, resulted in the blistering and burning of the superficial layers of Ivan's skin. The young boy's platelet count dropped to a fraction of what it should be; help was requested from specialists at nearby St. Jude's Children's Research Hospital before the problem righted itself.

Ivan's body was visibly taking a beating from the onslaught of complications and countering measures. He was bloated by fluids, bruised by needles, scarred by skin infections. Like a boxer programmed to thrash even as he is being pummeled against the ropes, Ivan's erratic flailing, unhealthy as it was, could be viewed as a sign of his resistance to the onslaught. With the sedatives he was on and the central nervous system damage he sustained, he could not communicate in any other way that he was fighting back.

"I was impressed with the child's desire to live. He just refused to give up. He was very, very ill at times throughout his stay in the ICU. He just would not give up on himself. That struck me as odd because of the number of severe complications he had," said Novick.

During the initial postoperative period Zdravka was understandably very shaken. "Some nights she wouldn't even have supper, she would go to her room, and on other nights she would just eat a little and go to her room," said Debbie. "It was obvious that she was upset and crying some nights." Even though she had the Petruseks, Dr. Sehic, Fr. Kerrigan, and a contingent of other concerned parishioners from Holy Spirit, Zdravka was ultimately on her own in these toughest moments. "She handled it all by herself. Whenever she thought about calling Dejan, she would sadly remember the time difference and go to sleep without being able to share what she was going through with someone who really understood her," said Debbie, who sensed that it was Zdravka's faith, and the strength that came with it, that got her through those hours. "She prayed a lot," she noted.

Zdravka established a routine of arriving at the hospital at the start of visiting hours at nine each morning and returning home at the shift change of ICU personnel at around six-thirty in the evening. Both in the hospital and on the phone at night, Zdravka relied on the invaluable support of Dr. Sehic, who acted as a medical liaison even though Ivan's care was not her specialty. For the early part of Ivan's hospitalization Zdravka also developed a vital friendship with compatriot Biserka Culjak, a mother from Ploce, whose two-year-old daughter Marija was struggling through her postoperative course during the first few weeks of Ivan's stay. Biserka was fluent in English, assertive with the doctors, and had already spent a week with her daughter in intensive care before Ivan arrived. Zdravka and Biserka huddled several times a day at each child's bed. They would meet for lunch to have a more thorough exchange about their lives and their children, and to occasionally pore over a Croatian magazine that one or the other had received in the mail. "Zdravka and I were trying to help and comfort each other," said Biserka. "She didn't know English, so I translated for her whenever she needed it, which was a lot because Ivan had a lot of complications. It meant a lot to me that somebody else from Croatia was there, and I also think that it meant a lot to Zdravka that I was there. Zdravka and I became very good friends. We still stay in touch and talk on the phone. We live far away and don't see each other, but I hope to someday."

Zdravka was happy for Biserka and Marija when Marija's improvement allowed mother and daughter to leave the hospital and return to
Croatia in early October, but she felt keenly the void created by their
departure. "I was very sad when I left Memphis for Croatia in October
because Zdravka had to stay and things were getting difficult for Ivan,"
recalled Biserka. "All I could do now was to call the United States a few
times to find out about Ivan's health."

Although briefed constantly on the clinical consequences of each
complication, "the important thing for Zdravka," Liz Christ pointed out,
"was that it took away Ivan as she knew him. The exact medical explana-
tions weren't as important to her as much as the fact that he was gone
long before he died."

This is not at all to say that Zdravka was indifferent to Ivan's medical
course. As her world collapsed into a single bed in an intensive-care
unit, she became acutely sensitive to the meaning of the numbers on
the monitoring equipment in that world: ventilator settings, the blood
oxygen-saturation level, resting heart rate, body temperature, and the
like. Over the weeks Zdravka's comprehension of the numbers was such
that she could read any shift in the figures and respond with hope,
dejection, or dismay, not unlike a gambler whose mood can be dictated
by the odds. The numbers, the only part of Ivan available to her, com-
manded vigilance.

After two months in the intensive-care unit and another life-threatening
infection, it was deemed urgent to have Dejan travel to Memphis in
November. "The next clinical event would have been cardiac arrest," said
Dr. Donald Watson at one particularly dire moment November 6. (Watson
cared for Ivan while Novick led a surgery team for two weeks in Kiev,
Ukraine.) A group of daily Mass participants at the Church of the Holy
Spirit raised the funds for Ivan's father in a matter of hours. "I was truly
confused when I came to Memphis," recounted Dejan. "Ivan was com-
pletely different. I saw him now as a sick baby, and when I returned to
Krapina I was lost. I became suspicious that things would not go well.
Before, I had faith in God. I believed that he would not let me down, since
he did not before. I was 100 percent positive that everything would go well.
But no more."

After Dejan's visit Zdravka's solitary routine resumed. "Get up, go to the hospital, stay there all day, and come home," said host Marty Petrusek. "Rarely did she change from that. She still held hope, or at least could not let Ivan go yet." A rocking chair was provided to make Zdravka more comfortable in her daily vigil at the bedside, but she was most at ease tending to Ivan, gently speaking to him, encouraging him, reminding him of her love, handling some of the light medical tasks, and caressing him. She would open and close her day in the ICU by making the sign of the cross over him; in the early afternoon she would pray a Rosary quietly in her chair. "Either God wants to welcome Ivan home or to help keep him on earth," was Zdravka's theological conclusion, expressed in words that reflected profound acceptance. "She never gave in to the bitterness, resentment, or anger—at God or others—that sometimes characterizes a parent's response to such a situation," said Kerrigan. "The unit had a complete turnover in patients from the time Ivan was first there; even some of the nurses had left. Not only was the outside world passing her by, but her new, sterilized existence of critical care was as well. If anybody had a right to rail against that world, it was Zdravka, but she never did." In these weeks, Zdravka gradually became more outgoing and available to others, lingering in the Petrusek kitchen to clean up or to chat in the evening, voicing concern about other members of their family. With gestures or a roll of the eyes, she began lightly to make fun of the people in the intensive-care unit or to comment on American culture—the ample waistlines, the abundance of cars, the lack of people on the Memphis streets, processed food, or the high price of clothing, for example. She was buoyed by the November arrivals of two other Croatian heart patients from Hrvatsko Zagorje and attended to them enthusiastically.

"As soon as you looked at her eyes, you could see that she was a very special person—kind, innocent, very caring for other people," said Sehic. "In spite of having a hard time, she was concerned for others. She even managed to find humor—'the operation was a success but the patient died' was what she said about Ivan. I think there are rare people who can handle that stressful situation as she did. We became close friends. She felt lonely at times, and not sure that everyone around her understood her, but she had great ability as a mother, and she had great strength."

The Petruseks experienced their own growth through Zdravka. "In twenty-seven years of marriage we never had had to deal with any real sickness in our families, chronic or traumatic, so we got to experience it, to see it in a different light," said Marty.

"It gave us an opportunity to give from our own need not just from our excess," added Debbie. "In the beginning I had it all planned out. I had a certain time allotted, and then it got out of control. Before Thanksgiving we were actually talking about letting Zdravka go to another host family, because her stay was starting to conflict with family life. But then I went to Mass one morning, and the gospel was about the widow's mite."

In the Lukan passage Jesus, noticing a widow placing two small coins in the Temple treasury, stated, "I tell you, truly, this poor widow put in more than all the rest; for those others have all made offerings from their surplus wealth, but she, from her poverty, has offered her whole livelihood" (Lk 21:3). Hearing this gospel, Debbie identified with the widow. Zdravka stayed.

Whenever Ivan's complications stabilized, discussion would begin about taking him back to Croatia, where at least the psychological aspects of his treatment could be better attended to. The hope was that in whatever rehabilitation he could make, Ivan would be spoken to and coached in his own language, in the presence of other family members. Additionally, in late November Ivan's neurological functions improved a bit; he showed improvement in eye contact and his mother could spoon-feed him small portions of applesauce and popsicles. Although he never returned to full consciousness, and there was a possibility that he would be ventilator-dependent for the rest of his life, there was enough long-term hope to start thinking seriously about taking Ivan home.

The talk began in earnest in late November, when Novick approached U.S. government officials about space on a military medical evacuation plane that would take Ivan and his mother from Memphis to Germany to Zagreb. A government air ambulance would cost the fledgling ICHF ten thousand dollars, while a place on a private medical plane would be a prohibitive fifty thousand dollars. In early December space on the twice-monthly Air Force flight out of Memphis appeared secure, but then the space was taken by another, more critical patient.

Zdravka and Ivan's plight received front-page attention in Memphis's daily newspaper, *The Commercial Appeal*, on December 5, 1994. The story, "Burning Within: Tot's Fight Reflects Croatian Agony," by David Waters, recounted Ivan's medical history in Memphis and the frustrated efforts to take him back to Croatia. A color photograph of Zdravka embracing Ivan in his hospital bed topped the story. "I believe in God much more now. Why? Now I think God is my friend. The people here have helped me.... God is my friend through other people," Zdravka was quoted as saying, publicly reflecting the unwavering faith she had displayed throughout the ordeal. Encouraging letters and contributions to Zdravka, from as far away as Arkansas, followed the article's publication. In response to the story, one person left an icon of St. Nicholas for Zdravka at the hospital on December 6, the feast of St. Nicholas.

In a follow-up article, December 13, James Brosnan from the *Appeal's* Washington bureau reported that State and Defense Department officials had "ruled that Ivan's condition isn't life-threatening and thus didn't qualify for a military ambulance under their guidelines." Hopes for a government-approved flight were growing dim.

But that same day the intervention of U.S. Congressman Harold E. Ford Sr., Democrat from Tennessee's ninth Congressional District, helped persuade the government to change its stance and agree to fly the Pozarics home. Ford and legislative assistant Mark Schuermann initiated a series of letters and phone calls to government officials in an effort to cut the red tape. "It's not going to cost the federal government any additional dollars, it would not place the federal government in any position it would feel uncomfortable with, and it certainly would be a great response to this kid and his family," said Ford in a television interview.

Ford's breakthrough and the Pozarics' good fortune made the news on a local television channel, as Zdravka expressed what a "big gift" it was to be able to go home. In an openly happy ICU atmosphere—alongside doctors, nurses, and technicians who had mostly been companions in bad news over the span of Ivan's hospitalization—Zdravka watched photographs of Ivan at play in Croatia flash on the television just a few feet from his bed.

"U.S. Relents, Will Fly Ill Croatian Boy, Mother Home From Memphis,"
stated the headline the next day in the *Appeal*. "Ivan Pozaric and his
mother will be going home for Christmas after all, on Air Force wings,"
reported Brosnan. "After a phone call Tuesday morning from Rep. Harold
Ford of Memphis, Assistant Secretary of Defense John Deutsch [who
would later become director of the Central Intelligence Agency] approved
the flights, overruling Pentagon officials who had said Ivan's condition
wasn't life-threatening enough to justify use of a military plane."

Ford said of his role, "We do this every day, but we don't always have a
case this complex." The congressman's words unknowingly summarized
what Novick, Kerrigan, and anyone else professionally involved with Ivan
knew quite well: there was nothing "everyday" about Ivan.

For Zdravka, the flurry of emotion around government approval for
Ivan's flight home led to as much anxiety as it did gratitude. Her gratitude for the tremendous outpouring of attention and support among
strangers was well-documented, but her anxiety about what lay ahead at
home stayed mostly private and hidden. Zdravka was acquainted enough
with both the seriousness of Ivan's condition and the level of health care
in Croatia to know that the homecoming was a tradeoff, and she spoke
often with Sehic and others to obtain reassurance that this was a com-
promise worth making. The hope that the psychological advantages of
rehabilitating Ivan at home would offset the medical disadvantage of
poorer health care was the prevailing factor.

Such weighty concerns did not prevent Zdravka from reaching out to
others. On the evening that she received the news about the flight home,
she stayed at the hospital until eleven o'clock, without having dinner, to
console another Croatian mother, Anka Kocijan, whose child Marina was
rushed to the operating room with postoperative bleeding. A member of
Marina's Memphis host family, a young woman who was Zdravka's age,
nearly fainted during the tense ordeal of several hours, and Zdravka
tended her, applying a cold compress and sitting with her in the waiting
room until she felt better.

"I'm lucky that people care about me. It's like a miracle," said
Zdravka in a *Commercial Appeal* editorial. The care was abundant in
Zdravka's hectic last days before the December 16 departure, as assorted

well-wishers said their goodbyes or assisted Zdravka to make hers by buying gifts or helping her pack. Kerrigan gave Zdravka a chain with a silver
cross that he had worn since early childhood; Ivan would be buried wearing it. A going-away party was thrown for her by parishioners at Holy
Spirit, at which time she received approximately six months' worth of
train fare for the two-hour round-trip commute from her home to Rebro
Hospital in Zagreb, where Ivan was to stay indefinitely.

Two television channels and a *Commercial Appeal* photographer joined
Zdravka and Ivan on the tarmac of the Memphis International Airport
under leaden late-afternoon skies as they awaited the U.S. Air Force
plane's arrival. Debbie and her daughter Corey were at the airport for the
Pozaric farewell. The final image Memphians had of mother and son was of
Zdravka waving a tearful goodbye as her son was carried, hooked to the
ever-present respirator, onto the plane. "Like a hero going home," said
Novick on television that night.

Meanwhile, for Elizabeth Christ, the story did not end with the closing of the military plane's door and the takeoff from Memphis on that
gloomy Friday. For her, the story was just beginning. Ivan's fate and
Zdravka's support were in her hands on the first leg of the trip, to Washington, D.C. She would be replaced by Novick for the rest of the mission.
"It was kind of scary," she said. "When the plane took off, I started realizing I would have to be the nurse *and* the respiratory therapist *and* the
doc.... It was different from anything I had ever done before and more
responsibility than I had ever had before. I was taking on this kid who
had been so sick, to whom so much had happened. He was also a symbol—one of the first kids everybody knew so well and who was there so
long. It was intimidating."

Although Christ was at Ivan's bedside in the postoperative hours and
had worked in the ICU for most of the four months that Ivan and
Zdravka were there, the young women did not formally meet until a
week before they took the flight together. Prior to their meeting Christ
had an ongoing, though distant, compassion for Zdravka. "I felt really
bad for her because she seemed so alone and so far from home. Everything was going so badly for Ivan, and whenever I saw her it made my
heart hurt. I couldn't imagine how hard it must have been for her."

Then, on call in the unit one December night, Christ was asked by nurses about sedating Ivan intravenously. "They had been putting two or three IVs a day in Ivan, and he looked like a pin cushion. His little veins were so fragile from being hospitalized so long," said the doctor. "I went in the room to see what was going on, and Zdravka got upset, started crying, and left the room. I didn't know why, so I followed her and she cried on my shoulder for a little while. Then I brought her back to the room and she tried to explain to me why she was upset. Ivan's ventilator settings had gone up during the day, and his movement disorder was worse. The combination overwhelmed her. I called Azra [Sehic], and through her we just talked a little bit. With Azra translating, I told her I liked her boots. She kind of laughed and said something in Croatian—she had seen mine a few weeks before, liked them, and bought a pair herself! That broke the ice, and since I was at the end of my shift, I asked if she wanted to go shopping. We went to a mall with that Croatian-English dictionary and discovered we were both Catholic, liked the same clothes, and overall felt that we had much in common."

In the air it was apparent to the young doctor that the military personnel on the plane "were nice and willing to help, but they expected us to take care of him, so I turned to Zdravka and told her it was *our* job to take care of Ivan." Three unscheduled stops turned the two-hour flight to Andrews Air Force Base in the suburbs of the nation's capital into a six-hour odyssey. One of the stops was because the oxygen on the plane was about to run out. All the plane's power was turned off, and oxygen was brought in by ambulances on the runway. Christ and Zdravka gave oxygen to Ivan with a bag, by flashlight, while mechanics refueled the oxygen system. "Then Ivan's fever went up," said Christ, "and we didn't have any Tylenol. Zdravka had some in her purse—adult Tylenol caplets—and we tried to smash one up and work it through his naso-gastric tube, but it clogged up. It was an eventful flight, but luckily he was stable the whole time."

Christ and Zdravka parted tearfully in Washington when Novick took the helm for the remainder of the journey: a trip from Washington to Ramstein military base in Germany, and the final leg from Ramstein to Zagreb. Things heated up for Novick before he reached Ramstein; he was trying to vanquish the fever that Ivan had developed, and he found himself dressed for winter in the summerlike climate of the Azores during a brief stopover.

Ivan went into cardiac arrest on the flight from Germany to Croatia. "The plane had taken off from Ramstein, and no sooner did the pilot announce that we were over Zagreb than the flight nurse told me there was something wrong with the EKG," said Novick. "I jumped out of my seat. There was nothing wrong with the EKG—Ivan's heart rhythm had degenerated to ventricular fibrillation." Ventricular fibrillation is a condition in which the electrical impulses of the heart are no longer coordinated. The result is that no blood is pumped from the heart, a situation that, if uncorrected, is fatal.

"This was terrible. I had a feeling of complete and utter frustration for about a minute," continued Novick. "Then it changed to a feeling of profound anger at fate. I felt frustrated that we had brought him all the way home and the little guy died before he could land in his own country. The moment his country was announced, he died! It took me about a minute while we were resuscitating him to get over that frustration and to be angry at the situation. I made up my mind that there was no way in hell he was going to die in the air over Croatia. The pilot asked, 'Do you want us to divert?' And I said, 'We're landing this plane. I'm coding [attempting to resuscitate] this kid all the way down, onto the runway, into the ambulance, and into the hospital if I have to!' And we resuscitated him and his heart picked back up about the time the landing gear locked into place. I could see the runway when all of a sudden the EKG picked back up. So he landed alive, and we shifted him over to the Croatian ambulance and got him to the hospital."

Ivan woke up in his homeland about thirty-six hours later. He had been heavily sedated for the trip, and the Zagreb doctors continued the sedation for an additional twenty-four hours. "We were able to stop all the cardiac support medicines, and he looked pretty good when he woke up," said Novick, who stayed at Rebro University Hospital for two days. "When I left, he was back to his usual state of wakefulness, and he was on no significant support medicines."

But that was to be the last medical comeback Ivan would muster. A few days after Christmas, Ivan developed pneumonia, a complication he was unable to shake. Seventeen days after returning home, he died. "Boy Who Was Local Heart Patient Dies In Croatia," stated the *Commercial Appeal* January 9 in a brief story that recapitulated Ivan's history.

Reaction to the boy's death from those closest to him in Memphis struck a common theme of sadness but relief.

Novick: "I felt depressed but relieved for both Ivan and his parents."

Debbie: "I felt sad for Zdravka and Dejan, but I also felt relief. Watching her watch him was grueling. Ivan needed to get back home, so his family could go through the process with him, and so Zdravka could have support."

Christ: "I felt terrible when he died, but by that time I expected it because he had coded several times. He had been through so much and hadn't gotten better."

Biserka: "I was very upset and sad because I was very far from Zdravka and I couldn't help her or come to the funeral. I told myself and her that the only thing I could do was to offer a Mass for Ivan."

Ivan was buried on a snowy hillside overlooking Krapina—in a grave replete with floral arrangements and plants—alongside his grandfather and great-grandfather, leaving Dejan the only living male of the Pozaric line. Pictures of the Croatian funeral and the Memphis memorial service were soon swapped across the ocean, and his American caregivers had the time—and the need—to reflect on their experience. Unlike the Croatians, who seem to handle death either by repressing their feelings or ritualizing them through the funeral liturgy, the careful tending and frequent visiting of the grave, and, for females, the donning of black clothing, for Americans, processing grief has an important verbal component.

"The worst part of this was that it was a scenario that you never want to see or hear about if it's your child: 'the operation was a success, but the patient died,' as Zdravka noted," said Novick. "This kid's heart would not stop; it wouldn't quit. It carried him through some hideous times. We had entertained the hope that the Croatians would be able to rehabilitate him slowly at home, but it stretched beyond the limits of what we are able to do in medicine. If you thought about fixing holes in anybody's heart years ago, people would've laughed at you. Now we've gotten to the point where we think we can do anything. Even though we have reached the point in surgical techniques and postoperative care where we can operate on just about anyone and expect to bring them to a successful end, you have to be reminded that you're only human. To me, Ivan's case is an example of a bit of medical/surgical arrogance, of thinking you can take a disaster and turn it around. Ivan just reminded me that humility and reality go hand-in-hand. The very moment you think you're capable of anything, God and the human body will humble you very quickly."

Liz Christ, who took advantage of some vacation time to travel to Croatia and visit the Pozarics just a month after Ivan's death, said this: "Zdravka had done most of her mourning when Ivan was still in the hospital. It was as if he had died long ago. She would still get sad intermittently—she would have a faraway look in her eyes, which was perfectly normal. But she had worked through a lot of it already.

"I think it's her strength not to be bitter, not to be angry—to just deal with everything. A lot of people wouldn't have handled it as well. They either would have fallen apart or become really angry with everyone, and she had good reason to be angry. She came over here to have her kid saved and he got worse. In retrospect, he would have been a lot better off if he had just stayed home until he died from his heart disease, but there's no way you could know that ahead of time. I think she had those thoughts and those doubts, but ultimately I think she knew she did what she had to do under the circumstances.

"I've been inspired and had my faith strengthened. A lot of parents have courage and their efforts are admirable, but to be in a whole new country and to have your baby not be as he once was is something else. I hope I could act as she did."

Kerrigan was also inspired through the Pozarics. He was motivated to take up the Croatian language. "After a few days at the hospital, to greet Zdravka with *dobar dan* ("good day") and *kako ste vi?* ("how are you?") or with a few words out of the dictionary didn't seem enough for me," he said. "There were intense medical and emotional moments over the weeks, but there were many hours of waiting as well, and that's when Zdravka would teach me her language." The priest also discovered a fund-raiser side of himself in his efforts to help meet some of Zdravka's needs. At the boy's death he got a tattoo on his left arm with Ivan's name, birth date, and death date inscribed, along with the motto of the Jesuits above it in Old English script: "A.M.D.G.," Latin initials for *ad majorem dei gloria* (for the greater glory of God). "The time with Ivan and Zdravka was a turning point in my life, a time to go from being a quiet, suburban priest to an advocate and chaplain for international families. The tattoo was a way to mark that for me and for others."

Kerrigan was still gaining insight two years later, through the death of another young Croatian boy, six-month-old Mario Rabuzin from Zagreb, a boy with a constricted aorta and an obstructed aortic valve who died in the operating room in Memphis. No one from Memphis was with Zdravka when Ivan died, but Mario's death gave Kerrigan a glimpse of what it may have been like for Zdravka:

"It was the first time since Ivan died that a child from Croatia died in Memphis, and it brought everything back for me," he said. "The way this mother, Antonija, reacted was deeply awesome and beautiful to behold, sad and tragic. After she was given the bad news by the anesthesiologist in the intensive-care waiting room, Antonija was enveloped with many embraces, condolences, and tears from the half-dozen or so people around her at the time. She then went with me to a private room to await the child's body. As she wept quietly, head in hands, in those interminable minutes of waiting, and then stroking and whispering to her deceased son once his body was brought in, I felt strangely close to her, even intrusively close, although I knew it was OK for me to be there. At the same time I felt distant and remote. 'Where is the source of this woman's love? Surely I don't have it within me,' I thought. She had gone to the end of the earth to save her son and had been defeated in a matter of minutes.

"As I sat with his mother, Antonija, I couldn't help but think of Zdravka and of the intense emotion that, at least in these two grieving women, was not released in wailing or an effusion of tears but seemed to compress and intensify as it was delivered in whispers and quiet sobs. It's only when I bring Mary, the mother of God, into things that it begins to make more sense. Zdravka and Antonija and others astound me by the sheer strength of their maternal love. But when I realize I am witnessing, in their actions, a reflection of what it must have been like for Mary at the cross of Christ, I am endlessly inspired. There's a commanding and knowing presence around these mothers at what has to be the most unwelcome moment in their lives, and their strength only makes sense if you consider that the cross is ever-present for them and directs their lives, as it did for Mary. It's a very energizing realization, too; I was more alive at Mario's death or in Ivan's suffering than I am most of the time, and if that's not a little burst of resurrection right there I don't know what is.

"By nature I'm not disposed to talk of apparitions and the like, but I would not hesitate to point to these special young mothers and their suffering sons as a great example of how Christ's redemption can take shape in everyday life. With the eyes of faith, you can really see a not-too-distant incarnation of the original."

The Marian analogy with Zdravka is not entirely out of line; in fact, one night earlier in the fall, when it appeared Ivan would succumb to an infection, Debbie Petrusek remarked that watching Zdravka was "like watching Mary at the foot of the cross." Like Mary, Zdravka had a peace and strength beyond her years; she knew what it was like to flee her homeland for the sake of her son, to struggle with forces greater than she; and she seemed to know instinctively that her son would die and that she would have to be a source of strength for him in his suffering. Like Mary, she accomplished this in a simple, silent manner, and she did so without her husband at her side. The unusual assortment of people who accompanied her—the Petruseks, Christ, Novick, Kerrigan, and Sehic—served remotely but analogously as the disciples.

Others found their own spiritual message. Cindy Pease, who was asked one day early in Ivan's hospitalization to "cover" for Kerrigan and the Petruseks and thereafter became a regular visitor, had this to say: "It was a time in my life I will never forget. I thank God for allowing all of us to have the opportunity to open our hearts not only to each other but to him—through this special child and his very brave, loving mother—in trusting and realizing there is always hope."

Eileen Carroll drove Zdravka the fifteen miles from the Petruseks to the hospital at least one morning each week. "After seeing Ivan, I would come home depressed, and one day my children said, 'If it bothers you so

much, why do it?' I decided that sometimes you get hurt and feel someone else's pain; if we are to be Christian we need to take those risks."

Azra Sehic added: "Looking at how she handled what was going on
with Ivan can teach us. We are sometimes concerned about our own
problems, and we need more strength and faith."

In the spring following Ivan's death Zdravka surprised many with the
news that she was pregnant. Mothers who have lost a child at an early age,
particularly under such traumatic circumstances, are usually fearful of con-
ceiving again for many months, if at all. Liz Christ, who was part of the
Zagreb surgical team in June, ventured to Krapina to see Zdravka and
Dejan. It was clear that Ivan had not been forgotten. She recounts this story:

"Zdravka told me that she had been out in the cornfield in the middle
of a hot day in the spring when she heard a child in the distance calling
'Mama.' It sounded like Ivan, she said, but when she turned around she
didn't see anybody. I was worried about her after that, and when I was
there I asked her about him, especially if she had had any more experiences like that. I told her it was normal for parents to think they've heard
their child call their name, especially since she said she had been working for a long time out in the sun and the heat. It was then that she told
me that she had been looking back on the whole thing. Yes, Ivan had
died, but being in Memphis had been a good experience. She had made
good friends and met people she wouldn't otherwise have met. She put
her hands out as in a balance—bad things happened but good things happened. I thought it was pretty impressive that only about four months
after she'd lost her child, she could have so much faith and resolve."

Zdravka returned to Memphis with Dejan in August 1995, almost a
year to the day after her first arrival. As Zdravka and Dejan toured and
visited friends, Zdravka remarked, "Everywhere I go, everything I see, I
think of the hospital." Even as the couple relaxed as the guests of Liz
Christ on a trip to New Orleans, a city that held no reminders of Ivan,
Sehic noted that Zdravka "looked sadder than I was used to seeing her."
Dr. Christ agreed. "You could tell a lot of times that she was sad," she
observed. "Whatever it is that people mean by 'closure,' I think there was
some of that in their visit."

Zdravka and Dejan reunited with Novick, Kerrigan, Sehic, the Petruseks, and others who had been by their side a year earlier. On a seething hot afternoon they watered a pear tree planted in Ivan's memory at the Church of the Holy Spirit. But Zdravka's new life was not forgotten during their stay. Debbie Petrusek threw a baby shower for Zdravka. "People were anxious to see her and to give gifts for the new baby," she said.

"Ivan's Mom Gives Birth In Croatia," was how a *Commercial Appeal* headline reported the birth of Iva Pozaric on December 18, 1995. The healthy girl, weighing seven and a half pounds at birth, was named for her deceased brother.

Even though Iva's birth gave the Pozarics and their friends more hope than had Ivan's return to Croatia the previous Christmas, for many the enduring point of departure was still the death of Ivan and what it had meant. "When we witness the human spirit not surrendering to such suffering, how can we keep from celebrating our firm hope and belief that Ivan, and all of us, will triumph over death as well?" concluded Kerrigan in his memorial service sermon for Ivan. "Today, throughout Christianity, churches celebrate the feast of the Epiphany, a strange word that means 'making public, shining forth.' The wise men of old followed a light to pay homage to Jesus. May we in our own way pay tribute to God through Ivan by shining forth, in our lives and actions, the hope that conquers all darkness."

Ivan Pozaric, together with the steadying presence of Zdravka, was a means for a small group of people to get in touch with their own hearts and with the heart of the gospel. That was the little boy's legacy. He lifted people out of their superficiality, their lack of awareness, or their fantasies about how childhood or surgery should unfold. Standing atop a hill before Ivan's marble headstone in Krapina, one can discern, as if by design, a reflected image of oneself and the surrounding countryside. Those most touched by the story of Ivan's life and death found therein another kind of reflected marker, a window, into God's deeper truths.

Immediately after the disciples ask who will be the greatest in the kingdom, Jesus says, "Unless you turn and become like children, you will not enter the kingdom of heaven" (Mt 18:3). Worldly greatness and importance are not gospel greatness, and Ivan Pozaric briefly lifted a variety of people beyond their worldly concerns. Through him they were drawn into the values of the gospel, not the least of which is solidarity—caring about others at least as much as about yourself, especially about those who are powerless and vulnerable. In the Mediterranean world of Jesus' time children were not doted on and spoiled as they are in American culture. The writings of the era look down upon children as examples of irrational behavior or simply as objects of instruction. In Aramaic the word for child is the same as that for servant. Yet Jesus showed how essential and priceless children, and thus all people, are. Ivan Pozaric was one of the latest who reflected that truth.

During a visit to Krapina in January 1997 Kerrigan asked Zdravka: "Does God close one door only to open another?"

"Yes, God gave me this wicked little girl," Zdravka laughingly replied, as one-year-old Iva rambled around the house. But maybe it was through the little girl that a fitting conclusion could be drawn: the toy Iva carried was playing "It's a Small World After All."

Ivan Pozaric stands in the meditation garden at the Church of the Holy Spirit. Before surgery the boy was engaging and precocious.

Marija Culjak and her mother, Biserka.

3
Marija Culjak

"Marija is my cross"
—Biserka Culjak

Like a restaurant wall adorned with framed, autographed portraits of celebrity diners, the International Children's Heart Foundation has its own display of photographs on portable door-size panels. The photos of patients, medical teams, and overseas trips travel to ICHF gatherings in the Memphis area, extending an invitation into the world of international pediatric heart care. A visual stroll through the display shows Novick happily towering over a newly healed patient, or a confused and frightened seven-year-old girl sitting upright in her hospital bed, or a grateful but still-disbelieving couple exchanging goodbyes with an American nurse as they take their child home from the hospital. The images reflect the life of the ICHF; the hope is that an emotional chord will be struck in the viewers.

Novick's photograph is uncharacteristic for the surgeon. He is captured face to face with a patient, no easy feat for any 6′5″ person, much less one who makes his living ministering to children who are usually horizontal and often unconscious while in his care. In the scene Novick and the patient, Marija Culjak (pronounced Chool-yak), a three-year-old girl from the Adriatic port city of Ploce, fill the left- and right-hand sides

of the photograph with their profiles as they lean toward the center of
the frame for a kiss.

"I felt like we were saying to each other, 'We're alive!'" said Novick of
the encounter, which occurred on the pediatric cardiology floor of Rebro
University Hospital in Zagreb, where Marija had come for a semiannual
checkup following surgery. "It's very difficult to explain the happiness I
felt. It's something like the feeling you have when you look into someone's eyes and you know that you love them but you don't have to tell
them that, and you get the same look in return. With Marija, it was even
a step up from that. It's not a look I have even gotten from my children
or my wife or anyone—it was more like the anticipation of the look and
the feeling that I hope to have when I meet God. I can't explain the
depth of that moment of real knowing, except to say that I was overjoyed
to see this child looking so good."

To appreciate Novick's reaction to Marija "looking so good" that June
1995 morning in Zagreb, one has to go back to Marija "looking so bad"
in August 1994, about six hours after a successful reconstructive heart
procedure in Memphis.

"Marija had developed a dangerously fast heart rate that could have
killed her," began Novick. "She was profoundly, gravely ill. We had given
her medicines to slow her heart down and convert it to the appropriate
rhythm, but they didn't work. Then we cooled her down, which is the
next treatment, and that didn't work; her heartbeat was still in the 220
range. She was stuck there for four hours and nothing was happening.
We had shocked her several times and that didn't help; it looked like she
was literally dying in front of us. Her blood pressure was 90 over 80, just
little bitty squirts of blood coming out. She was in what we call cardio-
genic shock.

"Then I did something very unusual. I disconnected one of her chest
tubes and had people from the O.R. bring over ice-cold sterile saline. I
cleaned the tube so it wouldn't be contaminated and took the saline and
injected it right into the tube to make her heart cold. Some might call it
stupid. You could make an argument for taking her back to the operating
room and cooling her heart by putting her on the bypass machine, but

frankly, I didn't think we could get her to the operating room. If I didn't do something immediately, it wouldn't matter.

"But that did it—the saline injection worked and we got control of her rhythm again." Marija was pulled back from death's portal.

Medical skill may explain Marija's physical recovery. From a theological perspective, however, all of the little girl's life may be best understood if it is placed at the gate where the world opens up to God, a gate that Christians call the cross.

Christianity has as its defining symbol the cross of Christ. Death and life, humanity and divinity, strength and weakness, humiliation and exaltation, solitude and solidarity—just a few of the many opposing pairs that intersect in the beams of the cross, personified in the death and resurrection of Jesus. Christian wayfarers are called continually to pass through the hopes and sufferings of life by way of the cross. "He who seeks not the cross of Christ seeks not the glory of Christ," the sixteenth-century mystic St. John of the Cross once wrote.[3]

The apostle Paul, in the Letter to the Philippians, uses a hymn to describe the dynamic of transformation undergone preeminently by Jesus on the cross. The core of the hymn reads, "Rather, he emptied himself, taking the form of a slave, coming in human likeness; and found human in appearance, he humbled himself, becoming obedient to death, even death on a cross. Because of this, God greatly exalted him and bestowed on him the name that is above every name, that at the name of Jesus every knee should bend, of those in heaven and on earth and under the earth" (Phil 2:7–10).

Perhaps in lived Christianity the cross is overly associated with suffering, heaviness, and obligation. Crosses are often worn around the neck like a chain or millstone, other symbols of servitude. People speak glibly and superficially of "the crosses they have to bear" or "the cross that God gave me." Not enough is said about the redeeming aspects of the cross and its power to convert and lift up.

There were many days in Marija Culjak's early years that the burdensome side of the cross was very much in evidence. But when the little girl's mother, Biserka, said simply and finally at the end of her daughter's medical odyssey, "Marija is my cross," she had more than enough cause to share in its redemptive side as well. The Culjaks could use as their song the triumphant Christian hymn "Lift High the Cross," the refrain of which goes, "Lift high the cross, the love of Christ proclaim, till all the world adore his sacred name."

As Pope John Paul II was celebrating the Catholic faith of the people of Croatia in a two-day visit to Zagreb in early September 1994, Biserka was still finding her faith being tested far from home in Memphis, as she and her daughter persevered in what was becoming an extended course at LeBonheur Children's Medical Center. Marija was now one month into her stay in the intensive-care unit, with no timetable for discharge. Besides the initial postoperative episode of tachycardia, the girl had not yet been weaned from the ventilator and had also experienced bouts of fever and feeding difficulties.

Biserka had come to terms with those death-defying first hours after the operation—"Marija's heart had been beating the wrong way for a long time, and after the surgery it wasn't yet used to the right way"—but she was having a more difficult time accepting the frustrations of the lengthy stay in ICU.

"I don't know why God gives me this," said Biserka, as she sat on the patio of the hospital's Physician Office Building. A petite woman with a taut face, olive skin, and large, dark, somber eyes, Biserka had the uncommon look of the Dalmatian woman, a look that prompts Croatians from all regions of the country to drop their provincialism and acknowledge that "the most beautiful women in the world are from Dalmatia." Biserka continued: "When Marija was born, they said she couldn't live, but God is doing the job and she still lives. We had the chance to come to Memphis and have surgery and that also is God's job, not mine, and I must believe in him. In the surgery room God was with Marija to help her make it through...." She broke off in the middle of her thought, unable to find words to explain the girl's condition.

If her words were lacking at that moment, the faith to which Biserka testified was apparent in her actions, at least to one veteran in the intensive-care unit. Staff nurse Cathy McCown is not someone easily won over. The forty-year-old nurse has closely cropped hair, fiery blue eyes, and a commanding expression. She can flush red with anger on a moment's notice as she wheels about the floor in a forthright, take-charge fashion. But, like a coach who can scare the daylights out of the team on the first day of practice only to be adored by all by season's end, McCown was deeply compassionate, warm, and sensitive. This combination of qualities served her well in her relationship with Biserka.

McCown originally encountered Biserka and Marija during the chaotic hours immediately following surgery, when she stayed with mother and daughter through the night, well past the end of her shift. The intensity of those first few hours forged a lasting friendship between the two. "Biserka came here with faith that her daughter would get the operation she needed, survive, and go home," she began. "With all the complications that occurred, there was still ongoing faith that no matter what happened, it would be OK. It was awe-inspiring. You would give her bad news, and she would ask the appropriate questions and want to know details, but she still had this faith that transcended everything.

"You have to remember, she was looking at her child, who had more holes in her body than when she was born—tubes and machines everywhere, no movement from the baby, temperature changes that she didn't understand—it's just overwhelming," McCown said. "There's a maternal urge to protect and you can't do that, but Biserka's simple acceptance made it much easier. She stayed at Marija's bedside every moment she could, she was very thoughtful and contemplative, and she didn't allow herself to be befuddled. She would say, 'I have to cry' and she would, and she would recover—that's one tough lady."

Her toughness was reminiscent of the following lines from C. S. Lewis:

Love is as hard as nails
Love is nails
Blunt, thick, hammered through
the medial nerves of One
who, having made us, knew
the thing He had done
Seeing (with all that is)
Our Cross, and His.[4]

It's a long way from the intensive-care unit at LeBonheur to Biserka's birthplace of Knin in southern Croatia. The lonely, mountainous outpost of Knin is a long way from anything, noted only as an important rail and road link between Zagreb and the Adriatic Coast.

Before the recent war Knin was just one of many towns and villages that had a significant population of Serbs. In a 1991 census 88 percent of Knin's forty-two thousand residents were listed as Serbians. It was in Knin that the Serbian Democratic Party was formed in February 1990, under the leadership of Milan Babic and Jovan Raskovic. Later that year the Serbs demanded autonomy and wrested control of the local government from Croatian authorities. Through this so-called Knin Rebellion the war in Croatia began. With the retaking of Knin in an assault by the Croatian military in August 1995, the war in Croatia ended.

Along the sparkling Adriatic on a warm, crystalline autumn afternoon in the fall of 1995, with water lapping at her feet, birds calling in the distance, and the breeze blowing her straight, shoulder-length, brown hair across her face, Biserka sat on rocks gently washed by the sea and recalled her life in straightforward, no-nonsense English. She was born in Knin in 1962 and lived there for her first eighteen years before going to college in Mostar, Herzegovina. Specializing in economics, she completed college and returned to her hometown as a schoolteacher. But she had some unfinished business in Mostar. "I met my husband, Goran, there, when I was finishing college. After two years of friendship, we married in 1986," she said.

For most of Biserka's life, expressions of religious faith had to remain private. "We had churches, but with the communist system you couldn't really go," she said. "I prayed by myself, and we would celebrate Christmas and Easter quietly at home. The priest would come to the house once a year for a blessing, and we would go to church to learn about religion from the priests." When she attended college in Mostar, where there was a healthy mix of Orthodox Serbs and Bosnian Muslims, it was "easier to go to church, because nobody knew you," but when the time came for her wedding in Ploce, where Goran lived, she opted not to have a church ceremony. She explained, "If you were married in a church at that time, you might lose your job."

The couple settled in Ploce, a small port town of thirteen thousand residents about halfway between Split and Dubrovnik. They settled into their careers—Goran with the railroad and Biserka keeping the books for a glass factory. Two years into their marriage, they celebrated the birth of their first child, Mario.

The war between the Serbs and Croats started in the summer of 1991. At the same time Biserka became pregnant with Marija. "That was the beginning of the hard part of our life," she reflected. "I know that it was not the best time to become pregnant, but I wanted a baby." Goran volunteered to serve in the army at the war's outset and was stationed in a small town, Ston, close to Dubrovnik. By September hostilities had escalated. "JNA [Yugoslav Peoples' Army] ships surrounded the town, and they turned the guns toward the city. You never knew when they would start shooting. Airplanes flew over the town all the time, and we spent a lot of time in the shelters, since we didn't know when they would start shooting."

Biserka was pregnant, and Mario was only three years old. They were living in a six-story apartment complex built in 1968, replete with concrete walls and terrazzo floors. The Culjaks' balcony overlooked the port and the rocky hills to the west and south. Twenty-four families lived in the building, four per floor, and the residents often had to go to the shelter in the cellar, carrying everything they needed for an extended stay. "It was very, very hard," she said in a subdued tone. "I was alone with Mario, Marija was in my womb, and Goran was fighting."

Beyond these immediate concerns, there were anxieties about her family back in Knin and Goran's family just outside Mostar, where "we were just waiting for the war to start there any minute." Close to the end of her pregnancy Biserka's family made it out of Knin and came to Ploce. One of the consequences of life in the new age of "ethnic cleansing" was the rise of an informal house-swapping network. For example, if you were a Croat and were displaced from your home, it was best to try to exchange your residence with one in another town formerly occupied by a Serb. Biserka's parents were successful in trading their house in Knin for one in Zadar, and not long after their arrival in Ploce they moved to Zadar and started living there. The violence in that coastal town seemed to have quieted down for the moment. In Mostar, where Goran's parents lived, such an arrangement was not possible, however, as the Culjak home was burned by Muslims. The family had no alternative but to flee to Goran and Biserka's small, two-bedroom apartment.

Before she gave birth to Marija, doctors told Biserka that the baby's size was not what it should be. They recommended that she go to a hospital in Split for further monitoring and also told her that she would probably give birth before the actual due date. Biserka's mother came to Ploce to take young Mario back to Zadar with her. Once Biserka was in the hospital, a sonogram showed that the baby was wrapped by the umbilical cord and could suffocate inside her mother. At the same time the Serbian siege of Sarajevo began only a day's drive away. Doctors decided to perform a cesarean section, and Marija was born on April 17, 1992. "Right after her birth, right after the surgery, they told me that she was tiny, like a little cat, but healthy," Biserka remembered. "But after two or three days Marija turned blue, and they saw something was wrong. They thought it was either the kidneys or the heart, but they finally decided that something was wrong with her heart." At the time it was impossible to go to Zagreb because of the war, and Marija spent one month in the hospital in Split, first in an incubator and then in a regular nursery.

When travel conditions improved, mother and child took the first Croatia Airlines flight that was available from Split to Zagreb and went immediately to Rebro University Hospital. Dr. Marinovic was waiting for them and performed a cardiac catheterization. "He said her situation was very complicated, that there was nobody in this world who could do this surgery because the arteries around her heart were very small," said Biserka. "I thought that he didn't believe she would survive."

Marija suffered from two major problems: pulmonary atresia and a ventricular septal defect (VSD). Normally, blue blood returns from the veins in the body into the right atrium. The blood is then pumped from the right atrium across the tricuspid valve, which functions like a one-way door into the right ventricle. Continuing its journey, the blood is ejected from the right ventricle through the pulmonary valve—another door—into the oxygen-rich lungs. The blood, now full of life and red in color, is returned to the heart through the arteries of the lungs to the left side of the heart, where it is pumped into the body, completing the circuit.

Pulmonary atresia has many faces, but the most common problem is that the blue blood from the right ventricle cannot get into the pulmonary arteries and is thus thwarted from obtaining oxygen replenishment in the lungs. Sometimes the door to the lungs cannot open (the pulmonary valve will not open), and sometimes the hallway to the lungs (the pulmonary artery) is not there. For the child to live, there must be some natural or manmade bypass that allows blood to get to the lungs to receive oxygen. Children with this defect, like Marija, appear cyanotic, or blue.

A ventricular septal defect is a hole in the muscular wall (ventricular septum) that divides the red-blood pumping chamber from the blue-blood pumping chamber. A VSD may be the only defect in a child's heart or, as with Marija, it may be found in combination with other defects. In Marija's case, and with many congenital heart disease patients, one defect helps to compensate for another. Her pulmonary atresia was compensated for by the persistence of a fetal connection. In the womb the child does not actually breathe, and the lungs do not expand with air. There is a bypass around the lungs called the patent ductus arteriosus. The child's first breath starts a reaction that leads to the closure of this bypass circuit. "You imagine how this bypass circuit can be beneficial to children with pulmonary atresia," said Novick. "The persistence of the patent ductus arteriosus may serve as the only source of pulmonary blood flow." In addition, the size of the PDA or other natural bypasses determines the amount of oxygen in the blood.

Marija was admitted to the Rebro hospital, where she was monitored for an additional two months, although there was some concern related to the lack of oxygen in her blood. Upon her discharge, Biserka was given an outlook with muted hope: if Marija improved and her arteries got bigger, then surgery could be done, but not in Croatia, where the expertise was not available.

Biserka took Marija home to Zadar for a few months. The major incentives for residing there were a pediatric cardiologist with a good reputation and the fresh air along the Adriatic. Marija's primary problem during this time was her poor appetite, but Biserka was resourceful. "I fed her at nighttime. While she was asleep, I would put a bottle in her mouth and she would swallow," she said. Incredibly, this was the feeding regimen for most of Marija's first year, and it resulted in the youngster's growth and prevented additional health problems. "On the one hand, the nightly feeding made sense, when you think about the tenacity of infants with their pacifiers," noted McCown. "On the other hand, how many mothers would ever think of that by themselves? It just shows how many hours Biserka must have spent watching her child."

After Marija's first birthday it was time to call upon Dr. Marinovic to chart the girl's progress. A catheterization revealed that the pulmonary arteries were indeed getting bigger. Surgery was now feasible. Even more encouraging was the news that a children's heart foundation was being formed in Memphis by a surgeon who had made a couple of trips to Zagreb. It would be possible for Marija to go to Tennessee for the surgery under the auspices of this foundation. On the down side, Marinovic cautioned Biserka that Marija's condition warranted immediate attention, and he reminded her that nothing more could be done for the girl in Zagreb.

The plan was for Marija to travel to Memphis in April 1994, right around the time of her second birthday. However, in January of that year her condition worsened. Marinovic felt that the little girl would not survive the trek to Memphis, and a shunt was inserted between the systemic circulation and the pulmonary artery to provide more blood to the lungs. Marija would need six months to recover from the procedure and get the clearance to fly to Memphis.

In August the Culjaks got the call to go to Memphis. The Croatian Ministry of Health paid ten thousand dollars toward the cost of the surgery, and Goran's railway company raised money for the airfare. There was one remaining matter to attend to, a visit to Medjugorje, the Catholic pilgrimage site set in the Herzegovinian hills about an hour's drive from Ploce. "Before going to Memphis, we went to Medjugorje to pray to Mary for help for Marija—that the surgery would go well and that we would come back healthy," recalled Biserka. "I named Marija after Mary, thinking that a mother is a mother. Mary knows what it means to love a child, and she is the only one who could understand me. I never asked God for a miracle. I asked for my child to stay alive, although I would accept any decision God would make. If he wanted to take Marija,

I would be all right with that. If he left Marija with me, I would be glad. But it is God's decision."

While Biserka may not have prayed for a miracle, a surgeon constantly aspires to the miraculous, or at least to do something that is not routine. "There is the excitement of using your hands and mind to design and conduct an operation, but certain operations provide an intellectual and artistic challenge that make you reach for the mountaintop," said Novick. "Unfortunately, those same operations can take you to the bottom of the Marianas Trench [the deepest spot in the world at over thirty-six thousand feet below sea level]."

The plan for Marija entailed two major parts: (1) a homograft, or human valve, to cover the space from the pulmonary ventricle to the pulmonary artery (dozens of these valves, each worth around five thousand dollars, have been donated for ICHF use by Cryolife); (2) widening the pulmonary artery, because the shunt had caused narrowing of the artery. The shunt would be tied off and the VSD closed to achieve the goal of the left ventricle ejecting blood into the aorta instead of the pulmonary artery.

This operation was introduced in 1965 by Gian Rastelli. The Rastelli operation, if conducted properly, is not difficult; Novick estimated that the entire operation could probably be completed in three hours or so, with the Rastelli portion taking approximately an hour. Time is a factor because when the clamp is placed on the aorta at the beginning of an operation, it causes an artificial heart attack. There is a limited amount of time to complete the work before the artificial heart attack causes life-threatening damage.

"What makes the Rastelli challenging is doing it on very small children, or when it has to be done with a lot of reconstruction of the pulmonary arteries, as with Marija," continued Novick. "Basically, all you're doing is opening the right ventricle and patching a hole shut, then sewing a valve conduit onto the pulmonary artery, and then sewing the conduit onto the ventricle. There are multiple opportunities to make a mistake, but by and large it's not a technically demanding operation."

For Biserka, the new surroundings and the reality facing her upon arrival in Memphis were challenging enough. "I was very scared, but I acted like everything was OK," she revealed. "What I felt inside was only for me and not for others around me." Biserka's fears were warranted. "This child was blue beyond blue when she got off the plane," said McCown. "It was remarkable that Marija lived long enough to get to Memphis."

After the victory over Marija's initial postoperative crisis, the list of setbacks and advances in her medical course was as sinuous and lengthy as the Adriatic coastal highway. For three days immediately following the tachycardia she was anesthetized to allow her kidneys and other functions to return to normal. Several days after she was stable enough to be awakened, an attempt was made to wean her from the ventilator. It was unsuccessful. Tests of her heart, lungs, and breathing failed to reveal anything awry, yet she was unable to come off the breathing machine. A fever followed, which led the medical team to believe that a low-grade pneumonia might be stalling her quest for independent breathing. After days of treating what would prove to be a phantom case of pneumonia, she was again unable to be weaned from the ventilator. Then, two weeks into her intensive-care stay, Marija began bleeding from her endotracheal tube, the tube bringing air to her lungs. A test of the airway passages, a bronchoscopy, was done, and again nothing was found wrong.

"I was starting to wonder why we couldn't come out of this," recalled Novick. "I had one more echocardiogram done, and I was told that maybe she still had a small hole in her heart. So I asked the cardiology department for a cardiac catheterization. And sure enough, a leftover VSD was found. A lot of people would argue that she probably had a residual VSD from the minute the operation was concluded, and that's why she had the tachycardia."

How could a ventricular septal defect be discovered now, when the girl's operation was to fix it in the first place? Novick explained: "You have a hole—that's the VSD—you get a piece of material and you cut it out the same size as the hole and sew it into place, and it's closed. Right? Wrong. It's closed right that second, but then the heart starts beating. If problems occur after the operation, you have to ask yourself, why is this happening? Did the string pull through the muscle? Did the muscle pull? Did it get infected? Did the child receive too much fluid, so the heart swelled up and the patch no longer fits? Or have I completely corrected this child's defect? Nobody knows.

"This was a straightforward operation—not one of those where you have to struggle and think that maybe you've left a hole and worry if the patch fits right. Boom, there's a hole, and boom, let's sew it shut. But there was a hole when we took her to the cath lab on her fifteenth day post-op."

Novick told Biserka that he didn't think Marija would come off the ventilator easily unless the VSD was fixed, and so the girl was taken back to the operating room. "My boss, Dr. Watson, told me that his boss had left children with holes like this and they went away. Maybe somebody with more experience wouldn't have taken her back to the operating room," said Novick. "But what we found in the O.R. was that about a third of the circumference of the patch had torn from the muscle. So we re-stitched it, and her blood flow improved.

"We made a decision after that operation that we wouldn't push her for a week. We would just give her tube feedings and see how she did. Only then did we start to try and wean her from the ventilator again. Fortunately, she responded this time."

As she began to breathe on her own, two-year-old Marija finally began to emerge as a person. Previously, she could only be described as a frail girl who remotely resembled her mother. "I did not see her awake or moving for three or four days after the initial operation. Because she had been through so much there was a question about her neurological status. Would she still be Marija when she woke up?" asked McCown, who had become Marija's primary nurse. "She was feisty, like a child is feisty when half asleep, but when she really woke up, she wouldn't move. She didn't cry; she would squint her eyes and whimper but not cry. She never smiled. But after a while, after seeing the same faces day in and day out, she began to respond."

Finally freed from breathing assistance, tiny Marija was very weak, and tube feeding was still being provided. Marija and Biserka were learning to be daughter and mother all over again, only this time, learning to be together included frequent changes in Marija's diet and medicines and a constant monitoring of her weight gain and activity level. "These were days of patience and fine-tuning," said McCown, "and Biserka kept vigil faithfully." Little by little the girl improved. Her blond hair and blue eyes seemed to brighten with her recovery. Marija's wan and washed-out look slowly took on more of her mother's intense expression.

Then a new problem emerged. Marija developed a buildup of fluids following the second operation. The fluids were fatty, containing a lot of lymph, white blood cells and fat that normally travel from the gut up to the neck so that it all can be put back into circulation. Fortunately the problem resolved on its own after ten days, just when the medical team was contemplating the possibility of a third operation on the girl. "Just when no one thought that the liquid would stop accumulating, it did," was Biserka's assessment.

On September 27, seven weeks after her admission to the hospital, Marija was sent home. She had spent a little over four weeks in ICU, one week in the transitional-care unit (a step-down care unit for children not quite ready for a regular bed but not sick enough to require ICU attention), and the rest of the time in a private room on the patient floor.

"She was a real challenge for me.... She had a stormy course, but it was very gratifying in the long run," concluded Novick. "The most gratifying thing about this child's whole trip took place in the hospital clinic during her last visit. Biserka and Marija were to leave for Croatia in a couple of days. Biserka was told that Marija would need another operation, probably in 1999–the graft would not be big enough for her after a few years. Like every mother whose child needs another operation, Biserka said she wanted to come back to America for the operation. Coming from Biserka, though, it meant more. She broke down in sort of a thankful cry and said no matter what anybody told her, there was only one place and one person for her child's next operation. That kind of faith brought tears to my eyes. I told her, 'Biserka, any competent pediatric heart surgeon in the world can replace your daughter's conduit.' Her comment was that the person who brought her daughter through all the difficulties was going to be the person to change the conduit. We exchanged a look of knowing awareness–she wasn't going to go anywhere else, and I would be more than happy, no matter when, where, or how, to do this for her daughter." For Novick, it was a moment most humans savor: the joy of seeing your best self reflected in the affirmation of another.

Upon returning to Croatia in October of 1994 Marija was fine for one month, and then she developed pneumonia and had to spend another month in Zagreb at Rebro. "In the beginning doctors were very scared that this could be a big complication," said Biserka. "But God was with us again, he helped Marija go through all that, and since then Marija hasn't had any problems. She's a really happy and healthy little girl."

There's a well-traveled story about a man who explained his spiritual conversion as follows: "Before I met God, I was lonely, depressed, angry. After I met God, I'm still lonely, depressed, angry. But, thanks be to God, loneliness is not the same anymore, depression is not the same anymore, anger is not the same anymore." Biserka gave the story her own spin: "Before Marija's illness we didn't have our own apartment, we didn't have a car, I wasn't working. After her birth her life was in danger, and that was the one and only problem. Now that Marija is a healthy child, we still have the other problems—we don't have a car, we don't have our own apartment, and I am not employed. We still think about those problems but in a very different way now. I was prepared for Marija's death at any moment, but after a long time of looking death in the eye a person starts to weigh things differently."

"God did the most in all of this—we did the least," Biserka said. The acknowledgment of God's role was never far from the family. A year after Marija's return to Ploce, Kerrigan joined the Culjaks—Biserka, Goran, Marija, and Mario—in a visit to Medjugorje. "Their determination to go to Medjugorje together and climb Apparition Hill to thank God for Marija's health impressed me," said the priest. "I know they prayed before, during, and after their ordeal, but I felt as though my arrival in their town was a call to prayer for them. It was like an Old Testament scene, maybe even a little like the dutiful faith of Abraham as he offered his son Isaac on the altar, only here were the Culjaks going up the mountain to offer thanks for all the great things God had done for them in Memphis." Marija wanted to walk up the hill by herself, but the steep and rocky hill would be very difficult for any child her age. She was carried up, complaining. Biserka and Goran let her walk down, however, and she did so uneventfully.

"Marija is feeling good. God decided that Marija could be with me, and I am very grateful to him for the decision," said Biserka. "I'm very glad that I can watch my daughter grow, and that I can try to make her happy. She is still my special contact with God.

"Marija looks like a very happy and healthy child right now—even though I still am scared sometimes, not all the time. I would like to forget all those hard times, but they are still present in my mind and still sometimes scare me. What else could happen? Sometimes I think, what else will God give us, what kind of adventures? I always try to calm myself with the thought that God will be with us. In Memphis I thought that God's messages could be read clearly even though what was happening to Marija was not always clear. Everyone has a cross. Marija is my cross, and God does not give a cross to anyone bigger than the person can carry. Right now, I think I am carrying the cross well, and I hope it will stay like this in the future. After all the hard times that we survived, a lot of things changed. I pray to God for her health and also for my family's health."

"Marija challenged all of us to the best of our abilities—Novick included," said McCown from her ten years' experience in the intensive-care unit. "She had God on our shoulders, and she would not have survived without God. Anybody who took care of Marija, especially during those early days, knows that it wasn't anything that we did."

"Christianity does not ask us to live in the shadow of the cross but in the fire of its creative action," Teilhard de Chardin once wrote. Look closely at a photograph of Novick and Marija, and perhaps you will sense that creative action of the cross at work in the space between doctor and patient. One thing is certain: Marija's heart shines forth as vivid testimony to the wondrous power of the cross governing the events of her life, and to the profound nurturing collaboration of a mother's steadfast love. May every heart resound accordingly!

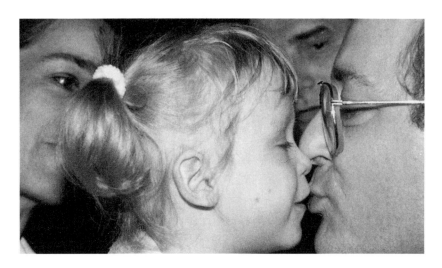

Marija Culjak and Novick exchange a kiss at Rebro University
Hospital in Zagreb.

Zvonimir Rak, surrounded by toys, and his mother, Snjezana, in his hospital room at LeBonheur Children's Medical Center. The boy had received lifesaving heart surgery just a few days earlier.

4
Zvonimir Rak

"Jinglebells"

In June 1995 Kerrigan's first stop on a seven-city, eleven-day journey
to Croatia and Bosnia-Herzegovina was the Croatian port city of Split,
located at the heart of the country's scenic Adriatic coast. Waiting for
him at the Split airport was three-year-old Zvonimir Rak (pronounced
Rahk) and his parents Snjezana (Snee-yeah-john-ah) and Grgo. Zvonimir,
a sandy-haired only child with a precocious and ever-present glint of mis-
chief in his eyes, had undergone successful corrective heart surgery at
LeBonheur Children's Medical Center just four months before. For Kerrigan, Zvonimir's continuing health was especially important to establish
from the trip's outset.

Zvonimir greeted the priest with a wide array of animal imitations he
couldn't wait to show off, and, like any youngster in an airport, he was
thrilled by the variety of airplanes and other vehicles present. "He's
good, he's healthy," said his thirty-one-year-old mother, Snjezana, whose
cheerfulness and hearty laughter was suggested by her full, rosy cheeks.
"He runs all day, trying to catch small turkeys and chickens in the yard,
and when he's not running he drives a toy car."

89

With Croatian nationalism on the rise during Snjezana's pregnancy, Zvonimir was an apt name for her firstborn. Loosely translated, *Zvonimir* means "ringing peacefully," or, as Snjezana would always introduce him, "Jinglebells." Many of the vehicles Zvonimir pointed to at the airport had "UN" lettering painted on them. In the days of United Nations peacekeeping, Split became one of the key transport points for convoys going to and from neighboring Bosnia; one could not travel very far in any direction in Croatia without encountering UN personnel or equipment. In the midst of Kerrigan's stay at the Rak's farm in Danilo, just outside Šibenik (pronounced She-bay-neek), the family interrupted farming activities to watch whenever UN helicopters whirred above the otherwise idyllic pastoral setting. In Šibenik the Cathedral of St. James the Apostle and other religious and cultural monuments have a Renaissance beauty from a distance, only to reveal unsightly shell-scarred walls upon closer inspection. The damage to the Šibenik cathedral is particularly galling; the church's dome, pierced by Serbian artillery in September 1991, was originally constructed in the fifteenth century by an elaborate process using grooved stone slabs.

The coastal geography, with its tough, mountainous, lunar features set against the deep, inviting blue of the Adriatic Sea, is perhaps the best symbol of the country's disparity. The U.S. military plane crash in Dubrovnik in April 1996, which took the lives of Commerce Secretary Ron Brown and thirty-four others, gave American viewers a glimpse of the terrain.

To Novick and Kerrigan the Croatian people are likewise drawn to contrasting extremes, not to moderation. On first impression the men and women appear very attractive or rather repulsive, with few in the middle. For every tall, dark, and exotically beautiful Croatian, there is another who is craggy, gnarled, and prematurely aged. The large, dark, and penetrating eyes of Croatians of all levels of beauty seem to be a national trait, but they can betray either a refreshing honesty and directness or a sinister spirit of lying and subterfuge—and sometimes a little of both. Croatians eat, drink, smoke, and entertain heartily when the hardships of war do not deprive them of such indulgences. They also seem to gravitate to either love or hate, freedom or imprisonment, boastfulness or humility, war or surrender—but not to peace, at least in the fullest sense of the term, the internationally bro-kered peace accord notwithstanding.

Zvonimir, too, behaved immoderately. He could usually be found either at the center of attention, launching into the rambling monologues characteristic of three-year-olds, or cowering in fear behind a stuffed toy bear or his parents' legs when he felt uncomfortable with strangers. Ask the youngster to "give you five" and hold out your palm for him, and he would either oblige energetically or blurt out "I will give you nothing." Zvonimir developed a fondness for American culture. During his stay in Memphis, hamburgers, French fries, and pizza quickly replaced eggs, onions, and ham as his favorites. By 1997, with a satellite dish now in place at his home, Zvonimir was learning English through the exploits of the Flintstones, Tom and Jerry, and other popular cartoon characters.

Zvonimir was born in November 1991 in Šibenik, a strategically placed coastal town of eighty-five thousand residents at the mouth of the Krka River, a little over an hour's drive from Split. He arrived during a brief period of peace after the first Serbian attacks on the town, though war was raging elsewhere in Croatia. "In the year before his birth we lived very tensely, looking forward anxiously to what would happen," said Snjezana in serviceable English. "In the summer of 1990 the Serbs blockaded our roads. They had guns from the Yugoslav Peoples' Army [JNA] to protect the unarmed Serbian people from the 'genocidal' Cro-atian people. But we had no guns at that time. My husband was needed to protect important places in Šibenik at night."

In the summer of 1991 the serious aggression started, first in Slovenia and then in Dalmatia. Snjezana recalled the first attack on Šibenik. "Inside of Šibenik the JNA had troops encamped—they attacked us from the sea, from inside of the city, from the air, and from hills on the north side. We went without water for twenty days, and for the next six months we would have water a few hours a day and the rest we would not. Many times we went without electricity."

It was difficult for Snjezana to become pregnant, and even when she did she recalls her gynecologist, Dr. Franje Mikulandra, constantly say-ing, "Mrs. Rak, be careful and take care of yourself. You know best how hard it was to get what you have."

"I was always thinking, 'What God gives God will protect,'" she said. "And I believed that all the time. I had no unusual problems during my pregnancy, but I had the flu in the sixth or seventh week."

Four days before her pregnancy was full-term, Snjezana was admitted to the Šibenik hospital and labor was induced; the doctors had been looking at the baby's heartbeat before he was born. "I noticed changes in the numbers on the instruments," Snjezana remembered. "But the doctor came and said, 'It is good.' After that I didn't worry about the heart."

After five hours of labor, Zvonimir Rak was born November 14. He weighed seven pounds, eleven ounces, and was twenty inches long. As Zvonimir's mother reported, "At first he had no problem and he didn't get any medical help." But upon breastfeeding the new baby in the hospital, Snjezana "heard him breathing strangely. Another mother in the room asked me about his breathing. When Zvonimir and I left the hospital, the pediatrician said: 'He has a heart murmur, but don't worry. Today they look after that very carefully and successfully. Come visit me after one month and I will send you to a heart specialist.' I went home peacefully."

When she went to visit Dr. Mikulandra, he again said: "Take care of what you have; you know best how hard it was to get what you have." The words were ominous, presaging a series of troubles. Zvonimir began to lose weight and turn blue, signs of inadequate oxygen in his blood. In cases like this, the child's energy is depleted and none is left for body fat and muscle; the bluish color is often the result of an insufficient amount of blood getting to the lungs. In addition, Zvonimir became fearful and cried a lot. He was admitted to the hospital. "A very young doctor listened to him with a stethoscope, and when he heard his heart he made me very nervous," said Snjezana. "He said to me: 'He has a heart murmur and you don't worry?' I was thinking, what does he mean? I am not a medical person and I don't know about heart murmurs. The doctor sent us to see a heart specialist, who said, 'I suspect what the diagnosis is, but I can't be 100 percent sure. Go to Zagreb, where they will do better tests.' It sounded impossible to me. I asked him, 'Must I go now?' He said, 'If you don't want to, you don't need to. I will give you two days to make a decision. Or you can come back here in a month.' But before two days were out I had to go see him again."

Zvonimir, who was discharged after the visit with the heart specialist, had to be readmitted; he had become bluer and his weight gain was inadequate. This time there were no options. Snjezana said: "The doctors told me: 'Tomorrow morning you must go to Zagreb. We will send an ambulance, and only one parent can go with him. You decide which of you will go, but we think it would be better if your husband went.' But my husband couldn't go. He was in the police and couldn't leave without special permission, and he was not able to obtain that. The next morning Zvonimir and I, along with one nurse and the ambulance driver, left Šibenik."

The trip went well. When the ambulance reached Zadar and Karlovac, two key Croatian towns in the conflict that had experienced major shelling, all was quiet. "We were lucky," said Snjezana. "When we reached Rebro Hospital, the nurses couldn't believe that we had made the trip. We went through the usual admitting procedures, and I was told: 'He looks very good. He has good weight. It isn't anything serious, he will be fine. Dr. Marinovic [pediatric cardiologist] will look after him, and he will have more to say.' My mother and I left the hospital to stay with my uncle in Zagreb."

But all was not well with Zvonimir. He was born with very complex defects, including only a single ventricle and an obstruction to blood flow to the lung. In addition, his heart was pointing toward the right instead of toward the left.

Snjezana got the bad news on her second day in Zagreb. "A doctor in the pediatric ward said to me: 'He is very seriously ill. The defect is very bad. Maybe he will need surgical correction immediately. In that case you will need to go to Šibenik and get papers for him and you and then you will wait—we will call you. But Dr. Marinovic still doesn't know for sure whether Zvonimir needs surgical correction immediately or whether he can wait. He is doing more tests and we will see. He will talk with you when he is finished, and he will tell you everything. After a few days we will know.'"

Zvonimir's defect, the absence of two functional pumping chambers, resulted in a mixing of red and blue blood, and this less-than-healthy mixture of blood was then exported to the body and lungs. Normally, the blue-blood chamber pumps blood into the pulmonary artery, which distributes the blue blood to the lungs so that oxygen can mix with it there and make it red. The red-blood chamber pumps oxygenated blood out of the aorta to all the parts of the body, which need oxygen to function. The two pumping chambers normally are separated by a thick wall of muscle (interventricular septum), so no mixing of red and blue blood occurs; each half of the body's blood circulation has a separate pumping chamber to push the blood along properly. The chaos that results when there is only one pumping chamber has obvious consequences to all aspects of health and can be immediately life-threatening for children like Zvonimir. The fact that such children survive birth and sometimes live for years without surgery is a testament to human adaptability and to a fortuitous combination of other defects that can occur with only one pumping chamber. In a sense Zvonimir and others like him are already miracles, even before surgical correction.

The trio of defects that affected Zvonimir were a double-outlet right ventricle (DORV), hypoplastic left ventricle (HLV), and pulmonary stenosis (PS) valvar and subvalvar. In lay terms DORV with HLV and PS is a condition where the main artery to the lung and the main artery to the body both function out of the right pumping chamber. The left pumping chamber is too small to function normally. An abnormal hole exists between the two pumping chambers and allows the red and blue blood mix to occur. The valve of the pulmonary artery is small and thereby prevents adequate flow of blue blood to the lungs, so it receives less oxygen. Although not the case with Zvonimir, children sometimes appear so blue that they resemble cartoon "Smurfs."

Surgical treatment for single pumping-chamber defects was first achieved in 1968 and reported in the surgical literature by 1971. Dr. Francis Fontan of France performed these operations, and the principles of his technique are the accepted form of treatment for this set of defects.

The Fontan Procedure was developed in part from several years of animal experimentation, which revealed that the blue-blood flow to the lungs could be provided by other actions of the body, such as walking or breathing, and that a blue-blood pumping chamber was not absolutely necessary for long-term survival. Of course, this abnormal circulation is fragile and can be upset by multiple factors. The observation of these factors over the last twenty-five years has led to modifications of Fontan's original operation. In terms of physiology and basic principles, the result is the same. As for the way the operation is conducted, there have been tremendous variations over the last twenty-five years.

In the most common modification of the Fontan operation the return of blue blood from the upper body and head bypasses the heart completely and goes directly to the pulmonary artery. The blue blood of the lower body is diverted through a tunnel of synthetic material that is constructed in the heart and that connects to the pulmonary artery. The single pumping chamber, whether right or left, is then directed to receive the red blood coming out of the lungs and pump it to the body.

In the United States most surgeons would have performed a bi-directional Glenn Procedure on Zvonimir first. In this, the surgeon undoes a shunt (a temporary routing procedure that connects part of the aorta to the pulmonary artery to increase blood flow), and then sews together the superior vena cava and the pulmonary artery so that the blue blood from the head and the arms goes directly into the pulmonary artery and gets oxygenated. The ventricle then carries much less blood per beat, since it no longer has to pump blood into both the pulmonary and systemic circulation. The heart is thus prepared for a completion procedure at a later date. As a surgical strategy, this two-stage Fontan has the advantage of breaking a complicated case down into manageable components.

According to Novick, a good surgeon can complete a Fontan—at least the important actions of sewing and connecting the vein bypasses to the pulmonary artery—in about twenty-five minutes. But for children such as Zvonimir, with single ventricles, those twenty-five minutes mean their only hope for life. Eventually, apart from the slim possibility of transplantation, these children would die.

Without knowing all the details, Snjezana was deeply troubled. "I couldn't believe this was happening. Why so difficult? Why so serious? He is ill, yes. But why so dangerously? I couldn't accept the truth. I started worrying about him. What if we have to go to surgery immediately, like our trip from Šibenik? What if he died and wasn't baptized? I took care of that the next afternoon in the hospital—I baptized him myself. The next day, when I came to see him in the hospital, he looked much better."

This religious matter-of-factness was noticed later in Memphis by her host, Annemie Miller. "I think she is someone who feels that if you go to church, pray the Rosary—all the things that we are taught as children—that's enough. Her belief in doing her duty was rock steady."

Snjezana finally met with Dr. Marinovic. "He talked with me very carefully. He took a model of the heart and made clear to me what was wrong with the heart of Zvonimir. He said: 'It is very, very serious. He needs two operations. I can't tell you when; it is up to Zvonimir. But for now he can wait.' He gave me instructions about medicine and the next steps. After a few days a nurse told me: 'You can go home soon. But Dr. Marinovic said you can stay here as long as you wish.' Even though the trip home wasn't safe, I wanted to go home."

On December 28, 1991, Zvonimir and Snjezana left Zagreb. The ambulance driver came from Šibenik to Zagreb to take the family back home. But the night before the Raks left Rebro, the driver called and said that they must be ready at eight the next morning, so they could make the ten-hour trip before nightfall. In the morning Snjezana could not find any doctors, especially Dr. Marinovic, to say goodbye to, and the nurses reluctantly let mother and son go home.

Snjezana described the trip. "We passed through Karlovac during the bombing. The roads were empty, full of torn pieces of earth and glass. Zvonimir was sleeping and he didn't know what was going on. I hope he never has to know what war is."

Back home the family enjoyed a period of happiness as 1992 arrived. Zvonimir was doing well, eating and growing. But in February, the three-month-old had to go to Zagreb again, accompanied by both mother and father. His blood tests showed that he wasn't getting enough oxygen to his blood, and so a shunt was performed to improve the blood flow to the lungs. This was palliative, intended to buy him time until the Fontan Procedure could be done. After fifteen days in the capital, the family returned home.

Every six months Zvonimir was taken to Zagreb to see Dr. Marinovic, and every time, according to Snjezana, the doctor said, "His heart has compensated and he is doing well." But in March 1994, Zvonimir, now two years old, began to do poorly on blood tests. First, Dr. Marinovic told Snjezana: "It is time to start thinking about surgical correction. He looks good, and I think he can get a lasting correction. I cannot tell you who will operate or where it will be, but first come to the hospital and then we will talk." But at their next meeting, Snjezana remembers, Dr. Marinovic looked unhappy. "He said to us, 'Zvonimir's heart isn't good. Nothing has changed for the better.... I don't know what we can do. I don't know what any surgeon will want to do. Here [in Croatia] I am sure nobody will do anything. In September a doctor from the United States will come and I will talk with him and we will see. If he says Zvonimir must go to the end of the world, nobody can stop you from going. Call me in September, and we will talk again.' I was so surprised. Zvonimir looked so good, and every time for the last two years I had heard: 'He is doing well.' I didn't expect the bad news—I thought it was past. I didn't forget that he had a serious heart defect, but I didn't expect to hear that maybe nobody could help. I returned home very disappointed. I threw all my childhood books in the trash, asking myself how life can be so cruel."

Nothing in Snjezana's life had prepared her for this. Growing up in Šibenik with her parents and two brothers, the dark-featured Croatian with intent eyes and thick eyebrows "didn't know what illness was," she once stated. Snjezana had enjoyed a tranquil, uneventful youth in the picturesque region lush with the beauty of mountains, valleys, and seas. The American dream reached into Šibenik around the time of Zvonimir's birth when a schoolmate of Snjezana's, Drazen Petrovic, went from hometown hero to national celebrity to NBA star.

In 1987 twenty-three-year-old Snjezana, a waitress in a Šibenik cafe, met her husband-to-be, Grgo, a handsome, slim, blue-eyed salesman of twenty-four from the nearby village of Danilo. When they married in 1990, they settled into a comfortable rural life at Grgo's parents' farm, tending to their poultry, sheep, gardens, and vineyards, selling whatever eggs, vegetables, and wine they could. They knew how fickle nature could be at times, particularly in the cultivation of their vineyard—an annual exercise in faith.

The ease of their life is symbolized by a bright orange curtain that blows freely with the wind in place of a front door at their house.

"It's one of the most relaxing homes I've ever stayed in," said Kerrigan after a second visit in October 1995. "When I was with them, I felt like I had a front-row seat to enjoy creation. In the ten days I was with them, I never saw so much as one cloud in the sky. The view of the hills is breathtaking, and there's an abundance of plant and animal life within arm's reach. The Raks' family life fits nicely within all that. After a while, my spirit felt as clear as that sky.

"Meals with them were the best. I never wanted to leave the table, as much for the good feeling as for the great food. We talk a lot in Catholicism about the sacred nature of food and fellowship, but there's something about the joy and calm the Raks have that brings it all home. Their space is simple and cramped, Zvonimir is always looking for attention, Snjezana and Grgo have to deal with Grgo's parents living with them, and the Croatian national television channel blares constantly from the corner of the kitchen. But around the table tucked in the side of the kitchen, with a sumptuous assortment of homemade cheese, homegrown onions, prosciutto, wine, and everything else, you can't help but hope this is what God had in mind when the scriptures present the kingdom as a great banquet."

September 1994 came, and Dr. Novick made his fourth trip to Zagreb. "Our TV and radio were talking about him, and for two days our telephone rang off the wall," said Snjezana. "All my relatives and friends called us and asked, 'Did you see that American doctor on TV?' After that I called Dr. Marinovic in Zagreb, and he told me that Dr. Novick would take Zvonimir to Memphis. I was very, very happy, and a little later Zvonimir even said, 'Mama is laughing more.'"

If Mama had known how Novick read her son's case, she would have had more reason to smile. "Zvonimir was palliated early; he got his shunt, and he didn't have that gaunt, undernourished look," he said. "The child didn't have to go through being cyanotic and out of breath. Size makes a difference in these kids. When they have poor results from their initial operation or when they have uncorrected cardiac disease and are in a growth spurt, they just don't have any energy left over—all their energy goes into breathing and their heart beat. He was a great candidate for surgery."

As 1995 began, Snjezana made preparations for the trip. The Croatian Ministry of Health informed her that it would pay ten thousand dollars for the surgery. The next hurdle was the trip itself. The Raks could have traveled free through a humanitarian agency in Germany but decided not to because the itinerary included a portion by ground, from Šibenik to Munich, that would be as long as the flight from Germany to the United States. Grgo worked for the local department store, Šibenik; however, like many workers in the country in the aftermath of the war, he did not receive his paychecks regularly. Still, the firm paid for the trip to Memphis, and many relatives and friends gave money, helping to shorten the travel time by almost one day.

At the airport February 3, the day their journey began, Zvonimir was "excited looking at the big planes and the small trucks that brought the luggage," said Snjezana. "He couldn't wait until we took off, but when we finally did he was sleeping."

The Raks arrived in Memphis on February 4 and were met by John and Nancy Dominis, who hosted them for their first weekend. "Zvonimir didn't understand what he was doing there. He asked me all the time: 'When will we go home?' I think he thought that once we got to America, we could then go home," said Snjezana.

Zvonimir began to get interested in his new surroundings. Snow fell one day, and although it didn't accumulate "Zvonimir liked that a lot, because we don't often have snow back home, sometimes only once in five years," said Snjezana. He played with his new host family, the Millers, and visited the interactive Children's Museum in Memphis, where little visitors can climb in the drivers' seats of child-sized cars, don firefighters' suits, and shop in a pint-sized, make-believe supermarket, among other attractions.

After some tests, surgery day arrived. "He was nervous and crying," recalled Snjezana. "When Dr. Michael Baron, the anesthesiologist, came and took him from me, I felt such emptiness. A nurse came and asked me how I was and took me outside in the hallway. After that, I went with [host mother] Annemie Miller to the hospital cafeteria and then to a hospital room where we waited."

Somewhere within two hours from the beginning of the surgery, Snjezana received a telephone call from the operating room: "Zvonimir is fine; everything is going well." Two hours later, another call: "Soon we will finish the surgery and you can go to the intensive-care waiting room." When she called her husband to relay the good news, she found Grgo so full of emotion he was unable to speak. Finally, when she saw Dr. Novick in the hallway, he said: "You have a remarkable son. He will be fine, and he will probably not need surgery again."

Zvonimir would not need additional surgery because Novick had opted not to do the Fontan in two stages. "I decided not to do that for him because his pressures were low and his red blood cell count was not real high," said Novick. "That means the shunt was functioning adequately and he was getting an adequate amount of oxygen to his blood." Lack of oxygen stimulates the bone marrow to make more red blood cells. This can be seen in people who live in the mountains, like the Peruvians in the Andes, and in people who smoke. Red blood cell production is the body's response to inadequate oxygen, since red blood cells are the ones that carry oxygen. Zvonimir's count wasn't particularly high, which indicated to Novick that he was in fairly good shape, even though he had a complicated defect for a single-stage Fontan. "As far as Fontans go, he behaved quite nicely," said Novick. "He didn't have any significant postoperative problems."

Snjezana saw the results for herself in the intensive-care unit. "I waited and waited and waited in the intensive-care waiting room. Finally I could go inside to see him. Fr. Kerrigan went with me, and when I saw my son I couldn't say anything. He looked so good. His skin had a nice pink color. A nurse, Cathy McCown, laughed and said: 'We don't like blue color here. Blue is good only for the sea.' I said, 'Only for the sea and sky.' She laughed again, and then she told me about the instruments used to monitor Zvonimir, but it didn't mean a lot to me because I was enjoying looking at Zvonimir."

Others in the ICHF were not able to enjoy the Raks' triumph fully. Two days after Zvonimir's operation, Ivan Ivic, a two-year-old Croatian from Djakovo, died suddenly following successful surgery. He was the second boy, along with Stjepan Goricki, to die within a month. Kerrigan recalls visiting Zvonimir a few hours after Ivic died. "He already had been moved to a private room on the seventh floor, but his mother was concerned that he wasn't eating and was moody," he said. "A few others by the bedside were pretty glum, and with Ivic's death weighing on me I was determined not to let Zvonimir go downhill. I don't know what possessed me, but I picked up a small cloth toy and flicked it at his bed, not far from his pillow. He always struck me as a kid with an attitude, and after a few more tosses he finally responded, and his impish grin returned. I knew then he would be OK."

The combination of Zvonimir's fearfulness and pugnacity were in evidence. Ironically, the child of the Adriatic developed a tremendous fear of water. "Whenever he would get bathed, he would be frightened," recalled Miller. "He must have been very sore; he would always sit with his shoulders hunched, as if he was afraid that he would get hurt. But yet, when he was upset and cried, it was always an angry cry—not sobbing, as in, 'I'm hurt,' but something more determined."

The determination became more noticeable as Zvonimir felt better. He provoked little confrontations with those around him, snatching things out of their hands and waiting for them to react. As Zvonimir became more combative, indicating his recovery, his mother's personality went in the other direction—more friendly, open, and revealing. "Before the operation Snjezana never talked about her family or anything personal," said Miller. "We knew she was married and all, but she was so totally focused on getting through the operation that it was almost uncanny. For them, I think coming to America meant seeing a doctor, having Zvonimir operated on, and going home. No nonsense. Get the job done to the best of your abilities. Period. I've been in the South too long, and everything is, 'Oh, honey,' 'Oh, darling,' everything is so wonderful, and then there's Snjezana's, 'I need food for Zvonimir—now' or 'I want such and such.' To me, it was very unusual. But once they got over the operation, she started to relax, cracking jokes, allowing herself to have a glass of wine at dinner—just totally different."

Zvonimir left the hospital quickly, and in his ornery way began the post-hospital treatment of walking, coughing, drinking fluids, and taking medication. As it was Kerrigan's custom at Holy Spirit to acknowledge successful heart patients, Zvonimir and Snjezana sat next to the priest, along with the altar servers, one Sunday during Mass, for what all hoped would be the Raks' public sendoff before returning to Croatia a few days later. But during the liturgy Zvonimir developed a cough that dramatically worsened, despite Snjezana's best efforts to alleviate her son's discomfort. Two physicians in the congregation stepped forward after the service to examine the boy, and he was taken to LeBonheur, where chest X rays revealed that Zvonimir had developed fluid in both his lungs. He had to be readmitted. "It was a frustrating little setback, more annoying than anything else, but because we all heard the cough and the congestion and knew what it meant, we weren't overly concerned," recalled Kerrigan. After a few days of successful treatment, Zvonimir was discharged and went home, at last, to Croatia.

Meanwhile two other foundation patients, Matei Marinic and Josip Špoljar, died in the next three weeks, leaving Zvonimir as the only survivor in the first three months of 1995. In a two-month period from early January to early March, four Croatian boys died in Memphis, along with Ivan Pozaric, who died during the same span in Zagreb. Snjezana and Zvonimir participated in the grieving and had the difficult mission of accompanying Matei Marinic's distraught mother, Slavica, back to Croatia. Before their operations Zvonimir and Matei were full of life, even having a brief fight at the Millers' house one night, and now one mother flew home with her son at her side while the other flew heavy-hearted and alone, with the grim knowledge that her son's body would be sent home on another flight.

Novick recalled: "Matei actually had a similar physiology, but he had a better situation than Zvonimir did. Matei's pressures were higher, but I thought since his anatomy was better maybe that would offset his physiology. It didn't, and he died. Sometimes you get surprised, but it's becoming more infrequent to be surprised in the operating room by catheterization data that is wrong or inadequate."

For Novick, the deaths outweighed the success of Zvonimir's operation:

"We had been riding on a high of seventeen kids or so. We had done difficult operations and had not lost a child. Then we lost two within two weeks of each other and were faced with a child [Zvonimir] who needed a Fontan and was only three years old with problematic anatomy, although he was an excellent candidate. I felt it was time to hit a home run. Yet we did just that with Ivic for the first two postoperative days—he was off the respirator, he looked great—but then he had a cardiac arrest and we couldn't pull him back. I was worried about stretching the limits then and considered doing the Fontan instead of the bi-directional Glenn on Zvonimir.

"Zvonimir's success was lost in the wake of the two subsequent deaths. Your latest result is your remembered result. You're only judged by what you've done most recently. That's fair because every child is the most important child you've operated on. The problem is, the success of Rak was lost as soon as the next child died. It's not lost to the parents, but in the grander scheme of things—Croatia, the program—Zvonimir got lost. Zvonimir was just another survivor.

"I've come to deal with the fact that it's extremely unusual to hear from a success. That's not to say you hear from the parents of a failure, but you do hear about a failure from your peers, who ask, 'What is the trend in mortality?' or, in assessing our program, 'What is the mortality rate compared with the norm?' The only times successes get brought up is in overall survival rates. As a pediatric heart surgeon, you are it. You are the last line of defense, the last responsible party for these kids. If they don't make it, it's nobody's fault but yours."

Novick is matter of fact in accepting the mantle of high expectations. "I think that's the way it should be; consequently, you've got to learn to deal with failure within yourself. If you're not capable of dealing with failure, I think it's extremely difficult to have a job where failure is under every stone. If you can't come to grips with failure as an individual, you shouldn't be a pediatric heart surgeon, because you will go crazy."

After a failure Novick replays the surgery, trying to find where the problem occurred. "Frequently I'm able to identify something that would have made a difference," he said. "I think that's part of experience in this profession." Novick talks with his partner and boss, Dr. Donald Watson. "Other people express their condolences, but the ability to sit down and talk about it is only possible between peers," he said. "You feel that you're speaking with someone who understands the situation, with at least the same if not more education about that particular child's problem, so you can discuss it on level ground. Otherwise, it's difficult to talk to other people—they don't understand. That's on a professional level. On a personal or psychological level, I go home and vent about the death of a child."

With a heart and mind filled with gratitude and renewed hope, Snjezana's spiritual life has changed for the better. Snjezana commented: "I used to go to church and pray because I was afraid Zvonimir would die. Now I know I need to go. Before I didn't go to church regularly—it depended on how I felt. The first six months of Zvonimir's life I didn't pray at all. Now I know what it is like to feel small under the stars and also what it is like to do whatever you want—but without the blessing of God you cannot do anything. Thank God we are not alone under the stars. We found very good people with great hearts in the United States. I got the impression that if I asked for a star from the sky someone could give it to me. Maybe they gave it to me with the life of my son. I hope his star will shine a long time."

Zvonimir's prognosis for the distant future is unknown. The Fontan Procedure performed on the boy is a modification that has only come into use over the last six years. Long-term data is not yet available. But it must be conceded that such a circulatory system reconstruction has to have long-term effects. In the short term, however, the particular operation that Zvonimir underwent provides him with a better and more consistent pulmonary blood supply. He can expect to have fewer abnormal heart rhythms and thus should live longer. As it stands right now, the best candidates with the best Fontan results have relatively good longevity, but Zvonimir is not in that group because of his anatomy; however, it was the only operation he could have had.

Nearly all objective studies of exercise capacity following the Fontan operation show a decrease, although patients frequently report they are able to maintain unrestricted activity in the absence of symptoms. Compared to their pre-operative exercise capacity, children such as Zvonimir are clearly improved but still below normal. "Can they go out and play with their friends?" Novick asked. "Sure. But they'll never be the best, unless they're playing with other kids with Fontans."

"He is now doing very well. He has nice skin color. He is in great spirits, catching chickens almost all day in the yard," reported Snjezana around the time of Zvonimir's fourth birthday in November 1995. "I hope tomorrow he will be just as successful catching girls." The hope Snjezana has for her son is now joined by one definite ray of sunshine; a second child, a healthy and happy girl named Suncica ("Sunshine") was born to Snjezana and Grgo in August 1996.

Zvonimir Rak ("Jinglebells") plays with his sister Suncica ("Sunshine") at the family home outside of Šibenik, Croatia.

Marina Kocijan with her mother, Anka, at the Church of the Holy
Spirit in Memphis, November 1994.

5
Marina Kocijan

"More tortuous than all else is the human heart"
—Jeremiah 17:9

A thin lane of asphalt cuts a winding path through thick fields of wizened cornstalks before reaching its end at the foot of a sleepy, baroque-style church. Along with a school building, the church sits atop a small hill. On a clear, crisp autumn Sunday a couple of hundred villagers emerge from their homes and stream quietly to the church on foot or bicycle. Inside, children of elementary-school age crowd around the altar for the Mass at half-past nine, as a religious sister strives mightily to maintain order among the squirming, mischievous little ones. The childrens' mothers and elderly men and women file into the front seats, while the back of the sanctuary is peopled mostly with young adults and men who, in their own weary indifference, appear as distracted as the children up front. Early in his sermon, a graying, avuncular priest halts to scold the unruly youngsters around him, but the scowl that remains on his face throughout the service fails to dissuade the boys and girls from giggling and other misbehavior. Their energy—even if a bit misdirected— sets the tone for the liturgy in song and prayer, overcoming the apathy and age elsewhere.

Like wild creatures released from a cage, the congregation vacates the church much more enthusiastically than it entered. The children run and cavort around the church grounds, while the adults linger around the front door to laugh and banter. Four children throw their arms around one another's shoulders and begin to careen down the hill. Two of them, each about nine years old, are dressed identically in denim jackets and brown corduroys, one a boy and the other a girl. At an intersection the quartet breaks up, and the boy and girl, both with straight, dirty-blond hair and brown eyes, head to the same house. Before reaching the front door, they wrestle in the yard. The girl, who is taller, playfully throws the boy to the ground and pins him without much struggle. Their energy happily spent, they scramble inside to the kitchen and seat themselves before a tableful of tasty assorted pastries.

Marina Kocijan (pronounced Koh-see-yon) may now be able to topple her twin brother, Bruno, in a wrestling match, she may be able to frolic freely with her school companions and enjoy the simple pleasures of an uncomplicated life on the outskirts of the city of Varazdin (pronounced Vahr-rahzh-dean) in northern Croatia, but for many years her life was anything but carefree. Rare even among congenital heart disease patients, Marina had the misfortune of being limited by an event commonly associated with the mortality of adulthood: a heart attack.

In his 1994 best seller, *How We Die*, Dr. Sherwin Nuland described a heart attack as follows: "It has been most commonly described by its sufferers as constricting or viselike. Sometimes it manifests itself as a crushing pressure, like an intolerable blunt weight forcing itself against the front of the chest and radiating down the left arm or up into the neck and jaw. The sensation is frightening even to those who have experienced it often, because each time it recurs it is accompanied by awareness of the possibility (and quite a realistic awareness it is) of impending death."[5]

Marina's attack happened within the first year of her life, and she has no memory of it. Because it occurred so early, no one can say what she was aware of and what she experienced. However, just the thought that someone so young could be subjected to something so traumatic is painful enough. The cruelty of heart attacks can be rationalized in the adult world as the price paid for survival on the planet for several decades. Often heart attacks can be seen as "justice" exacted upon persons with unhealthy diet, exercise, and/or smoking habits. *Did you enjoy that cheeseburger? You'll pay later.* A heart attack suffered by a child like Marina turns that kind of thinking on its ear. As expressed by Job: "It is all one! therefore I say: Both the innocent and the wicked he destroys" (Jb 9:22).

In another place in the Old Testament the prophet Jeremiah wrote: "More tortuous than all else is the human heart, beyond remedy; who can understand it?" (Jer 17:9). Who can fathom why Bruno was born healthy while Marina was not? The girl suffered from Bland-White-Garland syndrome, first described in 1886, exactly a hundred years before Marina and Bruno were born to Anka and Milan Kocijan in Varazdin.

In Marina's case the disease took the form of a misplaced left coronary artery, which formed at her pulmonary artery instead of her aorta. As a result, blood with an inadequate level of oxygen and at a very low pressure was delivered to the heart muscles on her left side. "A number of these children succumb to the condition at an early age, in the first year of their lives, when they have heart attacks," observed Novick. "Marina survived that. For children who survive the heart attack, the damage is pretty much done, and they develop collaterals, which function as a shunt for them. The blood flows backward from the coronary artery into the pulmonary artery. Medically, we see an increase in the oxygen saturation of their pulmonary artery, and they get a little better."

For a parent, shortness of breath and difficulty in feeding are typically the first things noticed in Bland-White-Garland children. The shortness of breath is a direct result of the insufficient level of oxygen that the child's heart is receiving, while the trouble in feeding is an indirect result of the same problem. "The children are working so hard to catch their breath that they don't want to take time to get nourished," noted the surgeon.

This is exactly how Anka, 38, a jovial woman with deep-brown eyes that match her hair, recalled her initial awareness of her daughter's problem. "A little before her first birthday, she was breathing hard and vomiting often and had a fast heartbeat," Anka said through a translator. "She was sent to the Varazdin hospital, and they told us that she had a heart defect." The diagnosis immediately halted the routine of the young family of four, who were settling into their new brick home in Sveti Ilija, a village near Varazdin. The capital of Croatia in the eighteenth century, Varazdin, a city of about ninety thousand inhabitants, has an air of both its former importance and its current quaintness in the mixture of churches, museums, and art galleries in the center of town. Today, the city is a Croatian textile and clothing center; many residents of the area, like Anka Kocijan, have found employment in one of the city's numerous factories.

The girl was sent to Zagreb and to cardiologist Branco Marinovic. "Marina was very interesting. We see a case like this maybe only once every five or six years," said the doctor. "She had the problems of an adult man, though she was a little child. We found that she had had a heart attack at about six months of age. Her defect was very unusual, but it could be taken care of since it had been discovered at an early age."

The defect could be taken care of, but not in the former Yugoslavia. The difficulty of the operation was beyond the capabilities of surgeons in Zagreb, Ljubljana, or Belgrade. Marina was sent home and referred to Ljubljana, where she underwent regular testing and drug management of her condition until 1992, when the six-year-old again developed shortness of breath and profound fatigue. Again it was decided that an operation could not be performed, but Dr. Marinovic promised to put her name on a list for international help. The hope was that the severity of her defect, along with the probability of a successful correction, would prompt an international surgeon to select her as a candidate. "I lived with high hopes, and I prayed to God and believed that Marina would be chosen," Anka said.

In the interim the Kocijans tried to find some normalcy in their daily life. Anka commuted by bus to her job at the Vartex textile factory, and Milan worked odd jobs near home, hoping that their small incomes would offset the effects of the country's high inflation. Anka's skill with fabric showed itself in the handmade tablecloths and curtains that dominated the interior of the Kocijan home. Milan tended to the young peach, pear, and cherry trees in the front of the house and an assortment of vegetables planted in the back. They lavished attention and love upon their twins, with a watchful eye on Marina's health. "She was a very happy little girl who liked to sing and play, only she tired very fast," Anka said.

In 1993 Marina started first grade. The school was almost two miles away, which proved a difficult distance for her to navigate. Her schooling was curtailed, but that did not prevent her from beginning to learn English. "One-two, pick up my shoe. Three-four, shut the door..." she recited often when she arrived a year later in Memphis.

The journey to Memphis was set in motion in September 1994, when Anka received a letter from Rebro Hospital, notifying her that Novick had accepted Marina for surgery in Memphis. "I don't know if I was excited because of happiness. I just knew that I was crying," said Anka. "Now we only had to wait for the call [to go to Memphis] and for the paperwork; those times were very hard for us. The thought that I had to go to America, the difficulty of surgery, everything was very hard. I awoke during the nights crying and praying."

Not long after the initial approval Dr. Marinovic called with the exact date that Marina was to leave for the United States. Milan and Anka were also told that they would have to cover the travel expenses, which they couldn't do on their own. Fortunately, there were others who were ready to assist. "My company and other good people helped, wanting to see Marina healthy," said Anka.

Across the Atlantic Ocean and unbeknown to the Kocijans, three more "good people" were poised to do their part to see Marina healthy. Jim and Cheryl Shields, along with their daughter Karen, age twenty-five, had opted to become a host family in the International Children's Heart Foundation program earlier in the fall. The Shieldses were longtime members of the Church of the Holy Spirit and lived in an ample two-story home in a quiet area less than a mile from the church. Over the years the family had been generous in volunteering for various church activities and participating in charities, and with bedrooms in the house now available since two older children had moved out, hosting Anka and Marina seemed the right thing to do.

One morning late in November, Anka and Marina left their darkened home at five in the morning, crying, with Milan, Bruno, and other family members accompanying them on the predawn drive to the Zagreb airport.

A few hours later they were in the air, from Zagreb to Frankfurt to Cincinnati to Memphis. "Marina met a little girl on the flight, and a few people from America, and we talked with them through a woman who happened to speak German and who translated for us. During the whole trip we played, talked, and had a good time," said Anka. "We arrived in Cincinnati, and another German translator helped us to get on a plane to Memphis. Marina slept from Cincinnati to Memphis. The flight was difficult because Memphis had just had a tornado and there was turbulence. Dr. Novick was there, with [translator] John Dominis and the Shields family."

During the first few days that the Kocijans were with the Shieldses, they were more like "visitors or guests," recalled Karen. "They were so quiet; their luggage did not arrive immediately and they were distracted. Marina was really shy and clung to her mom, which was funny because by the end of her stay the roles were reversed. Marina got bold enough to speak a little English, and Anka had to rely on Marina's translation."

Novick examined Marina as part of the pre-operative testing regimen. "By the time we saw this girl, she wasn't very active and tired quickly while playing with her peers," he observed. "She had severe mitral-valve regurgitation, and a gigantic left atrium as a consequence of that. The muscles that are responsible for tethering the valve become deadened, and so they scar and shrink and the valve doesn't operate properly. Such children tire easily, and they have shortness of breath upon exertion. Of those who survive to adulthood, about half have pain, or angina, with activity.

"When we looked at her heart valve, we found scarring throughout the entire distribution of her left coronary artery, so it had been a fairly serious heart attack. Her left ventricular ejection fraction, a measure of the ventricle's pumping ability, was estimated to be less than 20 percent; normal is about 70 percent.

"In 1990 she was a four-year-old with an abnormal electrocardiogram. But this was when things were starting to get tense in the former Yugoslavia. There wasn't a lot that could be done for her. The real evaluations started in 1992, when a peace agreement was brokered."

Before surgery Marina became sick with a mild stomach virus, and her surgery was postponed. The girl seemed to relax a bit; she had no idea that she was in Memphis for open-heart surgery! Anka had decided not to upset her daughter by telling her the full story; she only said that they were in Memphis so Dr. Novick and others could look at her heart. Since the surgery was postponed several times over a twelve-day interval, Anka maintained a pre-surgery ritual. "Every night we had to prepare mentally that the next morning Marina would have to get up and go to surgery," said Karen. "In anticipation of surgery, Anka and Marina excused themselves from the den each evening after dinner. Anka said the Rosary every night and stayed with Marina until late, when the lights finally went off."

The postponement had its benefits. "We had a lot of time to see the town," said Anka. "The days before Christmas were very beautiful. Karen became close to Marina and treated her like she was her own sister. She gave her a lot of things that I could never afford in Croatia."

On a Sunday, a few days before surgery, Marina went to the Church of the Holy Spirit and received holy communion for the first time. She would have received the sacrament earlier in Croatia had she not fallen behind her class. "Whenever someone is in danger of death, you want to pull out all the stops for them and for the community," said Kerrigan, noting that sometimes seminarians are ordained on their deathbed as a further means of conveying God's grace in a time of suffering. "In her life Marina had been singled out because of her limits—left behind in school activities and the like because of her heart defect, and I felt it was good to let her and the congregation know that God doesn't care about all that. Plus, her mother would not receive communion unless they have gone to confession right before the Mass, so Marina's communion was a good way to get her up to the altar, too."

"We could see how much Fr. Joe [Kerrigan] was trying to help us to feel better, to let us know that God would help us and that God would be with us," offered Anka.

One day Karen took Marina to the Discovery Zone, an indoor children's entertainment center replete with video arcade games, rides, and playground equipment. "When she saw it, she threw off her shoes and grabbed my hand as if I was her best friend and ran with me to the playground and all the slides," she said. Marina slid effortlessly through the bright red tunnel slide. It looked like a giant artery, and Karen couldn't help but hope that Marina's blood would soon flow strongly through her repaired artery. For now, Karen and Marina enjoyed their newfound friendship. "After the Discovery Zone, we were hooked. We went for pizza and to see Starry Nights [a drive-through display of Christmas lights in a large park in the city] and were inseparable for the rest of her stay."

In the gospels, stories of physical healings and life-changing conversions can be found side by side. Jesus' healing of sick people is often the catalyst that draws others to follow him. A good illustration is in chapters four and five of the gospel of Luke, where a series of healings (a demoniac, a woman with a severe fever, people "sick with various diseases," a leper, a paralytic) surrounds the call of the first disciples, Simon Peter, James, John, and Levi. In fact, before Simon Peter is called as the first disciple in Luke 5:1–11, his mother-in-law is cured of a fever (Lk 4:38–39).

Marina's treatment prompted Karen to leave her job and pursue a calling to be a pediatric nurse, the second Memphis woman to make a profound career change as a result of encountering a heart patient from Varazdin. Marina providentially came into Karen's life at a time when the tall, fair strawberry-blond was looking for a new direction. She had just broken off a five-year relationship with a college boyfriend and had moved back into her parents' house. As a commodities trader, her work days were filled with frenzied phone calls buying and selling millions of dollars' worth of cattle and hogs. "I knew that I had to get out of there and do something more fulfilling," she said. "When I saw the appreciation Anka and Marina had of everything in life, that clinched it for me. Seeing what they were going through began to change me. I saw how this mother-daughter relationship—they were all each had in America and were completely dependent on each other and on God—gave each of them the feeling that everything was going to be OK."

In the operating room Novick connected Marina's coronary artery to its proper place. He then turned his attention to the mitral valve. "We spent a fair amount of time trying to repair it," he said. "Here was an eight-year-old girl who at some point in her life would most likely want children. You don't want to put a mechanical valve in her if you don't have to. [Mechanical valves require anti-coagulation medicine, which causes birth defects.] But no matter how hard we worked on it, I couldn't make the valve work properly, so I took it out and put in an artificial valve. She came off bypass very easily and had good cardiac function."

Novick went to the waiting room to deliver the good news to Anka, while Marina was prepared for transfer to the intensive-care unit. "Dr. Novick told me that the surgery was successful, and I gave him a hug—I didn't know how to thank him," said the buoyant mother, who was able to shed more than eight years of guilt and twenty-four hours of superstition about Marina. From the first complications she experienced in her pregnancy with Marina and Bruno, Anka believed that because she was already thirty years old at the time of the pregnancy, she was to blame for the heart defect. Also, having an aversion to the number 13, she was anxious when the surgery was set for December 13.

The anxiety was eclipsed by the news of the successful surgery, followed by the invitation to see her daughter. "I was able to see Marina immediately, which was a big surprise to me, and I never moved from her," said Anka. "I followed her waking and I tried to make her feel more comfortable. I still get a little upset when I think about that time."

Karen got physically upset when she first saw Marina in the intensive-care unit. Leaning closely over the girl for a half hour, she grew faint and nauseated and had to be helped to the waiting room. Ivan Pozaric's mother, Zdravka, met her there. Zdravka had just received the news from the U.S. government a few hours earlier that her four-month odyssey in America was about to end, courtesy of a medical evacuation flight to Croatia for her and her son, Ivan. Equal to the task now before her, Zdravka settled Karen down and applied a cold cloth to her head.

Karen returned later in the evening to Marina's bedside. On the trading floor she handled the cacophony of ringing phones and shouting voices; the new noises in the ICU were something altogether different. "The machines kept beeping, and I had no idea what they meant," she said. "I would think, Oh, no, is her heart stopping? I was determined to know everything that was there, and I decided then to go into nursing."

A scary moment occurred when Marina was taken back into the

operating room to stop excessive bleeding from the surgical site. Novick reported: "After the initial repair was done, she went to the ICU, but she bled significantly and consistently within an hour after arriving. We took her back to the O.R., found the bleeding, and repaired it."

In open-heart surgery a crucial preparatory procedure is the removal of air from the heart after the muscle has been stopped and blood drained from it. If air remains in the heart when it is started again following cardiopulmonary bypass, there is a danger that the air will go to the brain and cause serious damage. The surgeon chooses a couple of places to punch holes in the heart to let the air out. "Most surgeons punch a hole in the aorta and then a vent site in the apex of the left ventricle and elevate the heart so that the air rises to the top and the blood slowly pushes the air out of the heart," said Novick. "We did that twice, using a different hole the second time. We sutured one of the holes shut. The other hole wasn't bleeding; we couldn't even see the spot we had punctured. We took her out of the operating room, and she didn't bleed initially, but after an hour it let loose. Bleeding like that can be serious if it is not found early, but we took her back to the operating room and fixed it. She came off the ventilator the next day and three days later she left the hospital."

Marina has an excellent long-term prognosis and can look forward to uninterrupted health throughout her adult life—with one exception. Novick envisions the following scenario for the girl during her childbearing years: "If and when she is ready to have children, we will take her current valve out and put a pig valve in. After three months she won't need the anti-coagulation medicine. She will have a window of maybe ten to twelve years [pig valves degenerate after that time span] to have all her children, at which point we would give her a mechanical valve." To parent or not to parent—a profound question in anyone's life. With Marina, parenting carries the risk of two added open-heart procedures.

Anka and Marina arrived back in Croatia on Christmas Eve, a storybook end for a tale that had had a most unkind beginning eight years earlier. Judging from the pictures that were sent from Varazdin over the subsequent few years, there has been no sign of a letup in her progress. In one photo Marina is licking an ice-cream cone while strolling through Varazdin's town square with Bruno and her parents on a sunny spring day, surrounded by teenage girls marching in bright red-and-white majorette outfits. In another shot, now with a maturing face and hair that has lengthened past her shoulders, she gleefully carves a jack-o'-lantern face at the kitchen table, even though Halloween is not celebrated in Croatia. In photos from Novick's social visit to the hospital in Varazdin in April 1996, Marina formally welcomes the surgeon with a kiss and an armful of flowers.

The priest and surgeon also found consolation in Marina's course. Novick said: "This was a case that the Croatian surgeons did not want to do, that their intensive-care doctors and cardiologists did not feel comfortable taking care of, so to overcome it was gratifying. The timing of her arrival in Memphis was interesting. Ivan's mom, Zdravka, was at the end of her rope in Memphis, yet fretful about going home; through Anka and Marina she was forced to channel all that energy in a positive way. And the whole ambiance of Christmas time was rewarding."

"A lot of healing took place through her healing," added Kerrigan. "Marina and Anka radiated simple joy and gratitude for life, and I think it rubbed off on a lot of us at the time between Thanksgiving and Christmas, when things can get out of focus. You could see the change in Karen, and Marina brought out Zdravka's compassion. The Kocijans were refreshing to almost anyone they met. They had an aura of God's presence about them, although I wouldn't have made the connection at the time. I'm reminded of a verse in the book of the prophet Hosea, 'Though I stooped to feed my child, they did not know that I was their healer'" (Hos 11:4).

Lest the importance of Marina's healing go inadequately expressed, Anka Kocijan stated, "Marina was born again in America. She was given a different life. My thanks to everybody for what they have done. I don't know the words to say how wonderful the people were."

"How are *you?*" answered Marina in perfect English when she recognized Kerrigan's voice on the phone one day in the spring of 1997. "I am super, really good," she volunteered. Marina was watching "Pop TV," a television show from Slovenia that features music and movie clips. With a hearty laugh Anka had another take on how Marina is really doing: "Bruno is my good child, he has the good heart. Marina, she's the other one—naughty." Ah, yes, to be young and innocent in rural Croatia. It seems that innocence is as fleeting there as it is anywhere else.

Marina Kocijan (far left) and her twin brother Bruno (far right) sandwich two of their friends on the road near their home in Varazdin, Croatia.

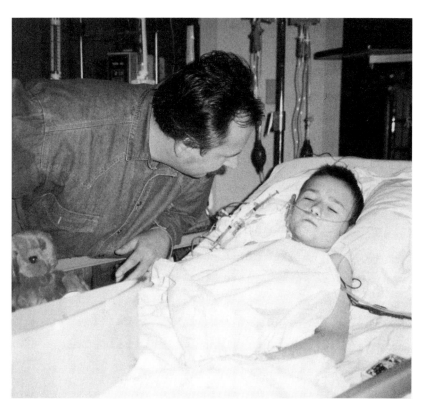

Krešo Cirkovic peers intently at his son, Krešimir, just after surgery at LeBonheur Children's Medical Center.

6
Krešimir Cirkovic

"Be Like Mike"

Poplar Avenue, the well-known and most-traveled Memphis thorough-fare, begins downtown at the Mississippi River and runs east for over a dozen chaotic miles of narrow lanes and commercial districts before crossing into the orderly, tranquil, and wealthy suburb of Germantown. There, spacious new brick houses with meticulously manicured lawns are placed at generous distances from one another on streets with such expansive names as Breezy Creek Road and Aspen Pine Cove.

Along Johnson Road, not far from Germantown's bustling Houston High School, the quiet of the early evening is breached in one backyard by four youngsters who casually banter, laugh, and scramble their way through the basketball game "21." The contest begins with players taking turns shooting at the basket from a distance of about a dozen feet. A successful toss is worth two points, and the shooter is rewarded with the opportunity to make another shot. The first player to score twenty-one points wins. On this night, however, under the floodlights of the drive-way, the frequent thud of wayward shots caroming off the backboard and rim is more frequent. Occasionally, among the clunk of the misses, is the swish of the ball as it passes through the net. The four players—three boys and one girl—range in age from eleven to fourteen, and because of their still-developing upper-body strength, a grunt of exertion sporadically accompanies a shot. Hit or miss, the proceedings are accompanied by the steady thumping of the bounced ball against the concrete driveway and the easy, friendly conversation among the participants.

A short while into the game, a father comes outside, visibly distressed. After a brief discussion the game resumes, only now with new rules. One boy is no longer running with the others for the rebounds and the loose balls. The boy, frail, with closely cropped brown hair, a broad forehead, and an intent but sad look in his eyes, stands on the edge of the driveway awaiting his turn while the others retrieve the ball for him.

The twelve-year-old boy suffers from more than errant shooting in basketball. He was born with a serious congenital heart defect. Now he is just a couple of days away from his fourth open-heart operation, each performed in a different country.

It would take more than heart disease and the approximately four-thousand-mile distance from Croatia to the United States to thwart Krešimir (pronounced Kresh-é-mere) Cirkovic from partaking in the same dreams as American boys. Krešimir's room in suburban Zagreb, Croatia, is indistinguishable from those of most of his twelve-year-old counterparts in the United States. A three-foot by four-foot poster of Chicago Bulls' superstar Michael Jordan is on the door. Inside the space that Krešimir shares with his three-year-old brother, Tomislav, the walls are filled with action posters of other American professional basketball stars—Reggie Miller, Scottie Pippen, Glenn Robinson, and Dennis Rodman. On the wood between the bunk beds there is a sticker of Drazen Petrovic, the Croatian-born guard who starred for the New Jersey Nets before his premature death in an automobile crash in 1993. The only non-basketball items on the wall—a large Coca-Cola calendar, promotional photos from the television series "The X-Files," and small posters of the Orlando-based pop band The Backstreet Boys—herald American culture in their own way. Atop Krešimir's desk sits a personal computer, wired to the Internet and used so often by the boy that his dad kept him off the machine for four months until his school grades improved. "Yesterday, Krešimir installed Windows 95," reported his father Krešo in the spring of 1996, a few months after the boy returned home from successful surgery in Memphis. "He loves computers. He wants to be a programmer–like Bill Gates."

The display in Krešimir's room attests to the pervasive power of American marketing, especially in the phenomenal success enjoyed by companies who use Michael Jordan to endorse their products. In 1991, to capitalize on Jordan's growing stature as a role model, Gatorade launched "Be like Mike" television commercials, but by that time millions of youngsters had already taken up that call. A year later the "Dream Team"–American professional basketball stars who represented the United States in the summer Olympics in Barcelona, Spain–gave them their best international exposure yet, bringing their images into bedrooms like Krešimir's.

That Krešimir can aspire to be the next Bill Gates is a tribute to the combination of medical competence and the tenacity of Krešimir and his family in combating his heart disease. The boy was born in June 1984, the first child of Krešimir and Ljerka Cirkovic. He was named after his father (who is called by his nickname, Krešo), who in turn was named after King Petar Krešimir IV, the strongest of the medieval Croatian kings.

At birth young Krešimir was found to have transposition of the great arteries, a ventricular septal defect (VSD), and severe pulmonary stenosis. "It was very difficult for us, you know, the first child," said Krešo, a broad-shouldered and slightly rumpled man in his mid-thirties with the intense eyes and broad forehead reflected in his son, but with a thick mustache and confident countenance that might cast him as an Eastern European police chief or mayor in a movie instead of his actual job as a customs agent for an import-export firm in Zagreb. "On the day he was born, they just told us that he had a heart problem. It was a maternity hospital, and the doctors didn't know exactly what was going on, so he was transferred to Rebro. We were very upset about it. 'How do we help him?' 'Who knows what's going on with him?' These were our constant thoughts."

The questions would not be fully resolved for Krešo and his wife, Ljerka, for a dozen years. The corrective surgery called for is the Rastelli operation (described in chapter 3), but it was not until Krešimir was twelve years old that he would undergo a successful Rastelli operation under the care of Dr. Novick in Memphis.

Krešimir's pilgrimage began a year after he was born in Ljubljana, in what was then the Slovenian republic of Yugoslavia. "We went to the Ljubljana center because they had more experienced doctors at that time," recalled Krešo in smooth English in his soft voice, a contrast to his rugged appearance. "The first operation in Ljubljana was to help him live to age three or four." The medical plan in Slovenia consisted of two procedures: the Blalock-Taussig and the Blalock-Hanlon. These operations were among the earliest surgical techniques perfected on congenital heart defects and can be done without cardiopulmonary bypass. In the Blalock-Hanlon operation an additional hole is created inside the heart to enhance the mixing of the blue blood and the red blood before they are ejected either into the aorta or the pulmonary artery. The Slovenian team next performed the Blalock-Taussig Procedure, creating a shunt between the pulmonary artery and the subclavian artery.

In 1987 three-year-old Krešimir was referred to a heart center in Munich, Germany, where he received what was thought to be a complete correction, the Rastelli Procedure. After surgery father and son met Dr. Ivan Malcic as he made rounds in the intensive-care unit in the Munich hospital where he was pursuing advanced studies. The meeting would prove fortuitous when Krešimir needed help again in Zagreb, and his parents would turn to Malcic as their cardiologist. Young Krešimir did reasonably well for three more years, before undergoing a cardiac catheterization that revealed a residual VSD as well as the start of some constriction in his right ventricular pulmonary conduit. These problems weren't serious enough to warrant another operation, although the boy was still in congestive heart failure and limited in his scope of activity. Medicines helped him compensate to some degree.

War came to Croatia in the summer of 1991. Ljerka's parents were routed from their home in Vinkovci, in eastern Slavonia, and were forced to stay with the Cirkovics in Zagreb for a few months before returning to

Vinkovci to rebuild. In 1992 Krešimir was found to have a worsening of the constriction in the conduit, and the VSD hole was still there. Another operation was prescribed, but he was now referred to Monaco. The Munich hospital was overloaded with cases from the former Yugoslavia, and Krešimir was sent to the resort country, where his conduit was replaced by a German surgeon. Less than three years later Krešimir was in heart failure again; he had a cardiac catheterization performed about the time Novick was visiting Zagreb in late 1995. His records were presented to the surgeon, whose attention was drawn by one anomaly among the data. "When they showed me his angiogram, it looked like his conduit had actually eroded through his sternum [breastbone]!" he exclaimed. "This is a very unusual situation, explained by the fact that the beating of the heart acted like sandpaper near his sternum—six thousand beats an hour—which is quite lot over two years. Now we were looking at a semi-urgent to emergency situation: the conduit was eroding, he was still in heart failure, and he had such severe stenosis that they couldn't even get the catheter to go across the pulmonary artery to measure the pressure. I said we would be happy to take the child as a patient."

Dr. Ivan Malcic, head of Croatia's Big Hearts for Little Hearts program for congenital-heart-disease patients, started the application process with the Croatian Health Insurance Agency to have the organization pay for part of the boy's treatment in the United States, but after four weeks there was no response. In fact, it would take over six months after the initial request. Concerned for their son's worsening condition, and able to raise the needed twenty thousand dollars, the Cirkovic family decided to come to Memphis on their own, without the sanction of the insurance agency. "We are middle class; we had some money," said Krešo. "The economy was OK for us. I work, my wife works, my father and mother are retired and get their pension."

Krešo and Ljerka took a chance by foregoing the opportunity to have the health fund pay for the procedure, but finances were secondary in their minds. According to Krešo, "The most important thing was that we believed Dr. Novick would do a really great operation and all this would be successful. When you speak with him and look at him, you are just sure—there is no doubt—that everything will be OK. We met him for the first time a few months before the operation, and he had no doubts. He encouraged us very much." Krešo's usually shy son commented on the decision: "I have been operated on in Munich, I've been operated on in Monaco, I've been operated on in Ljubljana, and now in America."

And so the boy was ready to come to Memphis. Because Krešo knew the language and young Tomislav was still attached to his mother, "we decided it was better for me to go," he said. So it was Krešo, and not Ljerka, who accompanied their son, one of the few times in the heart foundation's eighty-patient history that a father has been the travel companion instead of the mother. Ljerka had traveled with her son and husband for the previous three surgeries, so it was difficult for her not to go this time. "It is out of your reach—it must happen this way, I thought. It gives you feelings that you can't put into words," she said in Croatian, with her husband translating, a year after the trip to Memphis. "In one second, knowing I was not going to Memphis, I had hundreds of thoughts. I was alone in these thoughts, but God was with me."

To Novick, there is some difference when fathers are the primary caregivers through a surgery. "Fathers tend to be more stoic in public, and Krešo was that way. Fathers will question you, but not with the same level of questions that the mothers ask, not the questions that remind you that a piece of the mother's heart goes to the operating room. Fathers attempt to remain aloof from their own personal feelings for their children until something goes wrong. I didn't find Krešo different from most fathers I dealt with. They want you to understand that they have complete faith in what you are going to do, and that the outcome will be good."

It was remarkable that John and Sarah Mullis would be in a position to open their home to host Krešimir and Krešo for their trip to Memphis. Just fifteen months prior to the Cirkovics' arrival, the Mullis's home had been destroyed when a devastating tornado hit Germantown in late November 1994. An adjoining guest house on the property was miraculously spared, and this house served as the residence for the Mullises for over a year while their home was being rebuilt.

For the most part Memphis's weather, like its location in the United States, is somewhere in the middle. The city receives about an inch of rain a week, and the average temperature works out to a comfortable 61 degrees Fahrenheit, but on occasion Memphis can be subject to drought or flood, ice storms or tornadoes. On a Sunday afternoon during the Thanksgiving holiday weekend in 1994, the Mullises were shopping for a Christmas tree at the time the twister was unleashing its fury upon their neighborhood. Shoppers were handed pillows and herded into the center of the building in preparation for a direct hit. When the danger eased, and the family attempted to return home, their street was already cordoned off by police. Three people were killed in the twister, and nearly two dozen injured. About thirty houses in the affluent neighborhood were destroyed, while about three hundred sustained damage, adding up to an estimated fifty million dollars in property losses.

"I feel as though I'm under a black cloud," said John Mullis in December 1994. These are not the most comforting words to hear from an airline pilot, but given that the tornado struck just a couple of weekends beforehand, and that his brother Joseph, also a pilot, died in a plane crash two years prior to that, his feelings were understandable.

If John believed that he lived under a black cloud, his agreeable and soft-spoken personality disguised it well, as did that of his outgoing and energetic wife. Indeed, when the couple spoke in general terms about their lives, they spoke more from a profound sense of gratitude for their good fortune than to lament adversity. John, a North Carolina native, and Sarah, from Kansas, had both risen from humble backgrounds to fashion a very comfortable lifestyle for themselves and their three children, Andrew, Erin, and Colin.

Captain of a DC-10 for Federal Express, John flies about twenty days a month from the Memphis headquarters to cities such as Newark, Los Angeles, Seattle, Portland, and Minneapolis. A typical route finds John flying to one city with a delivery, then laying over briefly before returning to Memphis the same day, only to venture to another city that night. The airline industry brought John and Sarah together; they met in the mid-1970s when John was a pilot and Sarah a flight attendant. "I'm doing what I want to do and get paid well. I feel pretty lucky," said John. "I used to do the same thing in the Navy and got paid nothing in comparison!"

Aviation has also always carried with it a spiritual dimension for John. "One of the things I like about flying is breaking away from the ground and the wonder of all that—the sunsets, the night sky. It makes you realize how small you are."

"We've been blessed too much to not share it," said Sarah at the reconstructed Mullis home several months after Krešimir and Krešo left. "You need to make a return, to give back what you have gotten," interjected John, expressing a sentiment he said was instilled in him in sixteen years of Catholic education. A Catholic Relief Services' "Rice Bowl," used each year by Catholic families in the United States during the Lenten season to heighten awareness of the plight of the world's poor, sat in the center of their dinner table.

Although giving thanks to God for being spared from injury during the tornado may seem like an obvious reason for the Mullises to open their rebuilt house to families like the Cirkovics, their motivation actually predated the twister by a few years. "We knew we would do something with the guest house once we didn't need it anymore," said Sarah. "Originally we talked about using the house for pregnant girls who had no place to live." And then came the opportunity, through the Church of the Holy Spirit, to host Krešimir and Krešo.

"We all became good friends in a hurry. It was like an overseas military experience, where all you have is each other in a foreign environment and you want to make friends quickly," observed John. "Except that there was nothing military about Krešimir and us, only the bonding."

John Mullis's late brother Joseph once wrote to his brother as he began a military stint in Italy, "An ancient Indian definition of a friend is 'one who carries my burdens on his back.'" The Mullises became such friends for the Cirkovics.

The Croatian father and son spent their first full day in Memphis on Ash Wednesday, and, together with the Mullis family, attended a standing-room-only evening Mass at the Church of the Holy Spirit. They received ashes on their forehead from the two priests, Monsignor John Batson and Fr. Kerrigan, along with these words: "Remember, you are dust, and unto dust you shall return." One of the more sober days in the church year, Ash Wednesday is a day to reflect upon one's mortality and one's standing before God. But for Krešo, the church visit was an uplifting moment of welcome. "It was really an experience to go to church on

Ash Wednesday and see the people receiving ashes. I felt I belonged there—I don't have the words to express that moment, either in English or in Croatian. We felt that God was with us and that we were part of the church community. The man or the woman sitting beside us seemed an old friend—that we could rely on the community, know the people, and everybody would want to help." Krešimir had his religion class and family back home praying for him, but the feeling that came at Holy Spirit brought that prayerful protection very near in this strange country.

In his first experience at Holy Spirit, Krešo touched upon the parish's defining qualities. The sense of welcome and concern that he experienced at one Mass had been carefully crafted over many years. Nestled in a quiet subdivision that straddles the Memphis-Germantown line, the Church of the Holy Spirit was founded in 1975 as an alternative to the large suburban parishes flourishing in Memphis at the time. The warmhearted and savvy Batson, who retired in the summer of 1996, pastored the church for all but the first six months of its history. As a veteran of school administration and Catholic Charities, he put an accent on outreach and hospitality that quickly gave the parish its unique stamp. An intrepid group of parishioners, empowered by their progressive pastor, helped forge Holy Spirit's leadership in the Memphis diocese in social justice programs and outreach to alienated Catholics, and in creating a warm, welcoming environment for all to worship.

The gravity of hosting a child with a serious heart defect finally hit Sarah the next day, surgery day: "When they were getting ready to take Krešimir down to surgery, it was a very emotional time, with a lot of tense waiting. When they took him into the O.R., his dad stood with his hands against the window as long as he could. He sat down, put his head in his hands, and started to cry hard, shaking as he did so. At that moment I realized the importance of what we were doing as a host family."

At about that time Novick was donning his surgical garb and preparing for what he knew would not be an easy Rastelli Procedure because the boy's conduit was precariously placed under his sternum. "I was very concerned that the conduit would open when we opened his chest and that we would be inside his heart immediately, before we could put him on the bypass machine," said the surgeon. "In anticipation of that we prepared the large artery and vein in his leg and put him on bypass by this route, which is pretty unusual in children. When we began to open the sternum, we cut right into the heart, right into the conduit, and the sternum wasn't yet fully open! We had just made the cut into the front of the sternum. Had we not been prepared, he would have bled to death. But because we were on bypass and had cooled him down and had lowered his head—because he had a hole in his heart and we didn't want any air going to his brain—we went about the operation as though nothing had happened.

"Once we got his sternum opened, I closed the conduit, took it out, and closed his VSD. He got a new homograft conduit, and this time, to keep it from beating against his sternum, we put a Gore-Tex patch between the conduit and the sternum."

After an uneventful hospital stay, Krešimir was discharged and spent his recovery time indulging in American culture. "He loved fajitas, hot dogs, and hamburgers," recalled John. "Before he left, he had to have athletic shoes and a uniform jersey. When we left the store after making a few purchases, his dad said, 'God bless the man who invented plastic money.'"

As Krešo became more familiar with American customs, he made humorous observations. About speed bumps or potholes on Memphis streets: "We call them Russian traffic lights." On the difficulty he found in finding a place to smoke or to park a car: "America is a big intensive-care unit—no smoking, no parking, no people—you call this freedom? Is there any place I can smoke here?" On an information card he was given for the part of his son's heart that was replaced: "If it fails, do I get my money back or what?" About people who have double letters in their names, like the Mullises or Kerrigan or William Novick: "Why do you need the two? Is it in case you lose one?"

Upon their return to the Mullis residence, the Cirkovics also found their Zagreb neighbors, Marjan and Ljubica Haramija, along with their newborn son Fran, staying in the guest house. The two families live about sixty meters from each other in Gracani—a pleasant hilly neighborhood where comfortable two- and three-story concrete houses are set into the terrain as in a ski village, and where some of the most spectacular sunsets in Zagreb can be viewed over Mount Medvednica (Bear Mountain). The Haramijas had brought their son to Memphis for heart surgery, which also was successful. The two families would live on the Mullis property (Krešimir and father in the main house) for the last weeks of their stay in Memphis.

Grateful for the happy outcome and good experiences in the United States, the Cirkovics left for Zagreb in early March. "We didn't know to whom we would come in Memphis, how they lived, or if we would cause them any problems," concluded Krešo. "But everything was just great. Sarah herself spent almost the entire day every day with us. In the hospital, everybody was really great, very polite. I was surprised at how everybody treated us. Krešimir was just one patient, but they paid a lot of attention to us. Everything is so big, so clean. Nothing is missing. Maybe that's normal for you."

Krešimir resumed his life as a student. His school was within walking distance, a few blocks from home, but before the surgery in Memphis he was unable to make the short trek and had to rely on a ride from his father each day. Now, slowly, he was able to walk. But more important, he was able to enjoy what Krešo recalled from his own childhood as "the best time in your whole life, when you have no other. It's a time for playing and collecting posters for soccer and basketball. It's a time for enjoying the summers, when school is off, to go with the family to the country, to a little village in northern Croatia near Cakovec."

"I will meet you under the horse's tail," said Krešo, with more than a little bit of irreverence, as he arranged a meeting with Kerrigan in Zagreb in May 1996, two months after returning home with his son. "The horse's tail" referred to the statue of Ban Josip Jelacic, depicted triumphantly astride a horse in the center of Zagreb's main public square. Ban Jelacic Square (Republic Square during the Yugoslavian years) is not quite the size of an American city block. Bordered by nineteenth-century buildings that are alternately painted in muted tones of yellow, gray, and blue, and topped by garish illuminated advertisements on the roofs, the square is Zagreb's primary crossroads for trams and pedestrians. Just off it lie the magnificent St. Stephen's Cathedral, Zagreb's main open-air market, and the city's medieval Upper Town.

The same enthusiasts who would like to portray Jelacic as a Croatian

George Washington would also have you believe that Zagreb itself is another Vienna—the clean, well-to-do Austrian city of legendary attractiveness that boasts ornate buildings, museums, Baroque churches and palaces, along with numerous elegant hotels and cafes. "Some Croatians love to harp on the fact that they're 'Middle Europe,' but the *middle* it reminds me of is the Middle Ages," said Novick. "There's a drab quality to Zagreb that no amount of flowers or paint or street vendors will take away." Kerrigan added: "Without much imagination I can picture the sky, buildings, street, and people of Zagreb all blending into one steely gray mass. The one word I will always associate with Zagreb is *gray*."

Zagreb is a city that succeeds, as most provincial capitals do, by setting itself apart from others rather than by blending in. Zagreb ("Behind the Cliff") developed around Mount Medvednica a little more than nine hundred years ago; the city celebrated the nine-hundredth anniversary of its founding as an archdiocese in 1994, when Pope John Paul II visited. To the surprise of no one familiar with the region's history, strife was instrumental in Zagreb's founding. Two rival towns that served two different interests—Kaptol, the seat of the archdiocese, and Gradec, a fortress for Croatian nobility—united against the common enemy, the Turks.

Novick has noticed a vast improvement and a decided brightening in the city since his first visit in the spring of 1993. "My first impression will stay with me for the rest of my days," he began. "As we were flying there, it was really cloudy coming over the top of the Alps into Slovenia, and when we broke the cloud cover they announced that we were over Croatia. There are rolling hills, beautiful country—really gorgeous—but there was snow on the ground. As we dropped lower and lower and got closer to Zagreb, what stood out in my mind when the snow disappeared was that it was cloudy, and it was gray, and there were all these little bitty houses with red roofs. Everywhere you looked there were clay tile roofs. My first impression was of a dull, dreary, uniform place.

"When we landed, my suspicions were confirmed. Taxiing at the Zagreb airport, it was miserable—gray, overcast, cold, wet. When the plane touched down and went screeching past the airport terminal building, I thought, 'Oh, God, what are we doing here?' As we went farther down the runway, we passed a bunch of UN fighters, UN transport planes, helicopters, armored personnel carriers. It looked as though we landed in a military airport. The airport was exactly what you'd expect of a country that had been at war—dreary customs receiving room, dingy paneling on the walls, exposed pipes in the ceilings.

"It didn't get any better. We got out of the airport and up pulled this bright orange Volkswagen minibus, and I thought, 'If this is the only color in this country, we're in trouble.' The drive from the airport was more of the same—patchy snow; gray, overcast, misty, miserable weather; little houses with red roofs everywhere.

"We arrived in town and they took us to the Panorama Hotel, which was a refugee hotel. It is a tall hotel, maybe fifteen to twenty stories, but after looking at it for a bit you notice that the balconies look a little funny—some have clotheslines strung on them by the refugees; others have been made into sitting rooms by taping cardboard inside the railing.

"There were no street vendors, and maybe every fourth shop actually had merchandise in the window. There was one store—a household appliance shop—in which the entire display window consisted of a fruit crate with a single iron on it. That was the display. The buildings were all desolate and gray, there was an absence of material goods, and there were very few people on the streets.

"The sun finally came out, but the blooming flowers seemed incongruous with the surroundings—they were not patches of beauty but little islands that didn't fit. They were overwhelmed.

"It's a bright, happy, moving city now, at least superficially. Now you go over there in the spring and it's unusual to see drabness—everything is dressed up and painted. There are all kinds of happy people out in the streets anytime in the night or day—the downtown eateries and jazz clubs are open until the wee hours. It's a totally changed city in terms of its energy and in terms of the people's outlooks."

Krešimir Cirkovic's rosy cheeks and restored health reflect the improved energy and outlook of Zagreb. The danger pressing upon the boy's sternum had been removed, and Krešimir was now free to explore the adventure of youth in a land that was similarly finding its way in the fresh first years as an independent republic.

There was still some unfinished business over Krešimir's heart surgery in Memphis, but the arena had now shifted from operating room to courtroom. The family had appealed the Croatian Health Insurance Agency's September 1996 decision not to reimburse the cost of the boy's surgery. In January 1997 the agency again rejected their request. A letter from Stjepan Turek, superintendent of the agency, stated: "The parents have undertaken the entire risk regarding incurred costs because they did not take the time to wait for the Authority of the first instance to conclude the administrative procedure and refer Krešimir Cirkovic to the nearest foreign cardiology clinic which, according to its expert resources and experience, [would] guarantee the success of operation and according to costs of medical treatment would be more acceptable than those accepted by the American clinic." Novick was appalled that the agency did not recognize the urgency of the boy's condition and that Mr. Turek could state that another surgeon could guarantee the operation's success at a lower cost. In a letter to Krešo, Novick wrote, "Any surgeon who guarantees the success of a heart operation is unusual and perhaps should be the only person in the world performing heart surgery." Krešo and Ljerka have now begun a lawsuit against the insurance agency.

Legal battles notwithstanding, young Krešimir had come a long way from a period early in his life when friends and family feared that the inadequate blood flow through his heart would cause brain damage. "He has the same demands and needs as any other child, except he is not able to play basketball or soccer and he is skinny. That's it," retorted his father at the time. After his surgery in Memphis Krešimir is even trying a little basketball without restrictions, soccer, riding a bicycle, and playing normally with the other children. Most weekdays he can be found happily bounding down the streets with his schoolmates after class ends, garbed in the requisite Nike cap, jacket, and sneakers.

"Everything is fine, and we are very glad for that," said Krešo. "Surely God helped us in Memphis. God was following us in this period. The prayers were, 'Please help us to return with him healthy.' We have to thank him for all he has done. God is supposed to have a great heart for all of us, helping during our lives in the bad moments. We just have to believe, and if we do, everything is easier. Everything is now great. We believe that God is always helping, especially the children. And if God was leading us up to now, he won't let us down."

Krešo Cirkovic, his son, Krešimir, Sarah Mullis, and Ljubica, Fran, and Marjan Haramija at a Mexican restaurant in Memphis.

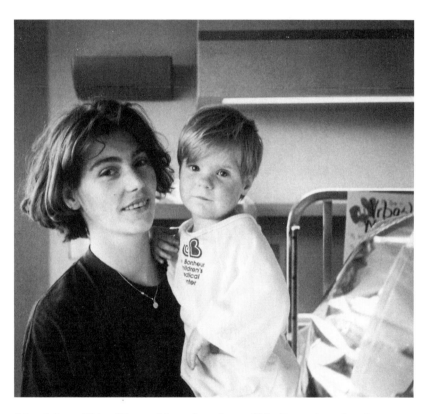

Magdalena Vrbašlija and her daughter, Nikolina, shortly after successful open-heart surgery at LeBonheur Children's Medical Center in the summer of 1994.

7
Nikolina Vrbašlija

"A simple child...What should it know of death?"
—Wordsworth

In the fall of 1995, on a typically gray, overcast, and drizzly morning in
Zagreb, Fr. Kerrigan set out along a major highway that follows the
course of the Sava River for more than two hundred miles before ending
at the Serbian capital, Belgrade. The highway, featureless and monoto-
nous, matched the drab weather. The priest was reminded of his native
New Jersey Turnpike, 150 miles of concrete and asphalt, also built after
World War II, with an emphasis on efficiency over aesthetics. It was hard
for Kerrigan to decide which engineers—the Yugoslav communists or the
New Jersey capitalists—had created the more numbing effect.

Despite the surroundings the priest's mood was upbeat as he anticipated his destination, the eastern Croatian city of Djakovo, little more
than halfway between Zagreb and Belgrade. He was especially eager to
meet one family in the city of forty thousand residents: Magdalena and
Nikolina Vrbašlija, the first Croatian mother-and-child pair that he had
worked with and had come to know well.

When Croatian children with congenital heart disease began to arrive
in Memphis in the spring of 1994, Kerrigan's volunteer chaplaincy

assumed a hit-or-miss quality. In general, once he received a message with a patient's name, hospital, and room number, the priest's routine was simple: get in the car and drive to the hospital as soon as possible. At the bedside with patients who were able to converse, Kerrigan's pastoral visits would span a range of small talk, prayer, and serious discussion about some of the personal issues illness evoked in the patient. Like most parish priests, unless the patient had some particular needs that required regular visits, Kerrigan would usually see a patient once or twice during a hospital stay. He would follow the patient's progress with updates from family members or church volunteers.

With the Croatian heart patients, however, making those one or two visits was another matter altogether. When a Croatian child was hospital-ized, Kerrigan did not receive word through his usual channels (a phone call from a family member, hospital representative, or the diocesan refer-ral program). Nor did he get word firsthand, as he would later, from Novick or from LeBonheur's cardiovascular surgery department. Instead, he usually heard about the new arrival from a nurse or doctor at the hospital, perhaps someone Kerrigan might have seen at church the previous weekend. Sometimes the information was not reliable or timely. More than once the priest arrived at LeBonheur to find that the child's surgery had been postponed or that the child already had been dis-charged. Once Kerrigan was in the same waiting room as the parents without even realizing it! Since his role in Novick's program was still unofficial, the priest did not take the mishaps too seriously. After a few more patients, he began to feel his way around the hospital and Novick's office and learned the protocol, but his experience with Magdalena and Nikolina motivated him to do more.

As he continued his three-hour drive along the rain-slicked road to Djakovo, Kerrigan had plenty of time to immerse himself in memories of his first encounter with the Vrbašlijas in the summer of 1994. He forgot exactly how he first learned of their presence in the hospital, but he remembered walking along the seventh-floor corridor at LeBonheur in search of the private room the child was placed in following her surgery. He knocked lightly on the open door but got no answer. He approached the bed and stood at its foot, with Magdalena hunched over at one side and attending to her daughter. Her back was to the priest. The next several seconds he would not soon forget.

"Magdalena stood up and turned around. She was tall, maybe 5 ′ 10 ″ or so, and she gave me a very piercing, intent look that disoriented me," said the priest. "It wasn't as if she were surprised or angry, or even reacting to me directly. It was more of a seasoned street glare, the acquired look of someone who has often had her privacy invaded but who maintains her pride and power with her eyes. I was now the latest one to cross her path.

"I would like to be able to say that in that moment I really saw for the first time the suffering and strength of people from the former Yugoslavia and that what I saw committed me more deeply to helping Croatian patients, but in all honesty I was too busy backpedaling from her look. I was thinking, 'What did I do wrong here?' and 'This doesn't feel right.' As a priest I had visited hundreds of patients before—patients who were disconsolate, patients who were angry with God, patients whom I mistakenly walked in on—but this was different, intimidating."

"I didn't see him walk into the room, and then he was right at the bed. 'What is he going to do?' I thought," Magdalena said later. "In Croatia our priests always wear black. I had no idea Fr. Joseph was a priest."

With temperatures in the nineties, Kerrigan had worn a white clerical shirt instead of the customary black. After his initial confusion over Magdalena's response, it occurred to him that she probably did not have a clue as to who he was, much less that he was a priest. At the same time he realized that, unlike his previous meetings with Croatian patients, he was alone in the room with the mother and daughter—there was no doctor, nurse, member of the host family, or translator to help ease his way into the conversation. Even the television, which diverts attention, was turned off.

Nikolina started to scream and cry, and Magdalena turned again to her daughter. "In that split second I probably could have just slipped out of the room," Kerrigan said, "but I couldn't. It was a moment of truth, a challenge that couldn't go unanswered. I felt I needed to understand the tension. Why was I in that room, really? What am I all about here with these Croatians, anyway? Just to smile and be sort of a token presence of the church for them? This was a different situation altogether. It was time to decide: do I want to deal with it or do I stay on the fringe?"

He broke the silence with, "Do you speak English?" Magdalena shook her head in the negative and pointed to a Croatian-English phrase book in the corner of the room. Kerrigan felt a little relieved at this brief interaction. As he opened the book and looked at the strange new words, however, he was again disconcerted. A priest who made his living with words—words of prayer, preaching, and conversation—now found himself at a loss for any words in this situation. Gamely, he tried to put together a few intelligible words in Croatian and, with the help of hand gestures, finally was able to communicate that he was a priest. He learned that Magdalena and Nikolina were Catholic. He interacted a bit with Nikolina, a chunky little girl with short blond hair and a square jaw; at her age she could even be mistaken for a boy. Kerrigan plucked a few more phrases from the book and tossed them at Magdalena, who was now becoming amused. Finally, he found the word for "tomorrow" (*sutra*), waved, and left, sweating profusely.

"By the time Fr. Joseph left the room, I had learned that he was a priest. I thought he was a nice man, too, but just to make sure I went to Silvija's room down the hall," said Magdalena. (Silvija Kubica, a seven-month-old Croatian girl, was also recovering from heart surgery at that time.) Silvija's mom, Lidija, the wife of a Baptist minister, corroborated Kerrigan's claim to be a priest. "In Croatia our priests and sisters are separate from the people. Usually all we get is a *'dovidjenja'* ['see you'] at the back of church from them," continued Magdalena. "Fr. Joseph was more like one of us."

Unlike her daughter, Magdalena was feminine in appearance. Her deep sable eyes, set in a lightly freckled, pale face, were difficult not to notice and were highlighted by long, thin eyebrows. Her lips appeared unnaturally full, but attractive, and her short brown hair accented her face nicely. Magdalena's figure was all limbs—her arms were particularly lanky.

Kerrigan returned to LeBonheur the very next day "because I wasn't satisfied, and I still felt there was something for me there." This time the host family, the Strummingers, presented gifts to Nikolina for her second birthday, and Kerrigan had a much more relaxed time on the sidelines. He was there again the following evening, just in time to point out to Magdalena and Nikolina the Fourth of July fireworks along the Mississippi

River, which could be seen from the hospital. A couple of days later there was yet another celebration, presented again by the Strummingers, for Magdalena's twenty-second birthday. Kerrigan assisted in Nikolina's rehabilitation by pulling the girl in a red wagon through the hospital's brandnew three-story atrium lobby, which has been likened to a pinball machine because of its bright colors, many angles, prominent pillars, streams of neon lights along the walls, and tiny white lights on the ceiling. When Nikolina was discharged from LeBonheur, the priest took the pair to the Church of the Holy Spirit for a weekday Mass. A group of parishioners handed Magdalena a couple of hundred dollars as she left the church. Afterward Kerrigan chauffeured mother and daughter to McDonald's for breakfast, and Nikolina enjoyed the playground that was attached to the restaurant. By the time the Vrbašlijas boarded the airplane back to Zagreb, the priest's Croatian vocabulary consisted of about a dozen words, and his "ministry" was more that of an activity director or a tour guide. Still, he felt he had made considerable strides as chaplain to the Croatian families.

"What is ministry?" he asked. "Making a good connection with someone, meeting a need, and relating it all to God and the church. I think I was there for Magdalena and Nikolina in this way."

Back on the Zagreb-Belgrade highway Kerrigan fast approached Djakovo, and the twin steeples of the city's cathedral began to dominate the modest buildings and flat landscape. Soaring nearly three hundred feet in the air, the steeples hinted at the grandeur of the neo-Romanesque and Gothic structure, which was built under the leadership of one of Croatia's most gifted religious and cultural leaders, Bishop Josip Juraj Strossmayer (1815–1905). At the age of thirty-six, Strossmayer was named bishop of Djakovo. He was acclaimed as an outstanding preacher and intellectual, a man who promoted the unity of the Roman Catholic and Orthodox churches at Vatican Council I, thereby courting opposition in his homeland from those who did not want the Catholic Croats and Orthodox Serbs to come together. At the council Strossmayer also fought unsuccessfully against the doctrine of papal infallibility; he felt the doctrine would thwart ecumenical progress with the Orthodox.

Numerous streets and monuments are dedicated to Strossmayer throughout the country, but the cathedral is by far the most impressive testimonial. Based on a style that originated in medieval needs for physical protection, the Djakovo cathedral is imposing with its large copper dome, dark brick exterior, and small number of windows. Inside, the church has a dark and haunting beauty, with round, vaulted ceilings and intricately ribbed arches that frame the doors, columns, and main sanctuary. Frescoes illuminate the space.

As he drove through the narrow city streets and neared the Vrbašlijas' neighborhood, Kerrigan felt as though he was about to reintroduce himself to the family. After all, in the year and a half since Magdalena and Nikolina traveled to Memphis, the priest had learned enough Croatian to carry himself in a conversation. "When I first tried to speak with Magdalena, the language sounded harsh, but there was a beauty to it," he said. "Look at a word like *vrt*, Croatian for 'park'–there's an 'r' as a vowel. Getting used to such words was a major effort, but I needed to pronounce them right away because the family's last name [Vrbašlija] used an 'r' for a vowel, as did the words for 'church' [*crkva*] and 'blood' [*krv*]. Croatian is like a strong drink that's hard to swallow, but there's just a little something enticing in it that makes you want another sip." For many, the region's special drink, *šlivovitz*, a plum brandy, fits that description perfectly.

Since Nikolina's surgery, Kerrigan had worked with more than two dozen patients, including some who had died. He had visited Croatia twice. He had acquired several Croatian prayer books, supplemental proof of his priestly identity for the times when he was not wearing the standard black clerical shirt. He was confident that the days of being dumbstruck by Magdalena were long forgotten.

He had little idea that the dreary drive to Djakovo, more than his language skills or work with other Croatian patients, was preparation for what he was actually to find there. The highway runs parallel to the Bosnian border, and the Vrbašlijas' saga parallels the suffering associated with Bosnia. Kerrigan was taken aback when he entered the Vrbašlijas' space.

"You know how a car feels when you get into it on a really hot day and all the air seems to be sucked out of it?" he said. "Their living space felt like that; it was about the size of a small American living room, except that this was for three people. There was a bed, a couch, a table, a few toys for Nikolina, a television, and a toilet. I don't remember much more.

"It reminded me of when I first came to work in Memphis several years ago. It was summertime and the temperatures were in the mid-nineties with high humidity. I was on a meals-on-wheels route in one of the inner-city housing developments, and in one of the first apartments I visited, I was hit by the suffocating lack of air in the apartment, similar to opening a closet that hadn't been opened in many years. Visiting the Vrbašlija family was odd because in Croatian homes I usually had just the opposite feeling, one of walking into easy, carefree homes with long, lingering dinners around the kitchen table."

If their living situation felt oppressive, the disheartening atmosphere may have been the biggest reason why. "Magdalena had lost her front teeth due to infection and had been without them for a while, so she had conditioned herself not to smile, while Goran [her husband] brooded with a blank stare," recalled the priest. "Nikolina was acting up and always having to be corrected by her parents—it was pretty bleak. To top it all off, it was the eve of All Saints' Day, a national holiday. In Croatia people throughout the country visit cemeteries to decorate family graves."

At least young Nikolina had an excuse if she felt the lack of air in her home. As an infant with transposition of the great arteries, she had been treated in Ljubljana with a palliative procedure, the Blalock-Hanlon operation, to enlarge the hole between the heart's two filling chambers, or atria, so that the blue and red blood could mix and allow oxygenated blood to enter the aorta.

This operation is performed with the patient on her side, and it is done across the right side of the patient's chest. To reach the heart from this angle, clamps are placed on the three veins leading from the right lung. When the operation is done, the clamps are released and the lungs operate properly again. In Nikolina's case one of the veins was damaged irreparably and could not service the middle portion of her lung properly. The blood that flowed into that lobe collected, as in a balloon, killing that part of the lung. The lobe had to be removed, and 20 percent of her lung volume was lost. Nikolina would thereafter be plagued by frequent coughs, colds, and assorted respiratory ailments. "She's always coughing, and she gets colds more than the rest of us," her mother reported in the summer of 1997.

> *A simple child,*
> *That lightly draws its breath*
> *And feels its life in every limb*
> *What should it know of death?*[26]

Unlike Wordsworth's verse, where breath and death only rhyme, Nikolina's lung condition complicated her overall outlook; her blue appearance was a constant reminder of her illness. The visit to Ljubljana was the latest in a series of unhappy events for her mother, Magdalena.

Magdalena was born in the village of Knezevi Vinogradi, a flat, vineyard-laden community that borders Serbia in the northwest corner of Croatia. The surrounding region, Baranja, was among the first taken by the Serbs in the war with Croatia in the summer of 1991. Magdalena avoided the danger by moving to Djakovo the previous year, as an eighteen-year-old. She relocated more out of boredom and a desire to live with friends than for any other reason. Taking a job as a waitress at a bar, she soon met her future husband, Goran, a truck driver who logged about sixty miles a day making deliveries of food and other goods to the villages surrounding Djakovo. Eight months after they began dating, Magdalena became pregnant. The social pressure in rural Croatia against unwed mothers forced her to wed quiet, handsome, sandy-haired, and blue-eyed Goran, who was nine years her senior. When she married, Magdalena hadn't finished school, her parents were divorced, she was pregnant, the country was at war—Goran for six months in the Croatian army—and one of her four brothers, who was also in the army, was jailed by his own superiors in Varazdin. The newlyweds occupied one room above Goran's parents, brother, and sister-in-law. "My life is without sense. I *had* to leave my home, I *had* to get married, and I gave birth to a sick child," she said bluntly. "I don't have a life, I don't do anything, I don't have my freedom."

Five days after Nikolina's birth in June of 1992 Magdalena realized that her daughter was not breathing right. She went to Zagreb for tests, and then to Ljubljana for the Blalock-Hanlon Procedure. The family had to pay one of the Zagreb doctors under the table for Nikolina to be referred to Ljubljana.

From the consistency of accounts given to us by parents, it is apparently not uncommon for Croatian doctors to ask for money from families in exchange for better care. This can occur at any time during the evaluation and referral process, and it is not limited to cardiologists or surgeons. Doctors also form kickback networks with other doctors for making referrals. There even have been rumors of foreign doctors asking for money from Croatian parents, knowing that the parents are accustomed to the practice. There are two major reasons Croatia's healthcare system has developed this unsavory practice. First, there are limited medical resources in the country. Where resources are limited, all the needs cannot be met. And if doctors are not well paid, there is a temptation for the doctors to establish their own criteria. They can give preferential treatment, and they can exclude patients from treatment altogether. Pediatric cardiology, a specialized area, lends itself to additional corruption because parents cannot change heart doctors as easily as they can pediatricians.

A second cause of this practice comes from the aftereffects of communism and the war. Immediately following the war, doctors were poorly paid. Doctors know that they hold the key to the child's life, and some exploit this for their own profit. There is no accountability or safeguards in the present system. "It is normal to be asked for money," a father said without emotion to Kerrigan.

In the United States, if one is wealthy enough, preferential treatment can be obtained. Unlike in Croatia, however, a patient will not be excluded because of poverty. Novick said: "In western Tennessee, at least, you will get into the healthcare system even if you fall through the cracks—you make too much money for state insurance but not enough for private health insurance. We write off thousands of dollars of charges a year for children in these in-between situations. Here you are more likely to find a chief executive officer's daughter in a hospital bed next to someone from a housing project. What happens in Croatia is not really an issue in the United States."

After Ljubljana the family needed additional and better assistance to make Nikolina's next operation possible. Kerrigan may have covered the last leg of Nikolina's pilgrimage to Memphis, but it was another priest who began helping the family several months beforehand. Fr. Evica Rebec worked for the Catholic social service agency Caritas in Djakovo and was known for helping Croatian children in Slavonia during the war. Nikolina's parish priest put the family in touch with Fr. Rebec, who began making the necessary contacts. One of his calls was to Diana Lohr-Matetic, a director of a humanitarian organization in Hamburg, Germany, that arranged transportation for patients in the former Yugoslavia. The organization would cover all travel expenses for Magdalena and Nikolina, and Lohr-Matetic would also frequently call Magdalena and encourage the young mother as she prepared for her American adventure. "Diana was super, always asking how I was doing," said Magdalena.

Having had their fill of their first cardiologist, the Vrbašlijas turned to Ivan Malcic, whose sense of justice was piqued by the family's plight. Malcic also recognized the severity of Nikolina's condition and alerted Novick when the surgeon visited Zagreb in April 1993. "There was a lot of concern about her," said Novick, "concern that a two-year-old might already have elevated pulmonary artery pressures, plus the fact that she lost her middle lobe in Ljubljana." Malcic and Novick decided that Nikolina was suitable for surgery in America. Even after he passed his clinical care over to Novick in Memphis, Malcic was determined to see Nikolina's surgery through to a successful finish, and when Magdalena and Nikolina returned to Zagreb, Malcic greeted them at the railroad station and celebrated by buying lunch for everyone.

At the time, Magdalena could not reflect on this sudden outpouring of goodwill from doctors, priests, and humanitarian workers. "I didn't have time to think about anything except Nikolina's health. I just ran around from hospital to hospital," she said.

Magdalena and Nikolina flew to Memphis in June 1994 and were met at the airport by their hosts, Laverne and Marvin Strumminger. Laverne volunteered in part because she had a more than fifty-year-old debt of gratitude that she was still making payments on. Born in Memphis in 1934, she had contracted rheumatic fever when she was five years old

and was bedridden for a year. Rheumatic fever is a complication of
"strep" infection. It can result in heart enlargement, murmurs, or heart
failure. The incidence of rheumatic fever has declined dramatically in
developed countries since Laverne's childhood, now that antibiotics have
conquered strep infections. At the time, however, rheumatic fever was
greatly feared; Laverne was told that she might not make it past her
teens. Having survived without any long-term effects, Laverne was par-
tial to any child with a heart condition. One day in the spring of 1994 she
came across a small article in *The Commercial Appeal* describing
Novick's work. The story also struck a chord with her husband, Marvin,
a Brooklyn, New York, native, whose late father liked to send anonymous
gifts when he saw a hard-luck story in the paper. "He never had much
financial security, but he would send them something," offered Marvin.

Marvin and Laverne, the parents of three adult children, were members of the Anshei-sphard Beth congregation of Orthodox Jews. Laverne
said, "We do something for others because we want to do it, and we hope
that someone would do the same for us."

Laverne tracked down Elizabeth Jameson, host coordinator for the
program, and had the Strummingers' name placed on the list of potential
host families. They first hosted a Jamaican child whose surgery was
scrubbed because of the boy's illness, and then they were assigned to
Magdalena and Nikolina.

Laverne, a warm, petite woman with light-brown hair, was raised in the
Lauderdale Courts housing project in downtown Memphis. Today the project stands half-abandoned in the shadows of the world-renowned St.
Judes Children's Research Hospital. Through her rabbi, Laverne met her
husband Marvin when he was stationed in the Memphis area during the
Korean War. As proprietor of the Lamp Shade House, a store for home
decorations, Marvin provided a comfortable lifestyle for Laverne in suburban east Memphis, but she could still relate to poverty when she saw it.
"When I saw that baby [Magdalena]—a very pretty girl, a natural beauty—
get off the plane with her baby, from clear across the world, without knowing anyone, I thought, 'O my God, how can I help this child?' And then I
saw that she only had a gym bag for the two of them. Altogether she had

jeans and the shoes on her feet, two blouses, and two changes of clothes for Nikolina. It was frightening."

Laverne approached the hosting task as if both she and Magdalena were twenty years younger. She protected Magdalena as if Magdalena was Nikolina's age, and she often referred to Magdalena as a child. "I was afraid to leave her alone at the hospital—I just couldn't let that child be by herself," said Laverne. Two other Croatian mothers and three Croatian physicians were in Memphis at the same time, but Laverne kept a close watch over her adult guest. When Magdalena developed a tooth infection, Laverne set up an appointment with a dentist. Unfortunately, Magdalena's infection did not subside in time for her to be treated, and her condition deteriorated when she returned to Croatia.

Laverne allowed Magdalena to take care of domestic needs around the Strumminger residence. Magdalena was adamant that Laverne not lift a finger at home on her behalf. "Once, after dinner, I went to pick up the plates to bring them to the washer, and she slapped my hand and took them herself," said Laverne. "She did the same thing one day with the vacuum cleaner. She took it right out of my hands." For recreation Magdalena would occasionally take a dip in the pool and hot tub.

For communication Laverne and Marvin used the same English-Croatian phrase book that Kerrigan found. "Magdalena and I would go through phrases, 'Where's the bathroom?' 'I have to mail a letter' 'I would like some ice cream,' and we just picked out the words we needed to communicate," said Laverne. Sometimes the phrase book was inadequate. Laverne recalls taking Magdalena to the bathroom to indicate the shower, toilet, and sink. There were some tense moments one evening when religion was the topic. Somehow, when the Strummingers were trying to make known that they were Jewish, Magdalena interpreted "not believing in Jesus" as "not believing in God," and she became unnerved. Laverne rushed to find one of the Croatian doctors the next morning to set things straight. "When he explained that I was Jewish, and that I believe in God and am not an atheist, Magdalena came up to me and gave me a big hug," said Laverne.

There was another hug at a memorable moment. "Magdalena never showed any emotion until the moment came for Nikolina to be taken for surgery, " said Laverne. "The nurses came for Nikolina, and Magdalena hesitated before she let her go. And then Magdalena grabbed me, hugged me, and cried like a baby. This was a frightened, scared-to-death type of hug. How could she know if she would see Nikolina alive again?"

The Strummingers stayed with Magdalena in the waiting room during the surgery. One of the Croatian doctors came out to tell Magdalena the good news of the successful surgery. Soon after, Magdalena saw her daughter in the intensive-care unit, alive and well again.

"Nikolina really did quite well. She went to the O.R., came off the respirator the next day, and then stayed in the hospital a few days after that without any problem," said Novick. "Her case was risky, but she did very well. We're delighted for her."

At the end of her stay in Memphis, Magdalena again gave Laverne a big hug, but this time joined with tears because it was so difficult to say goodbye. "My father was never there when we needed him," she said. "Laverne and Marvin became my family because they were there when I needed them the most. They were like family—gifts for our birthdays, hospital visits every day, always worrying about Nikolina and me."

Magdalena also was grateful for Novick's role in her daughter's healing. A couple of years after the operation the surgeon pulled a Christmas card from Nikolina's file. The card played "Jinglebells" and was accompanied by a terse message from Magdalena: "*Sretan Bozic, Sretan Nova godina* [Merry Christmas and Happy New Year]—you have done me a grand favor—Nikolina is OK—Mother."

How long will Nikolina be OK? Long-term survival for children like Nikolina—with transposition and no ventricular septal defect—who undergo a Senning operation is in the neighborhood of 80 percent. The Senning operation wasn't described until 1960; the longest-term survivor is only approaching forty years of age. Some patients develop right ventricular failure; others need to have their valves fixed. "Nikolina has a very good chance to do very well for a very long time," concluded the surgeon, "with a 15 percent chance that fifteen to twenty years down the road she will develop significant heart failure."

The prognosis for the family's happiness is more difficult to gauge. In one sense the family is an advertisement for immigration to America.

Emma Lazarus's inscription on the Statue of Liberty in New York Harbor seems specifically addressed to the family: "Give me your tired, your poor, your huddled masses, yearning to breathe free." When Kerrigan or others would call Djakovo to check on the family, Nikolina would ask, "When are we going to America?" But her family does not have the means or energy; they seem resigned to their meager existence in Djakovo. Another girl was added to the family when Daniela was born in August 1996. Says Laverne Strumminger, "I didn't know it when I was in poverty. If Magdalena didn't know she was in poverty before, now she does. And where she comes from, with the destruction, the shelling, the bombing, I have no hope that things will improve. I have the feeling that if she could get here, it would be a better life, but that seems so hard."

Djakovo and the surrounding Slavonia region represent the unfinished business of the war in Croatia, a place where the destruction was the worst and the embers of hatred and division burn the longest. If Croatia had an equivalent of America's aging northern industrial cities, dubbed collectively the Rust Belt, Slavonia would be it. At this writing, in the autumn of 1997, the easternmost part of Slavonia is still under United Nations administration, and issues of poverty and resettlement in Croatia are the worst in the area.

The symbolic importance of breathing in the spiritual life was not lost on the authors of the Hebrew and Christian scriptures. In the second creation account in Genesis, God "formed man out of the clay of the ground and blew into his nostrils the breath of life, and so man became a living being" (Gn 2:7). And in John's gospel, when the risen Christ gives the Spirit to his disciples, he does so with a breath: "He breathed on them and said, 'Receive the holy Spirit'" (Jn 20:22). Oxygen symbolizes spiritual revitalization. Is the lost portion of Nikolina's lung symbolic of the family's "shortness of breath" and their struggle to find room to breathe and retain their spirit?

The physician who discovered pulmonary circulation was also a theologian, the sixteenth-century Spaniard Michael Servetus. He tried to describe the relationship of the persons of the Trinity—Father, Son, and Spirit—in terms of the relationship between the heart, lungs, and blood. He said that people receive God's Spirit in the same way that oxygen circulates through the heart and lungs. Since he was burned at the stake as a heretic in 1553,

Dr. Novick and patient.

A sign warns visitors not to bring guns into Rebro University Hospital in Zagreb.

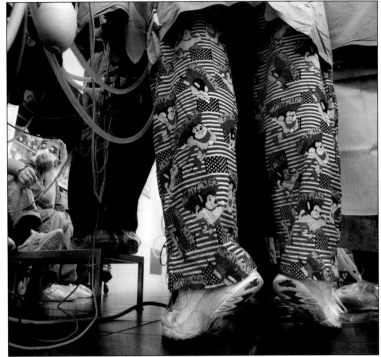

Dr. Novick wearing his Mighty Mouse scrubs as he works at the operating table in Rebro University Hospital in Zagreb.

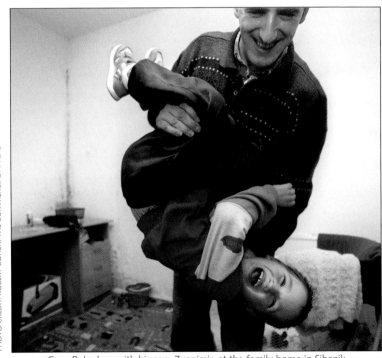

Grgo Rak plays with his son, Zvonimir, at the family home in Sibenik.

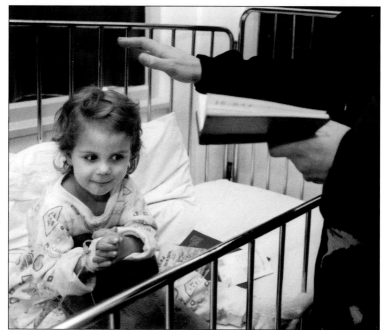

Fr. Kerrigan prays with Ivana Reljac, who has her hands clasped in prayer.

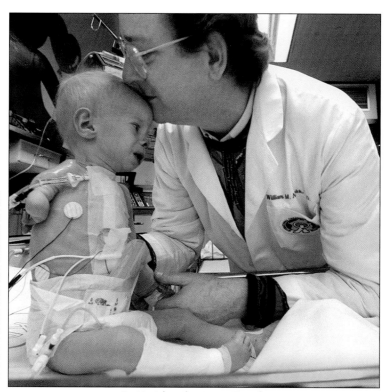

Dr. Novick and patient in Zagreb.

Fr. Joe Kerrigan anoints Ivana Lovric the day before her surgery in Zagreb.

The crucifix overlooks a medical team wheeling a patient from the operating room to the intensive care unit at Rebro University Hospital in Zagreb.

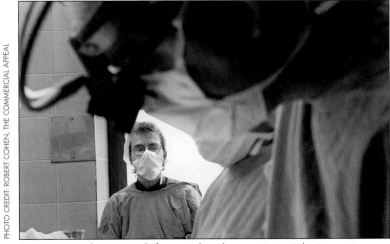

Fr. Kerrigan watches Dr. Novick (foreground) work on a patient in Rebro's operating room.

At Rebro University Hospital in January 1997, Kerrigan, Novick, and ICHF nurse Elizabeth Jameson surround Ljubica Haramnija and her son, Fran, who was treated for heart disease a year earlier in Memphis. Like many ICHF "alumni"—families who have had their children treated by the team—Ljubica and Fran greet the team whenever it returns to Croatia.

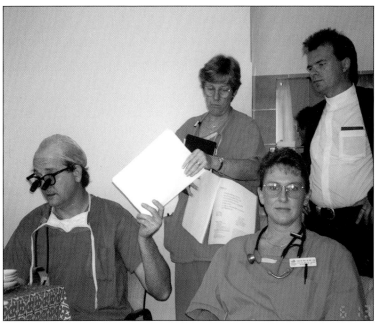

(left to right): Novick, ICHF nurses Rocky Thomas and Charlene Benz, and Kerrigan prepare for a day of surgery at Rebro University Hospital in Zagreb in June 1995.

Kerrigan is greeted by Franjo Cardinal Kuharic at the cardinal's residence in Zagreb, June 1995.

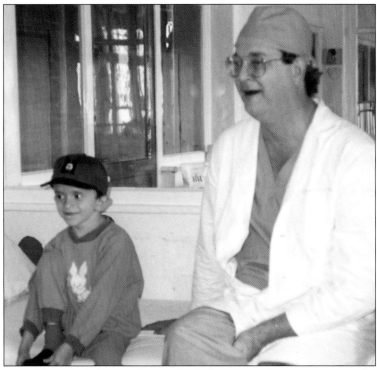

Novick has a bedside visit with an unidentified patient at Rebro University Hospital, Zagreb, during an ICHF trip.

Fr. Joe Kerrigan and Mišo Sirovina stand in front of Sacred Heart Cathedral in Sarajevo minutes before the arrival of Pope John Paul II on April 11, 1997.

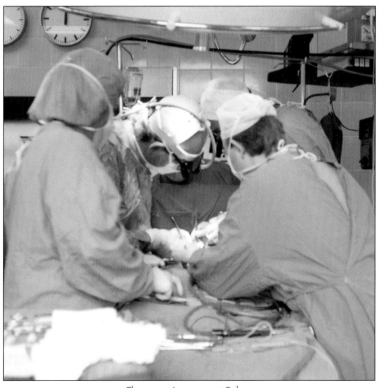

The operating room at Rebro.

Dr. Ivan Malcic and Dr. Novick in the cardiology office in Zagreb.

Dr. Novick wearing his Mighty Mouse scrubs.

his theological views did not fall on receptive ears, but he did write one thing that no one should object to: "He who really understands what is involved in the breathing of man has already sensed the breath of God." Somehow, Nikolina's lung deficit is related to the heavy-heartedness almost palpable among the Vrbašlijas.

Within many families the diagnosis of serious congenital heart disease in a child generates an all-consuming focus on efforts for a cure. Families—especially mothers—work, eat, breathe, and pray with the child's illness never too far from center stage. With Magdalena, we got another impression, the sense that her daughter's illness had value in diverting the focus away from the deeper unhappiness in the family's life. For several months Nikolina's disease gave Magdalena something more to her life than a feeling of being trapped in poverty and robbed of her youth through an obligatory marriage. The trip to America, in particular, gave her a brief glimpse of another kind of life. With a happy outcome at the end of treatment, families usually find themselves rejuvenated, energized, even spiritually reborn. Alas, Nikolina's successful surgery seems to have been only a palliative event in the big picture of the family's life. In Djakovo the look in Magdalena's eyes now registered fatigue and passivity rather than the intensity Kerrigan saw in Memphis. Poverty and hopelessness cannot be surgically repaired.

Goran drove Kerrigan back to Zagreb on a fog-shrouded evening that was even gloomier than the priest's entrance into Djakovo. His thoughts again turned to the New Jersey Turnpike and its soul-numbing expanse of asphalt and concrete.

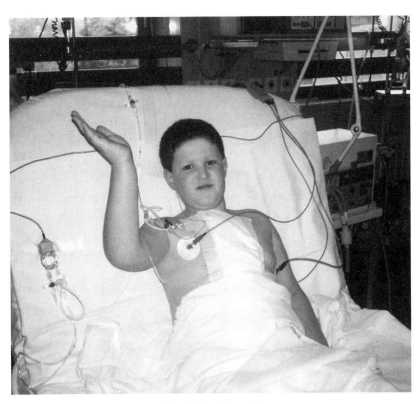

Tomislav Husnik

8
Tomislav Husnik

"A joyful heart is the health of the body"
—Proverbs 17:22

Children in the cardiology unit of Zagreb's Rebro University Hospital sleep four or five to a room in a spartan space encased by windows that run roughly from the height of an adult's waist to the ceiling. The rooms open into a heavily traveled corridor, through which people and equipment move almost constantly during the day. The glass and thin walls do little to buffer the patients from the incessant traffic, and the terrazzo floors of the hallway only amplify the cacophony. A door on the back wall of each cardiology room leads to a balcony with a panoramic view of Zagreb from the fourth and top floor of the hospital.

The children are grouped together because of lack of money and space for private rooms; the fourth floor of Rebro serves the same needs that a complete children's hospital would in the United States. The lack of space also prevents parents from having room to interact with their children. For all the disadvantages that this arrangement presents, especially the lack of privacy, there is one big advantage over American hospitals: the children can form a little community, talking and playing together, and sharing their hospital experiences. The rooms have a warm, alive feel, as opposed to the institutional sterility of American hospital rooms.

Early one winter evening in January 1997, during an International Children's Heart Foundation surgical team trip to Croatia, Kerrigan was visiting a patient room illuminated only by the flickering glow of the television set. Three patients, each about seven years old, were seated together on a bed, glued to the Croatian children's cartoon "Hugo." Hugo appeals to children with his big ears and eyes, curled hair, and odd way of speaking. The show's highlight is when the young viewers call in and use their touch-tone telephones to move Hugo around the screen. On this evening, however, the group's attention was occasionally diverted by a fourth child in the room, a boy who had arrived during the day. He coughed frequently in his bed in the opposite corner and seemed to be in discomfort.

Kerrigan went over and introduced himself to the young man. Tomislav was about five years older than the others in the room. After finding out why the boy was in the hospital (pneumonia) and asking if he needed anything for his cough ("the nurse just gave me something, thank you"), the priest asked where he was from. Tomislav said Karlovac, a city of about one hundred thousand inhabitants not far from Zagreb. Kerrigan asked if his last name was Husnik. Tomislav, looking surprised, said in English, "Yes, how did you know?" Kerrigan responded, "I've been looking for you for three years. You're in a book I'm writing with Dr. Novick!"

Indeed, Tomislav had made such a lasting impression on Novick and other doctors and nurses during a surgical trip to Zagreb in April 1993—before Novick had moved to Memphis, met Kerrigan, or formalized the outreach to Croatian children—that when it came time to choose patients for the book, Tomislav was selected without hesitation, even though much more was known about other Croatian children who came to Memphis and interacted at length with families, doctors, and nurses.

During the war, as a seven-year-old cardiology patient, Tomislav sang patriotic songs to fellow patients to cheer them up during air-raid alerts in Zagreb, in spite of his own suffering. After he was healed by Novick, he greeted the doctor by serenading him with thanks at the Zagreb airport, dressed in a traditional Croatian folk costume. In Isaiah's vision of perfect peace, often cited during the Christmas season, "the wolf shall be a guest of the lamb, and the leopard shall lie down with the kid; the calf and the young lion shall browse together, with a little child to guide them" (Is 11:6). Tomislav Husnik was a fine example of the child steering others through adversity—with aplomb.

Kerrigan was amazed by their meeting; the coincidence of the encounter was deepened by the fact that Tomislav was spending his first day in the hospital since that April 1993 stay. For his part, Tomislav was equally flabbergasted that this stranger from America knew so much about him. His round brown eyes beamed with each tidbit of information the priest related. A husky boy with chubby red checks and close-cropped brown hair atop a square head, Tomislav was polite to a fault, promptly adding "please" or "thank you" to every statement. His only hesitation came when, after telling Kerrigan that he still liked to sing, he was asked by the priest to demonstrate his ability. "There are so many songs that I don't know what to choose," he said. Finally, he cleared his throat and began singing in Croatian:

God save Croatia, my dear home
And the people who are blessed
In front of your altar.
If you need, my Lord
Here receive my testament
Take my life from me
And give it to Croatia.

By now the other three patients in the room had turned from the television character to the real-life one in their room, and they gave Tomislav a hearty round of applause for his rendition of the patriotic hymn.

It was with such spirit that Tomislav had charmed the Americans who cared for him in 1993, during the first of Novick's trips to Rebro University Hospital. Novick had led an eight-member team—one perfusionist (who runs the cardiopulmonary bypass machine), two scrub nurses, four intensive-care nurses—and brought an estimated $150,000 worth of donated drugs and equipment. Novick obtained the donations through his one-man telephone solicitation of companies like Medtronic, Cryolife, Siemens, and Nellcor. The Variety Club's International Lifeline Program sponsored the trip, with the exception of their hotel bill in

Zagreb, which was paid for by a Croatian cigarette company, Tvornica Duhana Zagreb.

The team was to have flown on Austrian Airlines from New York's John F. Kennedy International Airport to Vienna and then on to Zagreb. Upon arriving at JFK, however, they were informed that their flight to Vienna was postponed and that their travel to Europe would be delayed eight hours, a delay that would have postponed the first day of surgery. The team was transferred to Swiss Air, which brought them to Zagreb only fifteen minutes later than originally scheduled. The delegation of Croatians who would welcome the team at Zagreb's airport knew that the Austrian Air flight was canceled but did not know of the team's new arrangements, yet they came to the airport anyway. "Go figure," Novick mused.

The first trip was little more than a year after hostilities had ceased in Croatia, but the front lines were still in place around the country and there were occasional skirmishes in spite of the presence of the UN peacekeeping force, UNPROFOR. The Serbs occupied one-third of the new republic, and the territory they claimed nearly severed Croatia into two sections. Rocky Thomas, R.N., who had worked with Novick in Orlando and joined him on the first four Croatia trips, said, "While we never saw any battles waged, we frequently saw the results: orphaned children, children with mothers in detention camps, doctors being called away to care for wounded soldiers, and children forced to grow up too early."

Upon arrival in Zagreb Novick also perceived apprehension among the Croatian medical personnel. "They had just had a surgical group visit from another country in the last year that had had very bad results. The visiting team blamed the Croatians. After our mission unfolded successfully, we were told that before we came people were saying, 'It's going to be a bloodbath when the Americans get here.'

"During our team meeting the first morning, after we completed presenting and discussing our plan, Dr. Biocina, a junior cardiac surgeon from Rebro, announced that he hoped no children would die, because after their experience with the last visiting team, the Croatians had decided they would have to shoot someone from the team if a child died. He had an extremely dry sense of humor, but one of our nurses took him seriously and was petrified for days."

Like a church revival that seeks to provide a lasting spiritual boost to the life of a congregation in a short time, trips such as those undertaken by the International Children's Heart Foundation hope to focus and intensify surgical activity for the benefit of all who partake in the experience: patients and their families, host-country doctors and nurses, and the traveling team itself.

A church revival and an ICHF trip both build upon customary structures. Congregants typically hear about a half-hour's worth of preaching each Sunday, but in a church revival a missionary will preach for more than an hour a night over the course of an entire week. In the normal week of a pediatric heart surgeon, one or two operations are performed daily, but in trips to countries like Croatia, Novick may do as many as four a day. The itinerant preacher inspires churchgoers with an aura of the talented "outsider" who brings a new message of salvation, while the expertise of the surgical team, enhanced by the wizardry of new equipment, achieves the same uplifting objective within the hospital community. Over the course of several trips Novick rewrote pages of Croatia's surgical annals by introducing a number of complex operations to the country. "A truly impressive number of operations were performed for the first time in our clinic, and this should be seen as a historic event," noted Ivan Malcic.

To counter the fear often produced in children by the white coats of doctors, Novick wears custom-made, brightly colored surgical scrubs featuring cartoon characters, including the Tasmanian Devil, Bugs Bunny, and Mighty Mouse of "Here I come to save the day" fame. He makes spontaneous rounds on the floors for the children and parents to see him and to calm their anxieties. The Mighty Mouse slogan has meaning; it isn't as trite or as arrogant as it might first appear. According to Kerrigan: "There is a sense of salvation present on these trips, in terms of the all-out effort to heal as many people as possible. After a day or two it creates an energy that the routine of hospital life does not. Also, even though there are more operations than usual, each case takes on a greater and unique value. Momentum builds, and by the end it's as if the drama of surgery itself is restored to its original importance. In Zagreb my prayer life is very rich, because my days are so full of life. In fact, prayer is the only way I can direct all that I see during the day."

"The team in Croatia is more cohesive than a hospital group in America for the simple reason that there are no distractions," added Novick. "After a day of surgery, no one has to rush home to cook dinner or get a dog from the vet. Small talk does not take place as often, since there's no HBO or front-page news to talk about from the night before. Everyone is focused intensely on the child's progress."

The ICHF team in Croatia, traveling mostly with nurses trained in pediatric heart care, is even more focused than teams found in the United States, where children are frequently cared for in pediatric intensive-care units (PICU's) or in adult cardiac intensive-care units (CICU's). In a PICU there may be drowning victims, trauma patients, pneumonia cases, and others, so the nurses are not always specially trained to take care of the postoperative needs of heart patients. In a CICU children with heart defects are mixed with adults, and again the nurses have more general skills.

During a trip the emphasis is usually on what the team gives—the new life and health gained by the patients through the donation of time, talent, equipment, and drugs. No less real, however, is what the team members receive in the process: insight into different clinical approaches; a more direct, paperwork-free mode of treating patients; and the opportunity to collaborate with peers and form friendships with patients and families at a deeper level than usual. For some, the trips result in personal or professional transformations.

In the gospel of Matthew, Jesus promises an eternal reward to those who minister to those in material need: "Amen, I say to you, whatever you did for one of these least brothers of mine, you did for me" (Mt 25:40). Patients like Tomislav Husnik point to that reward in what they offer to their caregivers.

The boy's medical dossier was so challenging that a successful outcome would seem sufficient reward for those who treated him. Tomislav was born in 1984 (shortly after the Winter Olympics in Sarajevo) with transposition of the great arteries, a defect he shared with Karmen Koščak, Ivan Pozaric, Krešimir Cirkovic, and Nikolina Vrbašlija. Tomislav also had pulmonary stenosis and a ventricular septal defect (VSD). Nine days after his birth the heart disease was discovered and he was referred to Dr. Branco Marinovic at

Rebro. A catheterization was performed, and shortly after his first birthday he had a palliative operation in Zagreb. He developed normally until the corrective Rastelli operation in Munich in 1990.

"He had very complicated heart disease," said Malcic, who was overseeing Tomislav's care at the time of Novick's arrival in 1993. "The surgery in Germany was not the solution for his disease because calcification [a buildup of plaquelike material] developed between the right ventricle and pulmonary artery. This calcification was not expected for ten years, but in this child it came very quickly. He had very dangerous attacks of cyanosis and abnormal heartbeats. A few times he was in a very dangerous situation."

Although the use of valve conduits connecting the right ventricle to the pulmonary artery gives children like Tomislav near-normal physiology, they have problems. The conduits, made from either human or pig tissue, have a limited life span. They degenerate by calcification or the children simply outgrow them and need replacements. In Tomislav's case the calcium buildup came more quickly and heavily than expected, causing the arrhythmia.

Tomislav was also in a dangerous situation in his small village near Karlovac during the outbreak of war in Croatia in 1991. The fighting engulfed Karlovac and threatened Zagreb itself. "I remember the loud shots and terrifying detonations," the boy said. "A lot of people died near our church, and now there is a monument dedicated to them."

The ICHF team did not usually travel to Karlovac. On the second ICHF trip to Croatia in August 1993, the team was given a weekend break and went to the northern Adriatic coast, passing through Karlovac on the way out of Zagreb. The warning signs for grenades and rockets on the main road were sobering reminders of the fighting that had occurred there.

When Tomislav went to Rebro for checkups or for treatment of the effects of his heart disease during this time, there were always alarms sounding in the hospital. "We used to run to the basement because of the grenade warnings," the boy recalled. Tomislav's parents were not able to travel from Karlovac to visit, and the boy stayed in the hospital under the care of the nurses, who did his laundry and attended to his needs. "I would rather stay in Zagreb one month than in Karlovac for one week because I liked the nurses," he said. It was this group of nurses and patients that Tomislav first regaled with his patriotic singing.

"He was always a very nice young man," added Malcic. "Tomislav is a very happy young man, and he sang patriotic songs during his hospital stay because of the war. Children as well as adults were very agitated, and they sang patriotic songs. He is an only child, and I know the family well. They are poor, and the mother is sick; we had a big interest in saving the child."

Tomislav's condition worsened as the war ended in early 1992. By 1993 he was in need of another Rastelli operation, and the urgency coincided with the arrival of Novick and the American team in 1993. The situation was fraught with uncertainty. "This was very risky because it was a repeat operation and we were very afraid of the outcome," admitted Malcic.

"Tomislav was presented to us but not pushed on us," recalled Novick. "It was our first trip, and the Croatians did not know how much confidence to have in our abilities."

The Rastelli operation, a complicated reconstructive procedure, had never been performed in Croatia. But when the success of the trip was assured after the first few days proceeded without fatalities, Malcic asked Novick if he would operate on Tomislav. He did so on the trip's last day of surgery. The American team members would not be the only ones to look after him, however, because his hospital stay would extend past that of the team. This created concern.

"The Croatians had no experience in caring for children recovering from complex operations," said Novick. "We were reluctant to operate on complex cases late in our visit, but what choice was there? Without our expertise, they would not receive operations at all; without our post-operative management skills, they might not survive. My approach is somewhat radical: do the complex cases, do a good operation, and then try to get these children out of the intensive-care unit before we leave the country. It's emotionally difficult to do this and find out later that a child died in the hospital. At the start of our mission to Croatia, no child whom we left in the ICU on a ventilator survived. But we have not had a fatality in such a situation in the last two years. The ICU staff has learned a lot over the last four years."

Tomislav's parents went to the Zagreb cathedral while the operation was pending. His mother went to the front of the church and said quietly, "God, it's in your hands now—let your will be done—life or death, but no more suffering."

Tomislav was the last of the fourteen children selected for surgery. When he first met the American doctors and nurses, he said that if his heart was fixed, he would be as "happy as a kidney in fat," no doubt a Croatian variant on the American "happy as a pig in mud." Rocky Thomas said, "When I consider the courage of Tomislav and others like him, I look back with shame on my initial fear of going to Croatia."

During the week some patients became ill with fever or infection, and the surgical schedule was juggled. Tomislav saw the adjustments in the schedule through the eyes of his belly. "Dr. Malcic told me Dr. Novick was coming from America. In the ward the boys and girls were saying that somebody would be operated on, but we didn't know who. One day they gave me only sugar water and no breakfast because they thought I was going to be operated on. But in the afternoon I realized that I wasn't going to be operated on because they gave me lunch. After the day's surgery Dr. Novick came and chose me to be operated on the next day, and after that I felt much better. All I remember about what came next is Dr. Novick [after the operation]. He is tall and he took pictures and videos of me after the operation."

Novick has another recollection. "I will never forget making rounds on the day that we left the country. I was worried sick about Tomislav, and he was sitting there waving and talking to us. Most important, he was off the ventilator. He was the first Rastelli in Croatia, but that wasn't it, it was his spirit," concluded Novick. "We were all standing in the hall, and he was singing patriotic songs at the top of his lungs."

Close to four years after he won the hearts of the American team, Tomislav was still winning new fans among healthcare professionals. "He is the child I cannot forget. It was love at first sight," said Dr. Ruza Grizelj Šovagovic, a first-year pediatric resident at Rebro who, like Kerrigan, met Tomislav in January 1997. "One day in the hospital, Dr. Malcic said to me, 'This is Tomislav Husnik—go treat him.' He became my first case presentation."

Every week fifteen to twenty of the residents at Rebro have a meeting in which their cases are discussed and evaluated. Tomislav's pneumonia was not extraordinary; he was treated with antibiotics and left the hospital after about two weeks. The resident's interaction with the boy, on the other hand, was memorable.

"As I was taking care of him, I talked to him a lot," she began. "He was very optimistic, always walking around the hospital. He'd be in the endocrinology ward or in the playroom—always somewhere, always happy and extroverted wherever he was. When I would find him, I would say, 'Tomislav, I want to speak to you,' and he would say, 'Here I am, let's go,' and we would return to the cardiology floor. He took me very seriously. I think he's very serious and smart, and he's somehow grown-up. He's like a twenty-five-year-old but still a child."

Dr. Šovagovic, whose husband, Filip, is one of Croatia's leading film actors, was impressed by Tomislav's choice of a song when she learned of his performance for Kerrigan and the other patients in the room that night. "He chose a national song. People sing this to get confidence and strength. And I think this song came out of him, that he didn't choose it. It is a song of sacrifice, and either you have this sense of sacrifice or you don't. Tomislav has it already."

Tomislav was named after the first king of Croatia, who reigned from 910–928. He declared himself king of the Croats after successfully overcoming outside invaders. The connection between the country's founding king and Tomislav Husnik is not lost on Dr. Šovagovic. "For nine hundred years people tried to kill us, change our language, but we resisted," she said. "Tomislav is a sign that Croatia will always live. After three operations, he is so full of life inside—call it God—it is life and power.

"Children are innocent. I always get energy from a child, but I get more from Tomislav because it is rare to find people who can teach you something. You can think and learn and feel something from him. I admire him because he has had to overcome things that I'm not sure many people could. He has had three operations and still can sing and laugh and give to others."

The greatness of the child has a strong foundation in the Christian tradition: "The disciples approached Jesus and said, 'Who is the greatest in the kingdom of heaven?' He called a child over, placed it in their midst, and said, 'Amen, I say to you, unless you turn and become like children, you will not enter the kingdom of heaven. Whoever humbles himself like this child is the greatest in the kingdom of heaven. And whoever receives one child such as this in my name receives me'" (Mt 18:1–5).

Tomislav was not alone among Croatian children in the ability to give to others despite illness and hardship. Rocky Thomas said: "I never ceased to be amazed at how the children looked out for each other. Orphans or those whose parents could not travel to the hospital were cared for by other children. A thirteen-year-old girl with terminal liver disease endeared herself to us by translating for the Croatian-speaking parents. She had learned English in school and offered her services to us."

Tomislav was not alone among patients whose happy spirit seemed to facilitate physical healing. "A joyful heart is the health of the body," wrote the author of the book of Proverbs (17:22). In the adult world the connection between spirit and health was recently described more scientifically. A 1995 study of more than two hundred adult cardiovascular surgery patients at Dartmouth-Hitchcock Medical Center revealed that a patient's reliance on religious faith was an excellent predictor of survival. Patients without strong faith were three times more likely to die than patients with faith.[7]

For his part, Tomislav Husnik may perpetuate the enriching doctor-patient exchanges he has participated in over the years if he succeeds in his current goal to become a doctor. He has already adopted a medical student's work ethic. "When I get home, I first study, and if there is any time left, I play," he reported. When he plays, Tomislav can ride his bike and throw snowballs with the best of them. Tomislav is also not putting his singing talents to waste; he has joined the school choir and sings in church every Sunday. When the priest invites the congregation to "Lift up your hearts," Tomislav can respond better than most, "We have lifted them up to the Lord."

Tomislav Husnik encouraged his fellow patients by singing patriotic songs during the battle in Rebro.

Interlude

"The walls of my heart"
—Jeremiah 4:19

During the medical team's January 1997 trip to Croatia, fifteen-year-old Ivana Lovric was successfully treated for a rare defect. Her heart was literally too big. As a metaphor, this describes any number of Croatian patients. It seemed uniquely appropriate to Ivana, as though she needed an abnormally big heart to contain all the suffering she had endured in her young life.

My breast! My breast! how I suffer!
The walls of my heart!
My heart beats wildly, I cannot be still;
For I have heard the sound of the trumpet,
the alarm of war. (Jer 4:19)

The wall of Ivana's heart, the septum, was precisely where her problem lay. Her septum was too big, about forty millimeters in depth, whereas the usual is about six or seven millimeters. And Ivana, like Jeremiah, knew too well "the alarm of war," having been forcibly relocated during the war from her hometown of Ilok, in eastern Slavonia, to

Opatija, where she stayed with her sister and mother in a hotel that had been converted for displaced Croatians.

And yet, the war between the Serbs and the Croats saved her life. Shortly after she arrived in Opatija, Ivana went to England for seven months with her mother, sister, and two other family members. She contracted the flu, and a doctor who treated her heard a heart murmur. "Before that, I didn't know I had a heart problem," she said to Kerrigan in her hospital room before surgery, as he anointed her with the sacrament of the sick. She had thick brown hair and a steady, sober expression in her brown eyes. "That doctor was the one who found I had a problem."

She was diagnosed with idiopathic hypertrophic subaortic stenosis (IHSS), a defect where the outlet of the heart's left chamber is obstructed by an abnormal growth of muscle, so that when the heart pumps blood it meets the obstruction. A common result of the disease is sudden death. Ivana's father had died suddenly five years before her diagnosis, and although nobody knows for sure, Ivana now suspects he had a heart attack. Her defect can be hereditary. "It seemed to me that she was afraid she would die like her father," said Dr. Šovagovic, "and she was scared."

Novick treated Ivana with the Morrow operation, named after the doctor who developed it. "You cut a furrow in the muscle down to the point where the hypertrophy [abnormal growth] stops," said the surgeon. "Ivana had an extremely long segment of hypertrophy in her septum, extending almost to the apex of her left ventricle.

"Her recovery was very gratifying because her echocardiogram showed no obstruction. Unfortunately, the operation does not remove the risk of sudden death. Earlier this year there was a boy with the same problem who had to be resuscitated by his father at their home after his sudden 'death.' We had operated on him just a few months before."

Šovagovic witnessed Ivana's operation; it was the first time the twenty-eight-year-old doctor had been present for open-heart surgery. "It was strange to see Ivana after the operation, because all I was thinking about was her heart inside," she said. "I was looking at her in the eyes, but I was thinking of her heart. It was a strange feeling. When I saw a baby delivered for the first time, it was amazing, I didn't know what to do—

laugh or cry. I was so impressed that I was confused. A heart operation is different because the heart has meaning."

After the operation Ivana embodied yet another image from the verse from Jeremiah: her heart began beating wildly. She overcame the episode of tachycardia and recovered normally. Despite the surgery, however, the heart of Ivana's being was not made smaller. The experience of ethnic cleansing forged strength within her. "I heard that she was from Ilok, and when I heard that, I wanted to give her anything she wanted," said Šovagovic "And then she said that one day she would be back in Ilok, and I concluded that she is a girl with a brave heart."

Ivana's brave heart was formed in the crucible of eastern Slavonia, where the worst atrocities in the Serbian-Croatian conflict occurred. Ilok, a town rich in vineyards and fruit gardens, borders Serbia, and before the war it was populated equally by Croatians and Serbs. After her father's death Ivana and her sister lived with their grandmother from Monday through Friday, while their mother worked, and on weekends the girls stayed with their mother. Ivana went to school and had friends, including Serbs, with whom she would share her dolls. "I had a normal life, I went to church every Sunday...well, not every Sunday, actually," she corrected herself to Father Kerrigan, admitting that her mother was the one who made her to go to church.

In the fall of 1991 ten-year-old Ivana "felt that something was going to happen, war was in the air." Nearby, the city of Vukovar was under siege. One day in October, Serbian police went door-to-door ordering Croatians to leave town. Ivana, her sister, and her mother were forced to board a bus without knowing its destination. Her grandmother stayed in Ilok, where she died of breast cancer; treatment was unavailable during the Serbian occupation.

The bus first went to Serbia, where passengers faced harrowing threats and curses of Serbs along the streets. It next turned south and went through the Bosnian countryside. After many hours it arrived at Opatija, an Adriatic resort town that was frequented by wealthy Austrians before the first World War.

Ivana's experience in Opatija at the end of the century was much different from that of the elite Austrians at the beginning of the century. "It's very difficult to live in a hotel. We had only one room," she said.

Through it all, Ivana prayed every night and her faith remained solid. "God is not guilty because of all that has happened. God is never wrong. It is people who are too selfish."

Asked if God was in Vukovar, Ivana did not answer directly, only stating, "God is everywhere around us. Maybe God could be in Vukovar."

"One day we will go back to Ilok," Ivana predicted, in words that registered with Šovagovic, but in the interim she attends school in Rijeka and watches American movies, "especially ones with Brad Pitt and Mel Gibson." She had many friends in Ilok but only a few accompanied her to Opatija. "Some are in Zagreb or other towns, and I don't even know where the others are."

These days Ivana sometimes stops in the middle of what she is doing and listens to her heart. But if all goes well, her career plans will reveal her heart to others. Ivana wants to work with little children in Croatia's version of pre-kindergarten. "I love little children," she said. "I like to help them here in the hospital, and I can help them."

"You will never hear something as refreshing as you can hear from a child," concluded Šovagovic. "I love to speak with the children. I don't treat them by 'ooh-ing' and 'aah-ing'; they are people like we are, but they are more real and honest. I try to raise my four-year-old daughter, Klara, that way."

While Ivana suffered from her too large heart, many people involved with the program have found their own hearts expanding in new and fulfilling ways. As mentioned in the Introduction, some have made major life changes following their experiences with these children and their families. One of these is Christine Haines.

Fr. Kerrigan became acquainted with Novick and the Croatian children with heart disease in April 1994 through visiting Blake Haines, a four-year-old boy with a brain tumor. Blake was in an intensive-care unit bed next to that of Mario Miklosic, a Varazdin native and one of the first Croatian children sent to Memphis. Blake's mother, Christine, also began to undergo a transformation through her encounter with Mario and his mother, Vesna.

"I realized how fortunate I was. I had friends, family, the church, and the ability to communicate freely with the medical staff. It made me realize that I had something to give. 'Nobody should be that alone,' I kept think-ing. I guess I decided then that we should be a host family."

A year later Christine hosted Josip Špoljar, a month-old boy from Djakovo, and his mother. The boy died shortly after surgery, but Chris-tine continued to reach out. She helped organize a fund-raiser for con-genital heart disease patients which raised nearly twenty-five thousand dollars in its first two years. She volunteered to host another child, Mario Horvat from Novska, whose surgery was successful. Finally, Chris-tine, who nine years earlier had entered Auburn University in Alabama to pursue a career in fashion merchandising, enrolled in nursing school at the University of Memphis to become a pediatric nurse.

"Being a host family helped solidify a connection I first felt when Blake was in the hospital," she said. "After realizing that I could handle these intense experiences, I felt that nursing is the way that God has called me to reach out to people. Pediatric nursing, in particular, feels like it has a special calling within it to be there not only for the patient but for the family, whether things go well or not."

Christine's experience is reflected in that of other host families. The word *hospital* is from the same root as *hospitality*, and in the Interna-tional Children's Heart Foundation program, host families give excellent testimony to the important harmony that can happen between the hospi-tality of the host family and the health care of the hospital.

Dr. Novick remarked about three of the families that have been involved extensively in the program: "In my mind, the Rodriguezes, Antoinette and Ernesto, epitomize giving from the heart, without regard to personal problems, difficulties, or inconvenience. They are truly happy, giving volunteers, as are the Dominises and the Brickeys."

John Dominis, a retired native of the Croatian port city of Zadar, and his wife, Nancy, along with Art and Cherie Brickey, are the two other families cited by Novick. The three families are continually on call to host ICHF children. In addition, John Dominis and Antoinette Rodriguez lend their translating skills as needed.

"The walls of the heart," to use Jeremiah's phrase, expand with love as more and more people in Memphis open their hearts to these families from Croatia.

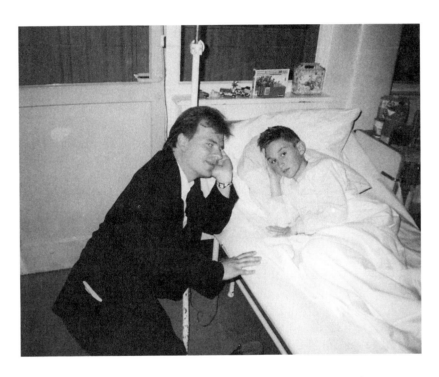

Kerrigan strikes a pose with Mario Bogdan after the boy's successful heart surgery in April 1996.

9
Mario Bogdan

"My heart is steadfast, O God"
–Psalm 108:2

It is April 1996, a little before nine in the morning. Novick prepares for a day of surgery at Rebro University Hospital in Zagreb. In Ivan Malcic's cardiology office Novick watches angiograms of the upcoming day's patients. Malcic operates the angiogram viewer, deftly reversing, stopping, and forwarding the black-and-white film. Novick comments to Malcic as he observes the images of the patients' blood flowing through their hearts. The mood in the makeshift theater is professional but relaxed. "As long as I'm in the dark, smoking cigarettes, drinking coffee, and watching films, I'm happy," Novick says. "Of course, I am happiest when I actually can work on the children in the operating room."

The surgeon has been awake for several hours. He began the day along with the rest of the eleven-member American surgical team with a big breakfast of assorted meats, cheeses, breads, and eggs at the team's hotel in Zagreb, the Panorama. "Don't forget the coffee, strong enough to stand a spoon in," added ICU nurse Rocky Thomas. In Memphis, Novick usually doesn't have breakfast, but in Zagreb he indulges, not knowing if he will eat again during the hectic day. After the hasty meal

the team piles into a bright red-orange Volkswagen van that careens
through Zagreb's rush-hour traffic to the hospital.

Rebro was built before World War II on top of a hill in a very green,
quiet, pleasant neighborhood in Zagreb, about four miles northeast of
the city's main square. Croatian hospitals are invariably found at a high
elevation, reflecting a belief that the air above street level is healthier.
Within easy walking distance of the hospital is Maksimir Park with its
broad meadows and several artificial lakes, along with the country's
largest zoo. Across the street from the zoo is Maksimir Soccer Stadium.
When matches are held, the din of the crowd can be heard inside Rebro.

The hospital complex is a bustling center of activity. The main hospital building is the hub of the campus, and the lobby of the hospital is the
crossroads for all the drama and emotion in the building. Unlike American hospitals, Rebro has no auxiliary emergency entrances, private
access doors for doctors, or special meeting areas for patients and their
loved ones; everyone and everything converges at the front door. "In
America you can't feel 'the real' in the hospital. There, in the lobby of
Rebro, there is life, there is everything," noted Dr. Ruza Grizelj
Šovagovic, pediatric resident at the hospital. A decal at the entrance
warns against bringing guns into the facility, but it's open season for
everything else to enter. In the lobby, patients, identified by their
bathrobes or fresh surgical scars, walk gingerly. Some are lined up at the
pay phones to call family or friends. A lone patient stares outside blankly
from under the haze of a freshly lit, unfiltered cigarette. Every so often
ambulance drivers rush a critically ill patient through the doors. Doctors
gather in the lobby to socialize or exchange notes before heading to the
parking lot. At the end of a corridor off the lobby, a large portrait of
Croatian President Franjo Tudjman gazes down on the proceedings.

Today, second in the three-patient surgical lineup, is eleven-year-old
Mario Bogdan from the Adriatic coastal city of Split.

Mario's patient information—the list that gives each child's name and
age, pluses and minuses of the heart condition, blood flow results, blood
and oxygen data, and a little bit of the patient's history—had attracted
Novick's attention. In Croatia, Novick always gets the moderately difficult
to very difficult cases. He chooses the first four to six children himself,

mentally arranging the list before the trip. As the operations unfold the schedule is adjusted frequently; some children have fevers or infections and must have their surgery delayed, while a newborn may arrive with an urgent condition.

Today is surgery day. Mario and his mother, Zorica, met with Novick yesterday. "I spoke with him briefly and I was very happy," she said. "I could see and feel success in his eyes and in his smile." But today Zorica is distraught. "I came to the hospital at 8:30 to see Mario before his operation and for him to see me," she says. "I did not find him in his room, and the nurses told me that he was already in surgery." By mistake, Zorica has been deprived of one of the most wrenching and important emotional experiences for a parent during a child's treatment—the goodbye before surgery. This parting is the moment of the most tears and pain among the parents. It is the moment when everything hits, when the parents realize the child is no longer under their protection. Mothers and fathers who up until this point have been placid and unemotional sometimes become inconsolable for a few minutes before steadying themselves and regaining composure.

Although Mario did not have his mother with him as he left the cardiology floor for surgery, he did not make the trip unaccompanied. When summoned to the operating room, the boy was with his nurse and fellow Split native, Helena Šimundza, who describes their exchange. "Imagine a situation where the child asks you before entering the operation room, 'Auntie, will I come out alive?' I squeezed his hand and answered, 'Mario, do not give up at the last second. Do not lose faith. Believe in God and all of us together will succeed.' He answered with characteristic strength, 'I will, Auntie.' I admire that child. Regardless of his small size and tiny heart, he expresses the most important things in life by showing me that he has a very big heart."

Mario has to undergo surgery because he suffers from a condition known as tetralogy of Fallot, named for the French physician who first described the disease in the nineteenth century. The condition is the most common heart defect among those that produce cyanosis, or a bluish appearance, in the patient. The condition accounts for about 10 percent of congenital heart defects. *Tetralogy* means "group of four," and this disease is made up of four defects: a ventricular septal defect (VSD), pulmonary stenosis, a displaced aorta, and an enlarged right ventricle. Because of the combination of defects, not enough blood flows to the lungs to receive oxygen from the lungs, causing the blue color that tetralogy of Fallot patients have. These children may also suffer from "Tet spells," frightening episodes of struggling for air, a very blue color, and sometimes loss of consciousness.

In order to feel better, tetralogy of Fallot patients instinctively squat, like a baseball catcher behind home plate. The increased resistance in the arteries of the leg and trunk increases blood flow to the lungs. Rocky Thomas says, "I have a wonderful memory of three eight-year-old Croatians whose tetralogy of Fallot had been corrected by Novick and who greeted us at the airport when we arrived for our third trip. All three squatted next to each other, to the side of the festivities. I guess old habits die hard."

Babies can manifest symptoms of tetralogy of Fallot within a couple of hours of birth and can even die as newborns, although with the diagnostic and treatment capabilities available this is almost unheard of in the United States. Zorica and Paško Bogdan got the news of their first and only child's condition a few days after what Zorica describes as "our happiest day," Mario's birth. A few days later that happiest day had dimmed considerably as Zorica noticed that "our son was unable to breastfeed and that he had a blue color."

Mario was taken to the pediatrician in the hospital, and the parents were told that he had tetralogy of Fallot. "At that time we asked the doctor what would be the best for our child," recalled Zorica, an expressive woman with a flushed face and broad cheeks. "They told us he would need an operation. However, that sort of operation is not done before the child is a year old.[8] All at once our life was turned around. We thought that the sun would never shine in our life again."

Mario stayed in the hospital in Split for a few days of evaluation. After his discharge his growth was slow and he had difficulties in feeding. He was referred to a cardiology center in Ljubljana, Slovenia.

"The first day we were in Ljubljana, Mario had a serious crisis," said Zorica. "The doctors said they needed to operate immediately. At that time he was seven months old, small and skinny. We thought that he would not survive the surgery, but thank God, our prayers and wishes were answered and the surgery was successful. We talked to the doctor after the surgery, and we found out that they did not perform a full correction of the heart defect. He would need another operation soon. That was another shock. We did not lose hope, because we are Catholic and pray every day for ourselves and the whole world."

Mario did not start walking until he was two years old, but he learned to speak quickly and to form sentences. "His intelligence was great, everything interested him, and he was lively," his mother recalled. "He was a happy and calm child, but I cannot say that he listened. We as parents gave him every little thing, and he took advantage more and more."

Mario had a second operation, again in Ljubljana, when he was two years old. By then he was stronger and the operation went well. A few days later, however, Paško was in a serious automobile accident. "His life hung by a thread," said his wife. "He was in a coma forty days. The doctors lost hope, but I believed that he would wake up. I prayed every day and I believed that God would not abandon me since I was willing to give my life. After forty days my husband woke up and regained consciousness. Now he is fine, and he suffers from no side effects. I realized that only God had saved him and returned him to our family."

After the second operation Mario started eating better and growing. He was less blue and less tired. Mario did not take it well when he saw other children running and playing soccer and he could not because he tired so easily. "Mario realized that he was different from healthy children. At that point it was not too hard for him to handle, but as he got older, it became harder and harder for him to cope," said his mother. "We enrolled him in kindergarten so that he could be around other children and play with children his own age. We also wanted him to shift his attention from his sickness. I have to say that due to his being constantly sick with various infections and viruses, we did not send him to class regularly.

"The time for the third operation was approaching, and we prepared Mario by telling him everything would be all right and he would be able to play and run after the operation. He always understood that these operations were necessary and that he would have to be brave. The third operation was when Mario was five years old, in Ljubljana. Again, the operation was successful and Mario healed very quickly. However, the doctors told us again that this was not the end and that they would have to repeat the procedure in a few years. We were mortified. Nevertheless, we were patient. We convinced ourselves that in the end everything would finish happily."

Mario went to first grade, a happy and cheerful boy with sandy brown hair and thoughtful brown eyes. "In the beginning he was a good student, but later he lost interest in school," continued Zorica. "My husband and I took him back and forth. His friends in school knew that he had had three operations, and they were cautious in how they acted around him. During recess Mario stayed in the classroom just to ensure that he would not get hurt while playing. This bothered him more and more. He was unhappy, but we talked to him and told him that it had to be that way and that he needed to be patient.

"Since our parents lived in Solin, three miles from Split, Paško and I took Mario every weekend out into the fresh air so that he could experience nature. He likes animals, children, computers, cars, but he especially loves flowers and nature and many other things. He does not like lies, wars, violent movies, and injustice. His wish is to train for soccer, and he asks very often when he can start practicing with his friends. During the war Mario got nervous and terrified with every alarm that went off. We were calm and told him that the war was not in Split; in fact, we hardly ever felt the war in Split."

Over the last few months before the operation, Mario walked slower, and he again became tired and was turning blue. When he found out that he was going to have a fourth operation, he became difficult to deal with. "He was crying, nervous, and became more aggressive," said Zorica. "Once he told us that he was scared of death. That was very hard for us to hear. My husband and I went to a psychologist to discuss Mario. We talked to Mario every day and took him out on walks, and that helped."

The three previous operations were preparation for the complete correction in this fourth and final operation on Mario, under Novick's care. In treating the boy's tetralogy of Fallot, the surgeon would follow a twofold strategy: the removal of the obstruction of blood flow to the lungs, and the closure of the VSD.

Novick leaves Malcic's office to work on his first patient for the day, thirteen-year-old Ivana Logarusic, who also suffers from tetralogy of Fallot. There are two operating rooms available to Novick at Rebro, so Mario is brought into the second room and prepared for surgery while work on Ivana continues.

Meanwhile, on the cardiology floor, the workday is in full swing. Ivan Malcic and Branco Marinovic usher a steady flow of families through their offices as they assess and diagnose various children. As cardiologists, the two men are meteorologists of the heart. They even use equipment whose images could be mistaken by the uninitiated for satellite weather photos. All too often Malcic and Marinovic have to report bad "weather and traffic conditions" within a child's heart: blood that flows in trickles instead of streams, unhealthy mixtures of red and blue blood, obstructions and chaotic rhythms. Their task is not without optimism, however. Taped to the echocardiogram machine is a poem written by Marinovic:

Let your heart be healthy
Strong like a terrifying lion
If, however, the heart needs to be fixed
It's not always a big deal
"Heartvision" looks at the heart
And keeps the disease in the distance.

Marinovic, Mario Bogdan's cardiologist, is chief of pediatric cardiology at Rebro and has worked in Zagreb for twenty-five years. During his medical studies he became interested in both adult and pediatric hearts. "The heart is a little secret organ that is special," he says. "It works while other organs sleep, and of course everyone knows that the heart is the center of life."

Marinovic, a tall, handsome man with a full head of salt-and-pepper hair, carries himself confidently. "I like to write poems, and I also like to read them to the patients during the hard times," he says. The cardiologist enjoys his work and his patients. He attributes this in part to an encounter he had as a young physician with a little girl from Dubrovnik. "She had inexplicable neurological problems," he recalls. "I was studying her and I wanted to understand her symptoms. One day I heard a noise in her brain, which led to a diagnosis of a brain tumor. The other doctors were surprised. Today she is fine and has two children. It turned my life around."

Helena Šimundza and the other Croatian nurses scurry on the floor attending to the needs of Marinovic, Malcic, and the patients. The nurses dress in two-piece, light-blue uniforms. For some, the outfit is the only thing that distinguishes them from their patients. Helena, at nineteen, is not much older than many of her pediatric patients. She decided to become a nurse when her older sister was hospitalized on the same floor in Rebro with juvenile rheumatoid arthritis a few years earlier.

"There in the hospital, with my sister and the other children, I felt the desire to work and dedicate my life to the recovery to health of these children," said Helena, a tall blond with deep-blue eyes and a husky voice. "I understand the severity of children's illnesses and what the parents go through because of what I experienced with my sick sister. I do not have many years under my belt, but I appreciate the meaning of life through the experiences that I have had. I usually tie myself emotionally to the children that come through the ward. That is why I have a hard time dealing with their suffering. This is the reason I pray and ask for the intercession of the Holy Spirit to heal and save the children. I love my job and what is most important is the compassion I feel for everything that can happen in this type of work," she added.

Professional pride and competence are also incentives for the Croatian nurses. "The nurses are a very important part of our team here," states Marinovic. "They help us, they boost our morale, and we gain a lot of motivation from them." This comes as a pleasant surprise to the Americans on the ICHF team. "When we first conceived of our role [on the trips], we anticipated doing all the bedside care," says Thomas. "Early on, we found it was not necessary and we rethought our role. The Croatian nurses are very capable, so instead of our doing it all, we became an international cooperative team. We each had something to offer. Rebro lacks extensive monitoring and laboratory equipment, but the nurses make up for it by being experts in assessment."

During most of the workday the American team leaves the cardiology floor to the Croatians and serves in three more acute arenas in the hospital: the pediatric intensive-care unit, the postoperative intensive-care unit, and the operating room.

Kerrigan is sometimes the only American on the cardiology floor, but he is not lonely. "This is where the patients first come into the hospital, and it's also where they leave the hospital from, so it makes a good base for ministry," he says. "A few times a day I make a sweep of the PICU, the ICU, the converted office that serves as the American team's temporary suite, and less often, the O.R. But the cardiology floor is where I have the most interactions. There I meet the parents and child before surgery to pray with them. It is also the place I work with the doctors and nurses.

"On my first trip to Croatia I was amazed that within a few days I was doing the same kind of work with the medical staff that I do in my parish office in Memphis—dealing with their personal issues, their relationships and rivalries, and with some who want to know more about Catholicism.

"Of course, I'm also always on the lookout for someone who may need more direct care. The day Mario was having surgery it was clear it would be a long and hard day for his mom, especially since she didn't have a chance to say goodbye to him. So I went up to her and said, 'I'll be in the operating room with Mario, and I'll be praying for him. I'll let you know how everything is going every hour or so.' I go into the O.R. when the family is really upset or when Bill [Novick] alerts me that the case might not go well."

Mario is now in the care of the anesthesiologist, American Mike Baron, for the approximately one-hour preparation for surgery. Baron directs the patient's care until the surgeon walks into the operating room. "I serve as the child's pediatrician and ICU doctor in the operating room," he says. "The surgeon is there for the technical correction, and the anesthesiologist is there to keep the child alive before and after."

Nurse Rocky Thomas is also with Mario in the second-floor operating room. "When the children are brought to the operating room and pre-pared for surgery, they are not pre-sedated, as is the practice in the United States, so one of us stays with the child," says Thomas. "None of us knows Croatian, and yet that never bothers the children. Having a hand to hold is often all they need."

Baron gives Mario a mild sedative and hypnotic drug and begins placing intravenous lines in the boy. A breathing tube is inserted, and Mario breathes with the help of the ventilator. Baron administers a morphine-like drug, as well as Valium and a neuromuscular blocking agent. Mario's blood pressure, heart rate, and ventilation settings are all displayed on monitors. The boy is placed on the operating table with his head back and his chest out. He is washed and a blue surgical drape is placed around him.

Baron turns up the volume of the pulse oximeter's signal sound, so Novick will be able to hear each pulse. (The pulse oximeter is a device placed on a finger or toe to detect pulsations in small arteries and to measure the oxygen saturation of the blood.) Although the instrument has a numerical display, Novick likes to hear the pulse because "listening to the tone and rate of the signals tells me a lot about the patient's condition," he says. The signal is a beep, high-pitched for high saturation levels and low-pitched for low ones.

The operation does not officially begin until the incision. The surgeon will say, "May I start?" or "The operation is starting." There will be four stages to Mario's heart surgery: First, the initial incision through the skin, soft tissue, and breastbone. Next, the preparation stage, when the sac around the heart (the pericardium) is cut and sewn to the edges of the skin. Third is the procedure itself, when the heart is exposed and the defect corrected. Fourth, the heart is restarted and the patient is taken off bypass.

In Zagreb, Novick arrives for the second stage, when the pericardial sac is entered, having entrusted the first stage to one of the other surgeons at Rebro. "The Rebro surgeons also search for and isolate the previous shunts to decrease the time I spend in the room," he said. "Then the surgeons call for me. As I scrub for the case, I review it again in my mind," he said. "Once I am gowned and in the O.R., I observe the patient's external anatomy to confirm my impressions from the X ray, echocardiogram, and catheterization. I am completely focused on this child's defect and care while he or she is in the O.R."

A key to making open-heart surgery possible is cardiopulmonary bypass, using the "heart-lung machine" first developed in the 1950s, popularized in the 1960s, and refined and improved ever since. Mike Solimine, perfusionist at LeBonheur Children's Medical Center, says he still finds people marveling at the machine he operates. "I was on an ICHF trip to Nicaragua, and there people reacted as if the heart-lung machine was a chariot and I was the driver," he said. "The machine is the most integral piece of equipment to the accomplishment of our surgical goal, but the successful completion of a procedure cannot be done without a total team effort."

Preparation for the cardiopulmonary bypass begins when the anesthesiologist gives the patient heparin, a natural substance that prevents the blood from clotting. The book of Leviticus expresses well the importance of blood for life—"The life of a living body is in its blood" (17:11). Its value can be quantified by clotting time, which is important in cardiopulmonary bypass. The average clotting time for humans is 120 seconds, but with heparin the average clotting time climbs to as much as 1000 seconds. A blood sample is drawn to determine the patient's clotting time. When it exceeds 480 seconds, the patient can be safely placed on cardiopulmonary bypass without great risk of a stroke, neurological damage, or injury to a major organ.

"It usually gets a little hairy when the heparin is administered," said Baron, whose impassive expression makes it hard to believe that he finds anything "hairy." "There are changes in blood pressure, the surgeons are cutting the pericardial sac, so I stand at the patient's head, making sure everything goes well."

A loop made of polyvinyl chloride tubing, is connected from the patient's heart to a pump (the "heart" in the heart-lung machine) and an artificial oxygenator ("lung") and back to the aorta. The surgeon first cuts the tubing, and the perfusionist sets the tightness of the rollers (occlusions) on the bypass machine. The surgeon next establishes the hookups for the arterial and venous side and makes sure that all air is removed from the inflow loop (air to the brain could cause a stroke) and that the connection will not produce excess trauma to the blood. Next, the surgeon puts pencil-thin cannulae (blood tubes or catheters) in the patient's vessels, and then connects the cannulae to the tubing from the pump by tying a stitch in the aorta and vena cava, completing the circuit. The aorta connection is always made first so that there is still control over the patient's life in case of a problem, like a hemorrhage, so blood can be delivered quickly and directly.

Another important step for facilitating open-heart surgery is cooling the patient's body and heart. Cooling protects the heart against the effects of no blood flow and decreased oxygen supply while it is stopped during surgery. The temperature drop works on the same principle that sometimes makes it possible for people who fall through the ice and drown to be resuscitated and to survive. In pediatric open-heart surgery body temperature is routinely lowered to around 75 degrees Fahrenheit, about twenty degrees cooler than normal; sometimes the temperature is dropped to around 65 degrees. A heater-cooler unit connected to the bypass machine's oxygenator provides the cooling and the warming before and after surgery.

Once the patient's temperature is low enough, the aorta is clamped between the cannula and coronary arteries, so the surgeon can operate on a bloodless, immobile heart. (The time between the initiation of bypass and stopping the heart is highly variable, says Novick, and depends upon each patient's defect.) This interrupts oxygenated blood flow to the heart, potentially giving the patient a heart attack. To prevent this from having long-term effects, the surgeon chooses to cool the heart topically and to infuse cardioplegia—a mixture of minerals and electrolytes at a very low temperature—into the heart to stop the beating.

Another option is not to use a clamp but to reduce the temperature to 82–90 degrees Fahrenheit, so the heart moves (fibrillates) without contracting and ejecting blood.

Novick stops Mario's heart by infusing cardioplegia. "We'll give additional doses of this solution every fifteen to twenty minutes while we work," he instructs.

"On bypass," says Novick. A switch is flipped and the bypass pump is activated by the perfusionist.

"Once on bypass, an irony overtakes me," says Novick. "On one hand

I am comforted about having control over the patient, but on the other I am concerned that all aspects of the bypass flow smoothly."

The perfusionist is ultimately responsible for the performance of the bypass machine. "Sometimes I just get a look or a grunt from the surgeon," says Solimine, "and we begin a 'symphony.' I do as many as ten things at once, checking the heating and cooling of the patient, making sure there is an adequate level of blood returning to and from the patient. I deliver oxygen; infuse cardioplegia as indicated; monitor pressures, urine output, blood gases, and other parameters. I go back and forth among watching Novick, the nurses, the monitors, and the equipment. The key is focus. These are critical moments. In some newborns as little as 10cc of extra blood pumped through the machine will distend their heart permanently, for example. My job is maintaining the patient's normal physiology during the stress of being on bypass and the stress of the heart operation itself, and, most important, knowing what to do when things don't go according to plan."

Novick is also alert to the bypass. "One must be ever attentive to the subtle changes that can occur and herald bypass difficulties," he adds. "The heart can fibrillate or over-distend. The inflow line pressures can be too high, indicating bad positioning of the cannulae. Attention to the heart and to the concerns of the perfusionist and the anesthesiologist are the keys to a smooth, successful bypass run."

Once bypass has started, the surgeon's repair of the heart defect is conducted without blood flow. The procedure should be completed as quickly as possible to avoid any complications. Novick comments: "Although I'm comforted by the state of control I have over the patient, I know that we need to perform a quick, complete, and accurate repair. The bypass machine causes harmful changes throughout the body that worsen the longer we have the patient on the machine." When the clamp is taken off the aorta, and warmer blood from the body flows into the heart, it warms up and beats again. Novick is acutely aware of the time the aorta is clamped, even though he doesn't wear a watch. "Clamp time is the only time that matters to me," he says. "Most cardiac surgeons have an internal clock in their heads. I check with the perfusionist every fifteen minutes, and I can usually tell within two to three minutes the actual clamp time."

The surgeon is as exacting of the team that joins him in the operating room as he is of himself. "I expect them all to have their responsibilities under control, and I constantly talk to people. The minute we go on bypass there is a plan, different for each operation. You don't conduct an operation for an ASD [atrial septal defect] the same way as for tetralogy."

Taped music is playing—Luciano Pavarotti, the Memphis blues, and old pop songs like "Strangers in the Night," "Somewhere Over the Rainbow," and "You've Lost That Loving Feeling"—as Novick conducts the operation on Mario. Eight people join the surgeon in the halogen-lit operating room: two people work the bypass machine, two surgeons and a nurse assist at the table, others behind the surgical drapes monitor the child's condition, and one or two other nurses get various things the scrub nurse needs. Kerrigan stands at Mario's feet to observe. He will take updates from Novick to Zorica, who waits in a chairless corridor outside the recovery room.

"Mario had three previous operations—one in each chest space and one through a median sternotomy [the breastbone]. This time we had to repeat the median sternotomy," said Novick, describing the procedure. "While I finished with Ivana, the first case for the day, Rebro surgeons reopened Mario's chest via the sternotomy. They took care to open the breastbone without cutting the heart. The normal soft tissues and sac surrounding the heart were disturbed by the previous operation, and scar tissue made the heart actually stick to the back of the sternum.

"Now we open the area of the heart where we know we can see and repair the defect. Mario has tetralogy of Fallot. We open his right atrium with scissors and place small retractors across his tricuspid valve to look into his right ventricle.

"I am always awed looking into a human heart and realizing that I am the only one with this view of this child.

"I know what this heart should look like on the inside, and I rigidly inspect the anatomy to confirm the diagnosis. We must close the VSD and somehow provide unobstructed blood flow out of his right ventricle to his pulmonary artery. I prefer to attack the obstruction first. With a knife and some delicate tissue forceps I carefully cut out the excess muscle until there is a clear unobstructed view of the pulmonary valve and its annulus [surrounding ring]. This takes about ten to fifteen minutes.

"In Mario's case the films and the external inspection indicate that his valve and annulus might be too small and will need enlargement. Once we cut the muscle away we measure the valve size with calibrated instruments. Indeed, his valve and annulus are too small to leave alone, so we have to enlarge them. I prefer to do this near the end of the procedure so we can take the clamp off and reestablish blood flow to the heart.

"Now we must return to assessing and sizing the VSD. I reposition the retractors so the VSD is easily seen. I take two tissue forceps and measure the VSD size, simultaneously noting its shape, which can be oval, round, or elliptical. The nurse places a sheet of Gore-Tex on the towels, and we draw the shape of the patch. We cut the shape as we would a paper doll. A fine suture, like fishing line, is used, and we sew the patch into the heart to close the VSD. The suture placement must be of the right depth and tension, otherwise the suture will cut through the muscle and leave a small VSD."

Kerrigan watches intently. "The heart is amazing to see in this state on the operating table," he says. "And then, in the midst of all this intricacy, a white patch is cut and sewn into place within a matter of minutes to become part of the heart. When I pray in the O.R., it's usually for the patient and the medical team, but even in the middle of the operation I look at the heart and I can't help but thank God for the awesomeness of creation. The artistry and knowledge that goes into the patch repair is part of the awesomeness."

Another dose of cardioplegia allows for the rest of the work. "A suture is placed in the anterior surface of the right ventricle to pull the pulmonary valve and proximal pulmonary artery into position," Novick says. "A knife is used to open the pulmonary artery just beyond the valve. I extend the incision up to the valve and look across the valve and annulus to make sure we have removed all the necessary muscle. In Mario's case, the valve and annulus are too small, so we continue to open this area, cutting across and splitting the annulus. The incision continues a short distance onto the anterior wall of the right ventricle. Once this area is opened up, we take a piece of the patient's pericardium and sew it into this opened area, like adding a roof."

"Next we remove the aortic clamp." The head of the operating table is lowered so the brain is below the feet, the needle in the aorta (used to administer the cardioplegia) is removed, the inflow from the pump is dropped very low, and the clamp is removed.

Novick tells Kerrigan he can leave the O.R. to tell Zorica that things are going well.

The needle hole for the cardioplegia allows air from the heart to leave the body rather than go to the brain. With the patient's head lowered, any air that might still be in the aorta is not likely to go to the brain. The pump is turned up, and Novick proceeds with the enlargement of the pulmonary valve and annulus.

"While completing this patch covering, I ask the perfusionist to rewarm the patient," said Novick. "Generally, about the time we finish sewing the patch, the heart starts to beat."

Mike Baron comes back into the room while the patient is warmed. He administers medicines to help strengthen the heartbeat. He also gives the patient more anesthetics. Temporary pacemaker wires are installed to assist the heart, if necessary. With a fine suture, Novick closes the atrium he opened to look inside the heart. Tubes are placed to drain blood from the chest cavity following the operation. Lines also may be inserted to monitor pressures inside the heart. "Once there is a stable blood pressure reading on the monitor and the patient has been adequately rewarmed, he or she can be slowly taken off the machine as machine support lessens," says Novick. "I insert a needle into the right ventricle, connected to the monitor by tubing, and measure the pressure. The pressure in the right ventricle should be no more than one-half of the blood pressure. That shows the repair is OK."

One of the most critical times in the operation is coming off bypass. "You're never really sure what will happen, " says Novick. "In your mind you box the variables within certain parameters. If the patient fits within the box, you take out the cannulae."

"At the end of the work on the heart, everything done to go on bypass is done in reverse," says Solimine. "For example, after the patient is rewarmed and the surgeon is satisfied with the patient's pressures and cardiac function, protamine, another naturally occurring substance, is given to reverse the effect of heparin." About halfway through the protamine dose, the cannula in the aorta is removed and the suture is tied. Novick makes a careful inspection of all the sites on the outside of the heart where sutures were placed to make sure there is no bleeding.

"Now it's 'hurry up and wait,'" adds Solimine. "We wait for all the patient's bleeding to come under control. There could be a hemorrhage or an arrhythmia—we have to be ready until the patient leaves the operating room."

A heightened vigil is maintained around the bed until the sternum is closed. The team is prepared to go back on bypass instantaneously if there is a problem with the heart. If all goes well—strong heart, normal pressures, and no bleeding—the patient's chest is closed with large sutures or wires.

"In a way, the closure of the wound is as important as the repair," observes Novick. "The parents won't see the repair; they'll see the wound. First, we bring together the sternum with stainless steel wires. The muscle and subcutaneous tissues are closed with an absorbable, dissolving suture. Finally, the skin is closed by placing a fine absorbable suture just below the epidermis. Dressings are placed over the wound, the drapes are removed from the patient, and preparations are made to transfer the child.

"We pull it together, put a large bandage over the wound, and transfer the patient to the ICU. Once I make sure the patient is OK," says the surgeon, "I'm through with the case and ready for the next one."

Making sure the patient is OK in the intensive-care unit is an art in itself. Novick explains: "I think all heart surgeons have a priority in what they look at. You scan the whole patient—it's something you learn over time that becomes second nature. The things that you spend so much time studying and memorizing when you're a student—the normal values for certain things—become second nature. You go into the ICU and you look at the heart rate, the blood pressure, the filling pressure, the blood-oxygen saturations, the color of the patient, and you put your hand on your patient's feet. If they're warm, they're well-perfused, they've got good pulses, their saturations are okay, and then you can say, 'All right, they look good.' When those things start to look abnormal, then the goodness starts to go away. And it's degrees of good.

"You must, in order to evaluate a patient adequately, consciously look at each one of these things, and ask yourself, 'I haven't forgotten anything, have I?' After a few years you just look at the patient in a way that may appear to be a superficial assessment, but it's not. Talking to the nurses is always very helpful, but you have to be able to filter the information the nurses give you. There's a difference—your 'she looks good' may be different from the nurse's. It's very relative."

Mario looks good. He is wheeled into the postoperative recovery room. "I Will Survive" plays in the unit. Nurses immediately begin to attend to his stabilization, an ungainly process.

"The child is rolled into the ICU and placed about five feet from the bed he will wind up in," says Elizabeth Jameson. "Then the patient is disconnected from the bags and pumps, carried to and put down on the bed. In the United States the patient is rolled next to the ICU bed and slid from one bed to the other. I watch the patient's condition during that time. You can usually tell within the first couple of hours, and sometimes in the first hour, if the patient is on the right track."

On the other side of the door to the unit, Zorica continues her all-day vigil.

"I have to thank Father Joe, who told me what was going on in the operating room," Zorica says later. "He was praying for the success of all the children being operated on.

At six o'clock Dr. Novick comes out of the operating room. He tells Zorica that everything is fine and that Mario is doing well.

"I was on top of the world," Zorica says. "After a few minutes I visited Mario in the ICU. He was no longer blue. The next day, when I came to the hospital, Mario's eyes were open and I talked to him a little bit."

The blond but no longer blue boy heals quickly and moves back upstairs to the fourth floor, again to the nursing care of Helena Šimundza. He gains over four pounds in the remaining two weeks he spends in the hospital and is discharged on April 30. "I feel only gratitude for Mario Bogdan," the nurse says. "In a very short time I became close to him and his mother. Mario told me that he likes and values his life, the people around him, nature, and everything God gives us. If only everyone could be like Mario, a small person with a big heart. This is what God expects of us."

There is a spectacular sunset behind the ancient Zagreb hills, but for Mario Bogdan, the sun is just beginning to rise.

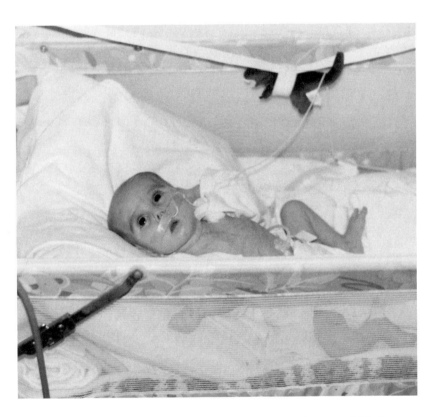

Four-month-old Marko Lukac in his crib at the home of his hosts, the Rodriguez family, in August 1997.

10
Marko Lukac

*"No other light or guide than the one that
burns in my heart"*
—John of the Cross

KLM Flight 8625 from Amsterdam touched down at Memphis International Airport on a hot, sticky Sunday evening in the thick of the 1997 summer travel season. Among the nearly three hundred passengers making the roughly five-thousand-mile trek, no doubt several were in need of healing for their hearts. Travel—even an international flight of this distance—to remedy a heart devastated by emotional or physical suffering is not uncommon. It would be difficult, however, to find anyone on that flight who had made a more arduous journey, or who needed his heart repaired as urgently, as four-month-old Marko Lukac, from Osijek in eastern Slavonia.

Novick, Kerrigan, ICHF nurse Elizabeth Jameson, and hosts Antoinette and Ernesto Rodriguez drove in separate cars to meet the flight. All five were veterans at greeting patients and families at the Memphis airport. If custom was followed, they would gather outside the staircase that leads from the U.S. Customs and Immigration checkpoint to await Marko, his mother, and the doctor accompanying them. "The ICHF families are almost always the last people off the plane, and they're almost always carrying a bluish child," said Jameson, describing how she finds a patient. But this was no ordinary arrival. The surgeon, the priest, and the nurse were called to board the KLM plane before the passengers exited the aircraft, while the Rodriguezes, both employed by Northwest Airlines, went to work behind the scenes to ensure the smooth transfer of the patient under peculiar circumstances.

When Novick, Kerrigan, and Jameson stepped onboard, they quickly found a handful of flight attendants standing around a row in the middle of the first-class cabin. Two women were seated with an infant carrier in the seat between them. Lying in the basket, with only his sleeping head visible, was Marko. The reason for all the special attention was visible: a breathing tube was in the boy's mouth, connected to an oxygen tank on the floor, and an IV hung from the ceiling above the infant's seat. The first-class cabin was Marko's air ambulance. Upon closer inspection, a shunt could be seen in the boy's brain; his color was unhealthy, somewhere between pale and blue.

Novick asked, "Who's the doctor?" "I am," replied the younger of the two women, Ruza Grizelj Šovagovic, a twenty-nine-year-old pediatric resident at Rebro University Hospital. Novick introduced himself and the group to the Croatians. Marko's thirty-three-year-old mother, Mirjana—pale, overwrought, and on the verge of tears—did not speak English and stayed on the periphery of the discussion.

"How was the trip?" continued Novick to Šovagovic.

"There were no problems; he was fine. The airplane had three liters of oxygen per minute for him, but we only needed two."

"Does the mother have any other children?" interrupted the surgeon, as he reached down to the basket where Marko was, examining him.

"Yes, two girls," said Šovagovic. Incredulity and anger swept over her face as she realized the grim implication of Novick's query; the surgeon was not optimistic. "You have a depressive personality! This child is fine!"

Novick didn't acknowledge the resident's impertinence, having made many such comments himself over the years on behalf of a patient. The surgeon turned to Jameson and directed Marko's transfer to the ambulance waiting on the tarmac. Jameson checked the boy's pulse and listened to his breathing before Novick carried him down the steps and into the ambulance. United States Customs and Immigration officials boarded the plane and interviewed the Croatian women at their seats. In an emotional moment the KLM flight attendants and the plane's pilot presented Mirjana Lukac with some small gifts and a bottle of champagne as tokens of their best wishes for the boy's good health. The grateful mother broke into sobs.

After everyone left the plane and Marko was taken to LeBonheur, Šovagovic stood by herself for a moment, apart from the others gathered just outside the jetway. Like a driver whose hands still grip an imaginary wheel long after finishing a harrowing ride, Šovagovic had not yet adjusted to the pleasantries and small talk around her. The Croatian doctor, still wearing an intense expression, looked fatigued. Her white linen shirt was rumpled, and her skin was clammy with perspiration. Šovagovic had not eaten during the sixteen-hour trip. The doctor's brown hair was pulled back tightly against her head, accentuating her dark skin, large brown eyes, and high cheekbones. Her face, even without the stress of the flight, was already severe in a classically Dalmatian or Herzegovinian way. Šovagovic's eyes were striking in their unblinking intensity, making her seem taller and larger than her medium build. In conversation her pupils didn't seem to move laterally as much as they seemed to wax and wane with alternating vigor. There was a solemn beauty to those eyes.

The stethoscope around her neck may have been the only visual cue to Šovagovic's profession, but once her raspy voice came to life in conversation, it was obvious that medicine was her passion. With Marko now in the intensive-care unit at LeBonheur and no longer under her exclusive care, Šovagovic began to recount the events leading to the boy's dramatic appearance in Memphis.

"It was a miracle that Marko is here, it was a miracle," she said in lightly accented English. "I felt the miracle. The day before I left Rebro with him, he was on the ventilator, pale-gray and sweaty with a 104° temperature. Nobody believed he would make it to Memphis. I entered the ICU and saw Marko in that condition. I took some holy water another child's parents had left—and I blessed Marko with it. Then I turned off the ventilator and put him on CPAP [continuous positive airway pressure] to see if he could breathe by himself. And he did!

"I stayed the whole night in the ICU with Marko. The next morning I left the hospital to pack my suitcase and to sleep for a few hours. I returned to Rebro to pack the medical stuff for the trip, and then we left. He traveled with an endotracheal tube in place because he needed secretions from his lung suctioned every two hours, he needed about six liters of oxygen per minute, and he had a central venous line through which I gave him eight doses of medication, including four antibiotics."

Marko needed the extra baggage and medicine for the flights from Zagreb to Memphis because he was saddled with four separate and serious defects in major organ systems. Šovagovic would say that the boy was born with an "occluding syndrome," since each of the defects involved obstructed pathways. At times in the course of the boy's treatment it also seemed that the way to Marko's survival was blocked by mishaps and misadventures.

Marko was born in Osijek on May 2, 1997, the third child and first boy in the family of Zeljko and Mirjana Lukac. Zeljko, a sawmill worker, fought against the Serbs as a soldier in the war from 1991–92 and became something of a local war hero for his bravery in combat. Three hours after Marko's birth, the infant also became a fighter for his own life, as he developed symptoms of suffocation. He was rushed to Rebro for emergency treatment of what was first diagnosed as atresia of the esophagus with tracheo-esophageal fistula. This meant that Marko's esophagus was obstructed, so food and saliva could not pass through to his stomach but instead went into his lungs. There was a fistula, or abnormal duct that needed closing, between the trachea and the lower portion of the esophagus, between the lungs and gastrointestinal tract.

Šovagovic and her mentor, Dr. Filipovic, met and treated Marko when he arrived at two in the morning on May 3. As was the case with almost everything involving Marko, it was easier to close things for him rather than open them up; this proved true in the treatment of his esophagus problem. Marko's fistula was surgically closed the same day he was brought to Rebro. Nearly two weeks later his esophagus was completely restructured and opened.

"After the second operation he started to vomit, became septic, and had a lung infection," reported Šovagovic. The boy's breathing was maintained by the ventilator for most of the first two months of his life, which were spent entirely in the ICU. Marko also suffered from gastrointestinal reflux and an enlarged liver. The nerve in the thoracic region responsible for pupil dilation and constriction was nudged during Marko's surgery and developed Horner's Syndrome, which caused the pupil in Marko's right eye to be bigger than the other. This emphasized the infant's large, alert brown eyes, which was the feature many people first noticed about him.

On July 4 the doctors found that Marko had a rare congenital heart defect, cortriatriatrum sinistrum. His left atrium was split into two compartments by a wall with a small opening that obstructed the blood flow from the pulmonary venous return. This, in turn, produced the life-threatening complications of pulmonary hypertension and pulmonary edema. This defect is usually detected at birth but inexplicably remained undiagnosed in Marko until he was two months old. Surgical correction is the only option.

Ivan Malcic made the diagnosis after Šovagovic, suspecting that something was wrong with Marko's heart, did an EKG that indicated a problem. "When Professor Malcic made the diagnosis, I felt like someone threw cold water on me," said the resident. "Malcic went to an ICU room to write down the diagnosis, and I went after him. I had never asked him for any favors before, but I told him then that only he could save the baby's life. I had never talked to him that way before. I didn't think about anything else in that moment. I was just fighting for this patient as I would for any."

Marko was about to become more than a patient to the young resident. Malcic listened to Šovagovic and made a phone call to Novick in Memphis. After the call the cardiologist approached the resident. "He told me, 'Everything is arranged. Marko is going to Memphis, and Dr. Novick will operate on him,'" she said, "and then he said, 'If the health ministry gives us the money, do you want to escort him to Memphis?'

"I thought of my husband, Filip, and my four-year-old daughter, Klara, who were waiting for me on [the Adriatic island of] Brac. They had been there for a few weeks already. But I wanted to go to Memphis, and Marko was scheduled to leave for America on July 20, the first day of my holiday. I recalled that when Klara was three she drew a picture of a house.

Her teacher admired it, but Klara ripped up the picture because she said there was no mommy in it. I had to choose: to have a holiday with my child, who needed me, or to try to save Marko. And there was the fact that I had been a resident for only seven months and had worked in ICU for only three months. Going with a sick child like that was a crazy thing to do; it made no sense. And what did I do? I didn't even take time to think. 'Yes' came from me very easily. I don't regret it now, despite everything I went through."

There was still much for Marko and Šovagovic to go through on their side of the Atlantic. On the very next day, July 5, another major organ occlusion was diagnosed. Marko suffered from hypertensive hydrocephaly—too much fluid in his brain. Physicians at Rebro thought he might have meningitis and were reluctant to operate on him. Šovagovic, becoming Marko's advocate, "didn't believe it, because I did a spinal tap and it was clear." Other doctors told the resident, "Marko is a lost cause, he is going to die," but they finally agreed to put a shunt in his brain to ease the congestion. Unfortunately, the neurosurgeon scheduled to operate on Marko crashed his car and fractured his knee on the same day of Marko's procedure, winding up in Rebro as a patient himself!

Šovagovic sought out her friend Dr. Krešimir Rotim, a neurosurgery resident, who agreed to operate. "If Marko was as bad as everyone believed, he would die on the operating table," said Šovagovic, giving the worst-case scenario. Closer to her heart was the feeling she expressed to Rotim when she asked him to operate: "Listen, he is not an ordinary case. He is a special child." Marko received the successful shunt on July 11, and the cerebral fluid flowed through the shunt into his abdominal cavity. "He improved greatly afterward," noted Šovagovic.

In her last few days before flying to Memphis, Šovagovic not only had her regular tasks to attend to but also the details that went along with traveling overseas with a sick child. She got passports for Marko and Mirjana, and visas for all three of them. She made arrangements with Croatia Airlines and with KLM for oxygen during the flight.

"I prayed to God that somebody else would go and not me. I was scared," she said. "I was told by others, 'He's going to die in the plane,' 'He's never going to make it,' and 'How will you give him medication if he needs it?' The only light in the dark for me was Malcic. One day, in English, he said to me simply, 'Don't cry, little baby,' and we both laughed. I felt better after that."

Although Mirjana and Zeljko visited Marko at Rebro constantly, the reduced visiting hours and the boy's grave condition prevented them from bonding with the boy as they might have normally. Mirjana had yet to hold Marko in her arms. On the other hand, Šovagovic was developing an attachment with Marko that helped fill the parental gap. The boy had ceased being part of her job, someone who fit neatly into her working hours and required tasks, and had been absorbed into her vocation, her life. "Newborn babies can make a big impression," she said. "Marko was still alive despite everything; he was phenomenal. I have had to live with Marko. I sleep with him always on my mind. I search the Internet for clues to his disease and make other investigations. Both medically and emotionally I feel about him as if he were mine. Actually, he *is* mine in a small way. I said to myself that if the parents didn't want him, then I would take him home."

It was this dedication that Šovagovic took along with Marko as she left everything that was familiar to her at Rebro. The sixteenth-century Spanish mystic, St. John of the Cross, wrote, "I have no other light or guide than the one that burns in my heart." In many ways that was all that the resident had as she began her pilgrimage with the infant. No institution can replace the human heart in its ability to make a difference. And the resident's heart was passionately with Marko.

Traveling in the ambulance from Rebro to the Zagreb airport, the full weight of the journey ahead began to hit Šovagovic. "I was thinking, from this moment on, I am going to be alone with him. I am going to be the nurse and the doctor, but who will encourage me? I was aware of the dangerous situation. Marko could stop breathing, and I would only have a little bit of oxygen on the plane. Where was the resuscitation medicine? Where would I put the baby on the plane? We didn't even have a seat for him. Then I was filled with optimism: Everything would be all right. I knew what to do. There was no reason for Marko to get worse on the plane. I felt he would be just fine."

Marko was all right as the plane took off from Zagreb—as much as an emaciated, feverish, seriously ill infant could be. However, as the plane landed in the Adriatic resort city of Pula, the oxygen bottle that Marko was using fell to the floor and fluid from the tank got into his breathing tube and lungs. Marko turned blue. Šovagovic pulled the tube from the oxygen bottle and ran from the plane with Marko, with Mirjana following, to find a first-aid station. There she got assistance to suction Marko's lungs. The medical personnel on duty were not equipped to handle the boy's needs, so Šovagovic suctioned him herself. After about half an hour Marko improved; the infant, doctor, and mother climbed aboard for the journey's next leg—to Amsterdam. "It was pretty dramatic," the resident said of the incident.

In Amsterdam, while the three Croatians waited in an airport lounge for an ambulance whose equipment Šovagovic would use to suction Marko during the four-hour layover, a KLM representative saw him and said, "This child cannot travel to Memphis in this condition." Šovagovic responded that she had briefed the KLM doctor and had medical clearance to fly, that arrangements had been made for oxygen. "She wasn't friendly at all," recalled the resident. "I didn't know if she was a doctor, but I knew she was a problem that we would have to overcome." Šovagovic offered her some Bajadera, Croatia's exquisite cream-filled chocolate. The chocolate opened the door. Within a short while Šovagovic was given three liters of oxygen per minute, was allowed to call Rebro, and was offered extra coffee.

"Everyone has a way to their heart," said Šovagovic of the successful chocolate overture. "You just have to find the way, and then you will find the goodness in them."

Šovagovic would not have to resort to such methods when she met the host family in Memphis. Antoinette and Ernesto Rodriguez wear their hearts on their sleeves with their cheerful, generous dispositions, only appearing unhappy when they don't have someone to help. Marko Lukac was the sixth baby, but the first from Europe, to be hosted by Ernesto and Antoinette in the International Children's Heart Foundation program. No other ICHF volunteer family had hosted more. The Rodriguezes seemed to reflect the innocence and simplicity of an earlier age. Natives of Pueblo, Colorado, and high-school sweethearts, Ernesto recalls the day the two first met. "I was eighteen, she was sixteen," began Ernesto, who at forty-two is ruggedly handsome with thick, black hair, a mustache, and broad shoulders and rippling muscles from weight lifting, his hobby. "Antie was sitting on the steps of a restaurant she worked in, and I was drinking beer on the other side of the street. As soon as I saw her I said to myself, 'I'm going to marry that girl.' She went to college in Denver, but we still spent time together and saw each other. We grew up as a couple and as individuals, and after eight years we got married."

The couple has spent the last nine years in Memphis working for Northwest Airlines. They own a comfortable three-bedroom home about fifteen minutes from the airport. Their friends call their home Hotel Rodriguez, and indeed, even during the stay of Marko, Mirjana, and Šovagovic, Ernesto and Antoinette took in a fellow employee who was having difficulties.

Novick found Antoinette and Ernesto when he needed a Spanish inter-preter for patients from Central and South America. He remembered that the Rodriguezes had been the host family for a Nicaraguan heart patient. Another connection developed later when a nearby Church of Christ com-munity invited Antoinette to speak about the International Children's Heart Foundation at a community service evening. She made many con-tacts there who would serve Marko well during his stay.

Meanwhile, at LeBonheur, Marko joined the hospital's intensive-care unit, which already had two other Croatian patients: Petra Begovic and Ivan Majic, both a year old and both from the Zagreb area. When Marko was admitted, Petra was having a rough time recovering from her open-heart operation (she would not be discharged from the hospital until August 30), and Ivan had also just undergone surgery the previous week. Petra's mother, Anka, along with Ivan's parents, Petar and Manda, were all anxious and upset, and at week's end, Kerrigan called them together, along with Šovagovic and Mirjana, for a special Mass in Croatian at the cathedral parish of the Immaculate Conception, where he was now stationed.

"Everyone had had a rough week, and the three families were going through the same anxieties and fears, so the Mass seemed like a good idea," said Kerrigan. The gospel for the day (July 25, the feast of the apostle James) was the story of the mother of James and John, who asked Jesus for a special place of honor for her sons in the kingdom (Mt 20:20–28). Jesus responded by asking if the sons could "drink the cup that I am going to drink?"—an allusion to his suffering and death. "Like the mother of James and John, you seek the best for your children," Kerrigan told the parents in his homily, "but Jesus again responds by offering a share of the cross. You are not alone in your suffering. You are not alone in light of those who have gone before you, and you are not alone now. If we can be strong and bear this cross for Marko, for Ivan, and for Petra, we will see that this cross will mysteriously bring us to that kingdom we seek."

It was in those first few days in Memphis that the diagnosis of a fourth major defect was made on Marko: pyloric stenosis, an occlusion of the stomach. "The pylorus is the last part of the stomach before it connects with the intestines," explained Novick. "In certain children the surrounding muscle swells unnaturally and closes the outlet. When that happens, very little gets out of the stomach. The child eats and then throws up." Marko was taken to the radiology suite, where a feeding tube was inserted around the obstruction to hold the problem in abeyance until after the heart surgery.

Although she had plenty of expert assistance, Dr. Šovagovic was unflagging in her dedication to Marko. She relaxed each day by walking to the University of Tennessee medical bookstore down the street from the hospital to flip through the latest in medical literature. Antoinette Rodriguez commented: "I got positive energy just from watching her work all day and all night with Marko." The young doctor responded: "Treating a child is like chess. You must know your moves from the beginning, sometimes even in utero. I love medicine, it's such an adventure. I'm so happy I chose this way of life."

In Marko's third week in Memphis his condition improved; his feedings were better and he began to gain weight, and his fever and infections went down. The boy, however, did not improve enough to be ready for surgery before Novick and his ICHF surgical team left for Kazakhstan on August 2 for two weeks. The surgeon devised a plan to send the child home to the Rodriguezes. A combination of Šovagovic's continued vigilant care and the round-the-clock presence of Mirjana would help keep Marko on the right path, and maybe even fatten him up a little, in preparation for heart surgery upon Novick's return. "Marko had already been through two pre-vious operations, and we felt his ability to withstand a third would improve if we improved his nutrition," said the surgeon. "The child was skin and bones; he was so thin you could see every bone in his body."

At the time, Šovagovic, Kerrigan, and the Rodriguezes had already developed their own jargon for expressing their confidence in Marko's prognosis. Marko was now Marko the Man, Marko the Miracle, or, with the Croatian word for miracle, Marko Cudo. Though Marko was still a long way from being a picture of health, he grew more alert and active with each day. The sporadic fevers and ongoing lung secretions had become so much a part of his daily routine that they seemed normal to Kerrigan and the Rodriguezes. And now there was a goal to rally around: to have Marko healthy when Novick returned August 17. Only Mirjana, who was still as quiet and on the fringe of her son's care as when she arrived, did not get caught up in the enthusiasm. "Mirjana and I were able to communicate with our eyes and gestures, but she was really scared by it all, especially when Marko came home and we had to provide twenty-four-hour care," said Antoinette.

It was on August 7, seventeen days after his arrival in Memphis and a lit-tle more than three months after his birth, that Marko was discharged from the hospital to spend his first night in a real home. Kerrigan was the ner-vous chauffeur for the drive from LeBonheur to the Rodriguez home, dri-ving with uncharacteristic caution on the Interstate 240 loop around Memphis. The priest hardly ever had any passengers in his two-door Grand Am, but now he was taking Marko for the first non-ambulance ride of his life, along with Mirjana and Šovagovic, who quietly observed the boy.

A number of minor highlights marked the infant's first few days with Ernesto and Antoinette. One of the visiting nurses reported that the boy smiled at him; it was the first time anyone had ever seen him smile. He was given some toys that captured his attention more pleasantly than the suctioning equipment, thermometers, and respiratory therapy that he was accustomed to. He was taken outside and saw the grass, trees, and insects for the first time on August 11, the feast of St. Clare of Assisi, foundress of the Poor Clares order, who was influenced by that famous friend of nature, St. Francis of Assisi.

There was a down side to the home care. Despite the volunteer efforts of doctors and nurses who would sit with Marko while Šovagovic slept, more often than not she would stay awake the entire night with Marko and grab only a few hours of restless sleep during the day, again at the infant's bedside. The fevers and lung infections did not subside, either; they came and went in waves of varying degree of severity.

On the evening of August 14 Kerrigan volunteered to assist the resident in an all-night vigil. Elsewhere in the city, up to seventy-five thousand people were preparing to hold a candlelight vigil at Graceland to commemorate the twentieth anniversary of Elvis Presley's death. Dressed in a white T-shirt with the slogan "You Can Trust Me—I'm a Doctor," Šovagovic conducted her semi-hourly routine of checking the boy's temperature, applying cold cloths to his head and chest if he had a fever, suctioning his lungs of secretions, tapping his chest to help unclog the secretions, and holding a medicinal mist spray to his nose to assist his breathing. In between these checkups, Šovagovic sat in her chair and listened to the sounds of Marko's breathing as if she were trying to tune in a far-distant AM radio station.

Suddenly, while Šovagovic was in the kitchen for a moment, Kerrigan heard a gurgling sound he hadn't noted before. The resident returned to discover that the boy was choking on saliva or food. He started to turn blue. Through a quick combination of turning the boy over and pounding on his back and then using the suction machine to vacuum out unwanted fluid, Marko's color and breathing returned to normal. Calm was restored, for the moment.

"Does this happen every night?" asked Kerrigan a few minutes later.

"This was the first time for anything like this," said Šovagovic, still a bit shaken. Marko was unsettled for the rest of the night, with a high fever and a lot of congestion. He was brought to the hospital the next afternoon, given another antibiotic, and returned to the Rodriguez home.

On Saturday evening, August 16, Kerrigan decided to drop in at Ernesto and Antoinette's after dinner. It was about ten o'clock, and Hotel Rodriguez was quieting down for the evening. Marko was alert and looking good, although the congestion seemed worse. Antoinette held him for the first time, and Kerrigan had his picture taken with the boy in his arms.

"Antoinette and Ernesto had just gone to sleep, and I was getting ready to leave after I had helped Ruza [Šovagovic] prepare Marko for sleep," began Kerrigan. "I helped with a couple of rounds of suctioning, tapping and inhalation therapy, and we turned away from Marko for just a moment. I went back to put Marko in a more comfortable position for sleep, and something seemed odd. I darted my fingers past his eyes, and he didn't respond."

"Ruza, come here. Something's wrong," said the priest.

"Oh, my God, he's in cardiac arrest!" shouted the doctor as she turned to the bed. "Quick, call Antie and Ernesto and call 911!"

"I remember Fr. Joe knocking on our door and saying that Marko was in cardiac arrest, to call 911," said Antoinette. "I wasn't in shock, but we had just been with Marko and I had held him for the first time. I'm not a doctor, but he looked good, and all of a sudden he was gone."

"I remember the panic of trying to find an oxygen mask or something for Marko, going through things to find it. We never did," said Ernesto.

It was a helpless, chaotic scene as Šovagovic desperately tried to restart Marko's halted heart, while Ernesto and Kerrigan tried to answer the doctor's requests for emergency items. Antoinette was on a portable phone talking to the 911 dispatcher. In the commotion Mirjana awoke and began to cry but stayed in the background. After what seemed an eternity but was actually only a few minutes, the ambulance arrived.

"I still had hope on the way to the hospital," said Antoinette. "I was saying the Our Father the whole drive and telling Mirjana that he was going to make it. I was really conscious of the time, and it took only twenty-three minutes from the time we called 911 to the time we got to the hospital."

"I had a bad feeling from the first second everything started happening," said Kerrigan. "During the ambulance ride I was in the front seat, and I saw all the activity in the back. But I didn't see anything in Ruza's face that gave me hope. Yeah, I was praying, but all I remember from that is something that told me, 'accept this.'

"The emergency room was the worst. The doctor made a cursory exam of Marko, and a half-dozen or so people around Marko seemed poised to do something, but then the doctor looked at his watch and declared him dead, just like that. Then he said: "How long has this child been dead—five hours? Why did you bring him here?" At the same instant Ruza and I both bolted out of there. I don't know why she left, but I couldn't take it. It was chilling, deadly, just awful."

Antoinette, Ernesto, and Mirjana arrived in the emergency room just seconds after Kerrigan and Šovagovic had left it. "I thought they were working on him in the emergency room, but they had already declared him dead," said Antoinette.

The shock and disbelief of Marko's passing hit everyone hard. Looking more dead than alive themselves, Šovagovic and Kerrigan sat motionless a few feet apart from each other on the curb outside the emergency room. Mirjana began a mournful, unremitting wail in a hospital conference room, while Antoinette tried to comfort her. Ernesto went back and forth between the two groups of people.

By the time Marko's body was prepared for viewing, it was about two in the morning, the same hour that Šovagovic first met Marko in May at Rebro. The resident stayed silent long after the others feebly tried to verbalize their emotions. She was bedraggled with sweat, emotion, and the spent energy of her attempt to save Marko. The five mourners gathered in an examination room off the emergency room to pray and to hold him one last time. Afterward Šovagovic did not want to leave the emergency room through the same door that Marko had entered. Instead, she walked with Kerrigan around the block to the parking lot. The full moon hung in the western sky.

At the hour of Marko's passing Novick and his twenty-six-member ICHF team were in the air on their way home from a successful surgical trip to Kazakhstan, where twenty-four children had been operated on. In Kazakhstan that day the big news was that the crew from the troubled Mir space station had just landed. Little did Novick know that his precarious patient, Marko, had just crashed. It would be the unhappy duty of Kerrigan, Šovagovic, and Ernesto and Antoinette to greet the surgeon at the airport with the bad news.

"I thought it was very strange that Antoinette met us even before we went through customs, so I was alerted to the fact that she had bad news," said Novick about his arrival in Memphis.

"Antoinette had a terrible look on her face, and she said, 'There's something I need to tell you,'" added Jameson, who had been in Kazakhstan as well. "I knew right away what she was going to say. At that point I felt worse for Antoinette, who said, 'You know how it is—you see death a lot.' I said, 'I don't know how it is to have a child die at home.'"

As they went up the staircase to the terminal, both Novick and Jameson sensed anger in Šovagovic. "The first feeling I sensed was the anger emanating from Ruza, with her crossed arms and her facial expression," said Jameson. "I said, 'I'm really sorry.' She said, 'Well, he's dead.' She wasn't angry at us, but she had to go back to a bunch of people who would say 'I told you so.' She felt she had failed, and she was emotional."

"Many doctors don't think of their patients this way, but I think of Marko as a real loss," said Šovagovic. "Marko 'checkmated' me, and I feel like a failure. Maybe I can only hope to compensate by doing great things in medicine."

Novick could relate to the resident's resolve following Marko's death; after all, the International Children's Heart Foundation owes its origin to the Nigerian girl Novick was unable to heal when he was a resident at the University of Alabama-Birmingham. "The girl and her mother had flown thousands of miles with the hope and belief that the child would receive corrective surgery," he recalled. "When they found that the girl's disease had progressed to the point where she was no longer a candidate for the surgery, they were still very appreciative and grateful. It seemed inconceivable to me that someone could travel that distance, receive a virtual death sentence, and still be as thankful as they were. For several weeks I had dreams about that child—nightmares—and that stimulated in me the thought of how we could help children in third-world countries by providing education and equipment to their physicians and nurses so that they could receive appropriate therapy earlier in life. After several weeks I resolved to try to make a difference somehow, though I wasn't sure how.

"The 'how' came when two Colombian surgery resident friends came to Alabama to learn about congenital heart disease. The last night we were together, they invited me to come to Bogotá to operate with them. When I went, I found two very different situations. One friend worked for the most successful group of heart surgeons in Bogotá. They had a nice hospital, good equipment, good physicians, and they operated on paying patients. The other friend's hospital, although relatively new, ran on a shoestring budget and operated on the children who were on Colombia's equivalent of Medicaid. There were always more children on the list than could be operated on. When I operated over at the well-heeled hospital, I felt as if I were just a visiting friend. When I operated at the welfare hospital, I felt better about what I was doing. I felt that I was really making a difference. That's when I determined to try to find a way to make a difference in the lives of children like these."

The Tuesday evening after Marko's death an impromptu memorial service was held for the boy in an east Memphis funeral home. As was the case in the deaths of other Croatian children in Memphis, Marko's body was placed in a parlor for viewing rather than in a regular chapel. Over thirty people crowded into the room, from a wide range of backgrounds. There was a large contingent of volunteers from the Church of Christ, who had provided nursing care, translating services, and food for Mirjana and Šovagovic; a college student from Croatia, who had met Marko only in the last week of his life, was there with her boyfriend; a doctor from Chile, who had driven Mirjana and Šovagovic to the hospital each day, was also there. The group stayed to pray and reflect long after the funeral home's other services had ended. Mirjana addressed the group, thanking them for giving Marko a home and a family after so much time in the hospital.

Mirjana left for Croatia the next morning to prepare for the funeral, but Marko's body remained in Memphis. His death occurred in the midst of a strike by United Parcel Service. The strike caused an overload of the overnight delivery system in the country, and it was not certain whether the paperwork on Marko's death could be relayed between the Croatian embassy in Washington, D.C., and the funeral home in Memphis before week's end. Antoinette, Ernesto, Kerrigan, and Šovagovic decided to take matters into their own hands and used the Rodriguezes' flying privileges with Northwest to fly to Washington themselves to expedite the paperwork. The night before their meeting at the embassy, the group drove to Baltimore, where Šovagovic wanted to make two brief stops: one at the grave of Edgar Allan Poe, whose prose and poetry seemed especially appropriate to the last few days, and the other at Johns Hopkins University Hospital.

Šovagovic left Memphis with Marko's body on her name day, August 23, the feast of St. Rose of Lima. Ruza's namesake (ruza is "rose" in Croatian), who lived from 1586–1617, heard Christ tell her, "Let all men know that grace comes after tribulation. Let them know that without the burden of afflictions it is impossible to reach the height of grace. Let them know that the gifts of grace increase as the struggles increase. Let men take care not to stray and be deceived. This is the only sure stairway to paradise, and without the cross they can find no road to climb to heaven." It was a timely message for the Croatian Ruza.

Kerrigan was officiating at a wedding when Šovagovic's plane left town, and so he missed the emotional farewell with her, Ernesto, and Antoinette. As he came out of the front door of the cathedral at the end of the wedding, he heard a plane overhead and checked his watch. It could have been Šovagovic's flight to Amsterdam. He silently wished her well.

When all was said and done, Novick, whose first comment when he saw Marko—"does the mother have any other children?"—proved prophetic, was as frustrated as anyone with the infant's death. " I felt we were dealt a very bad hand. We tried to make the best of it, but unfortunately the child never got to the point where he could be operated on," he reflected. "The child had multiple lung infections and had already had two operations. He arrived in bad shape, and his infections never cleared up.

"He started out with one diagnosis: tracheo-esophogeal fistula. He got operated on, but the Croatian physicians couldn't get him off the ventilator. So they looked for other problems. They checked out his heart and found a problem. He had obstructive hydrocephalus, and they had to put in a shunt in his brain. He had heart disease, brain disease, gastrointestinal disease—three major organ system defects. In the middle of all this we found we couldn't feed the child, and then we discovered that he had pyloric stenosis. It was a frustrating combination and a frustrating feeling, especially for his family, because we were the last, great hope, and they traveled this distance. In the end, what good did we do this child?"

"What good did that baby do for everybody else, that's the question," said Ernesto. "That boy touched us with his eyes alone, when he looked at us and knew us." Antoinette added: "He had to struggle just to get here, to be accepted on the flight. I have never seen or known such special treatment as was given to Marko. He fought for every inch, and seeing that made it easier not to complain about things as I normally would. He brought so many different people together in such a short period of time. Marko even brought Ernesto and me closer together, and we were close already. We don't take anything for granted now."

"I never met Marko until he was brought home from the hospital, and I was impressed by his courage," said Ernesto. "He would never cry, except when the suctioning hurt him, but I never saw him cry for attention. I only saw that one other time, when my mother was dying from cancer."

After seeing Marko's problems, the Rodriguezes' house guest who was going through hard times decided to return to his job and family. "I can never give up my life and family. What's there to complain about?" he said.

Marko's funeral was held in Vrpolje, Croatia, on August 26. He was laid to rest in a cemetery in the same town that gave birth to Croatia's greatest sculptor and acclaimed native son, Ivan Mestrovic (1883–1962). On the same day as Marko's funeral Kerrigan flew to New Jersey for a few days with his family. Driving on the Garden State Parkway, he looked at his watch. Marko's funeral was long completed, and Dr. Šovagovic should have returned to Zagreb by now. He pulled into a rest stop and used a pay phone to call the doctor at home and ask about the funeral.

"Hello?" she answered.

"How was it?" he began without introduction or greeting.

"Sad. Very sad," she replied. "But the worst was when I went to work in the ICU today. The beds were full of children, except in the corner where Marko had been. That space was empty."

Kerrigan didn't respond; he was thinking about the empty space within him that was for Marko, and about all the spaces Marko had created in other people's lives that were now empty. Those spaces may remain empty for some time, but somehow, someday, they will be transformed for the good. Easter, after all, began from an empty tomb.

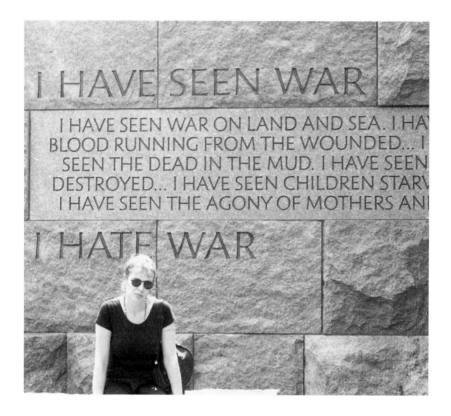

Dr. Ruza Grizelj Šovagovic, one of Marko Lukac's caretakers, at the Franklin Delano Roosevelt memorial in Washington, D.C. The poignant quotation is from Roosevelt.

Rebro nurse, Anela Bosnjak, baby Tea Rajic, and Nedja Rajic at the hospital in June 1995.

11
Tea Rajic

*"Do not neglect hospitality, for through it some
have unknowingly entertained angels"*
–Hebrews 13:2

ICHF nurses Elizabeth Jameson and Rocky Thomas exchanged
remarks as they headed a get-acquainted session with children scheduled
for surgery over the course of a two-week International Children's Heart
Foundation trip to Zagreb in June 1995. As they worked their way
through the pediatric cardiology ward, the nurses tried to match the
unpronounceable names and complicated heart defects on their surgical
list with the children seated or lying on the beds in front of them. In
these introductions, pertinent personal details about a patient occasionally surface. For example, earlier the nurses had met a two-year-old girl
from Banja Luka, Bosnia. They learned that Suzana Anusic's father had
been killed in the war; her mother was rumored to be in a detention
camp somewhere in Bosnia. Suzana was on their list.

"Hey, who's this?" one of the nurses remarked as they moved on
through the ward.

"She's blue as a Smurf!"

"Blue as a Smurf" is an overworked expression to describe a child's
cyanosis, but in this case it was an understatement. "She was the bluest
child I've ever seen," recalled Jameson, who has examined hundreds of

children with congenital heart disease over the years. The girl, an infant of five months, had a chubby, porcelain-doll face that would be described as pretty or cute if it wasn't overshadowed by the telltale blue pallor of a serious oxygenation problem. "As we walked through the ward, we started seeing patients who were on the surgical list. Then we saw this little girl, the bluest one, with oxygen saturations in the forties [normal is in the high nineties]. Where was she on the list?" asked Jameson.

The child wasn't on the list. The nurses called Kerrigan over, so he could use his shaky Croatian language skills on the mother, a disconsolate and painfully thin woman who wept as she held her baby. The priest learned that the baby's name was Tea (pronounced Tay-uh), and the mother was Nedja Rajic (pronounced Nay-juh Rah-each). They were from the outskirts of Capljina (Chap-lean-ya) in Herzegovina. Tea was not on the list, Nedja said, because the doctors had told her that "there are a lot of children who need surgery."

The ICHF asked around among their friends at Rebro and heard, "She's probably a Muslim from a small village—that's how it is around here." Sometimes they only got a knowing roll of the eyes in response. While nobody could point to a specific person or reason that Tea was off the list, murmured responses indicated that the family's poverty and Muslim origin were likely reasons. Novick was informed, and a strategy was devised. The team would work its way up the Rebro chain of command if need be, starting with the girl's cardiologist, to find out where the problem was. The team members would confront it and do their best to get the girl on the schedule.

As the one who might best be able to accomplish this inoffensively, Kerrigan was instructed by Novick to approach Dr. Branco Marinovic, Tea's cardiologist, and ask about the girl. "We were all looking at Tea Rajic and noticed how blue she is," the priest said to the cardiologist. "We were curious about her condition. Dr. Novick was interested in seeing the girl's records. I wonder if you could give them to him?" Marinovic agreed, but it turned out to be a couple of days before the angiograms and other records were given to Novick. Only then was Tea in the loop. With her records in hand, Novick could argue for her case among the Rebro doctors in the daily jostling of patients in the surgical schedule. Novick had an advantage: he was the surgeon, and, as such, the referee. Tea was put on the surgical schedule. "The downside is that we had to bump another child off the list," said Novick. "The schedule is a living, breathing thing. We found the least urgent child on the list and offered the option of either coming to Memphis or waiting for our next trip."

Patient advocacy, usually the domain of social workers and chaplains in American hospitals, falls heavily on the shoulders of Novick and others on the ICHF team during their trips abroad. When team members fight to include a child on a list, they are championing a patient at a deeper level than even social workers and chaplains do in America. "I've been an advocate for Down's syndrome patients who otherwise would not get treated, for patients who are on the wrong side of the ethnic fence, for children who have been deemed inoperable, and for children who have been called a waste of available resources," said Novick, listing some situations where he is called on to blow the whistle on what he views as injustice. "There are political, financial, and educational reasons why doctors pick certain patients. Sometimes a patient is chosen strictly as a teaching case. The child will have a definite diagnosis of heart disease but doesn't have the other qualifications that would put him or her on the list above sixty-five other patients. When we ask the doctors, they say, 'Yes, but we have never seen this operation before.'

"When you feel you have to be an advocate, it increases the pressure and responsibility on you and the team for that child to have a successful outcome. Using the American civil rights movement as a model, you can't take the 'Robert Kennedy' mentality over the 'George Wallace' and not have it work out. That student better do well in the integrated school. And that patient better survive.

"Once you become an advocate for a child, the reality is that someone else falls off the list. No one runs faster to the child's mother or father than the guy you just ran over with the advocacy truck, the cardiologist or the doctor who wanted that child on the list."

Nurses are also called to practice the art of advocacy. For example, in Croatia, as Jameson observed on her first trip, Croatian doctors "never let the parents in the ICU to visit the children. When we first asked the Croatians about it, the doctors just said, 'the parents can't come in.'

'What do you mean they can't come in?' we said. We were incredulous. 'What if the children die?' we asked. 'Then the parents would not see them.' 'We're bringing them in,' we said. 'They must be dressed up,' the doctors said. 'Fine, we'll put the gowns on them.' Over the years they have become very easy about that."

Skirmishes have also been fought over the custom Croatian physicians have of not visiting with patients or parents before surgery (Novick always asks to see both) and over parents not being allowed to see their children after they die. "The parents are an afterthought, and I think it has to do with a mentality left over from communism," said Novick. "Everything is for the motherland. No individual is important, only the motherland, as if they believe, 'What can the loss of one child mean in the grander picture of the motherland?' I can't think of another reason why we only see this on our trips to former Eastern-bloc republics. It's not true when we travel to South or Central America or to the Caribbean. And it's not a peculiarity of Central or Eastern European culture, because all the parents who come to Memphis don't follow that thinking. When a Croatian child dies in Memphis, the parents don't refuse to see him, saying, 'The child died for the benefit of the motherland.' When we inform parents that they can visit their child virtually all day in the ICU, no one says, 'Thanks, but I'll stay outside the door. My presence at the bedside is not as important as yours.' "

"No one really looks out for parent needs in these situations," added Kerrigan. "For example, there is no waiting room outside the operating room. Families stand in a hallway, where a doctor may or may not appear to give word of an operation's progress."

With Tea now on the surgical list the ICHF team continued with its hospital duties. Kerrigan made his rounds anointing and praying with the children, including Tea, before surgery. A very tall—over six feet—nurse turned in his direction and approached the bed where he was about to anoint a child. Kerrigan anticipated a "what do you think you're doing here?" inquiry and then a polite or not-so-polite invitation to leave the room. It was, after all, his first time traveling with an ICHF surgical team and perhaps his idea of hospital chaplaincy differed greatly from what the host hospital staff expected or wanted. But something completely different happened: the nurse stepped in front of the patient, extended her palms to the priest, and asked to be anointed herself!

"I don't know if I will live tomorrow," said Anela Bosnjak after Kerrigan anointed her and asked why she wanted the sacrament.

"Really? That's very interesting. I'd like to talk about it," said Kerrigan.

"Tomorrow, after work, we can go for coffee," said the nurse.

"OK, tomorrow—if we're alive."

Bosnjak was born in Mostar, the capital of Herzegovina, in 1975, and lived there until 1992, when she came to Zagreb. "My life in Mostar was beautiful," she said at a café near Rebro. Mostar, a city of about 200,000 inhabitants before the war, is on the Neretva River and was known for its beauty and rich multi-ethnic heritage. The city's Old Bridge, built in 1566 during the Turkish empire, was a staple on former Yugoslav postcards and symbolized the ideal of ethnic harmony. Ivo Andric, the late Bosnian Nobel Prize winner wrote: "All over the world, wherever my thoughts wander or pause, they come upon mute and faithful bridges, as upon the eternal and eternally unfulfilled human desire to tie, to reconcile and to link everything that our spirits, our eyes or feet suddenly find themselves faced with—so that there shall be no separations, no contradictions or partings."[9]

"We were all the same," Bosnjak continued. "We went to school together and worked together. We celebrated our Catholic feasts, but also the Orthodox Christmas and the Muslim Bajram. But things started changing in 1991, when the war started to spread.

"I didn't think anything would happen because of the three religions. But everything changed overnight. One afternoon I went out with my friends, and we heard a detonation. My apartment was damaged. People were afraid; some were in shock. We took our things and fled to nearby villages. After a couple of days we went back to our homes. We started cleaning and continued with our everyday lives. And then the Serbs attacked us. We spent so much time in shelters, we ran short on food and had to leave. Our family was trying to decide between Split and Zagreb, and we chose Zagreb because we had a relative there. But still, we thought that was only for a short time—a month, maybe."

Alone and afraid, "like poor little kittens," according to Bosnjak, she began a life in Croatia's capital along with her mother, brother, and sister. (Anela's father left to find work in Germany, common among refugee families.) "For a month, we lived at my mother's cousin's house. We just sat around in shock," she said. Bosnjak finished school in Zagreb, found some new friends, but noticed differences from the people she was trying to blend in with. "Everyone in Croatia suffered, but it was different for us, who came from Vukovar and Herzegovina," she said. "We were different, a little bit more mature. We never laughed. In school they called me Aunt Anela because I was always like a mother. My life was different. I had had to leave my life."

When she left Mostar, Bosnjak's best girlfriend was a Serb, and Bosnjak owes her recovery from life-threatening gastrointestinal problems to a Serbian doctor in Mostar who operated on her shortly before the war broke out.

"When I was fifteen, I had a pain in my stomach that I didn't pay much attention to," she said. "Suddenly, one day when I came home from school, my stomach really started hurting, and my mom took me to a hospital. A doctor said my appendix should be removed. So, they did that—took out the appendix and I went home.

"It seemed that the surgery went well, but one morning the pain in my stomach was unbearable. I had cramps and couldn't move at all. I started screaming, because I couldn't stand the pain anymore, and I ended up in intensive care. Part of my appendix had not been removed, and it was festering.

"Twelve days after this second surgery I went home, but three weeks later I felt the same kind of pain. So, for the third time I ended up in a hospital. I had a small bowel obstruction. A Serbian surgeon operated on me, and I haven't experienced any pain of that type since. I wish I had had the chance to thank him for saving my life."

When the Croatian-Serbian violence stopped, the Bosnjak family did not return to Mostar because Croatian-Muslim violence began in 1993. "That was the worst, because more of my friends, both Muslims and Croats, died," she said. "My uncle was killed by a sniper; he left three little children behind. That's why the great hatred exists, but I cannot hate anyone."

In November 1993 Mostar's Old Bridge, after repeated shelling by Bosnian Croats, shattered and fell into the Neretva. The perpetrators had no better reason to destroy it than nationalist pride. The government of Bosnia-Herzegovina announced a national day of mourning.

Five years after her departure from Herzegovina, Bosnjak is still in Zagreb, splitting her time as a nurse between the pediatric neurology and cardiology wards. Like many young adults, Bosnjak retains a remarkable innocence amid the sobering ambiance of war. Her locker at work is papered with pictures of the American film star Brad Pitt, and when her shift ends she usually looks forward to going to a café with some of her girlfriends. Every night Bosnjak prays with her entire family, who have worshiped in Franciscan parishes in Mostar and now Zagreb. Pointing to her shoulder, she said, "St. Anthony is here. He is my guardian."

Bosnjak was Tea's nurse, although Nedja caught nearly as much of her attention. "Nedja is a wonderful and loving person; she looked at her baby with such great love that I thought at first that Tea was her first child," she said. "She cried and feared for Tea a lot. She didn't eat and was so skinny. Because of all the love she showed, I assumed she had gotten married early and waited at least ten years to have children. But later I found out that Tea was one of four children."

Bosnjak may live not knowing whether or not there will be a tomorrow, but thanks to a successful operation under Novick's hands at Rebro, Tea gained a better prognosis for her future on the first day of summer in 1995. "She did very well following that, and we were happy for her," said Novick. The bi-directional Glenn performed on Tea created a bypass that bought her some time before the completion, the Fontan, was performed.

Little Suzana Anusic also did well, and she was reunited with her mother, who managed to cross the Croatian border and come to Rebro with the International Red Cross to see her daughter. "Suzana recognized her mother and we all cried—doctors and nurses alike," reported Dr. Irena Senecic, pediatric resident at the hospital, who frequently assisted the ICHF team. "You don't have to make up the stories here, life makes them."

A few months later, Kerrigan found out more about Tea Rajic's family, and about the Herzegovina where both the Rajics and Bosnjak have their origin, when the priest visited Capljina. The terrain shifts in harsh increments along the Neretva River valley as one drives north from the granite hills of the Adriatic coastal region. The bright green river, lined by modest homes, remains the only constant as the rocky, rough beauty of Herzegovina presents itself in varying forms. Surprising tufts of colorful growth sprout from the rocks and hills, and literally no stone seems to go unturned in the pursuit of planting a vineyard or orchard. Farther inland and northward uniquely recent landmarks emerge: the shells of fire-bombed homes and vehicles, destroyed bridges, tangled power lines. The sights of war are as vivid to the senses here as anything else the Herzegovinian countryside offers. Kerrigan could see why Bosnjak was unsure about her future; Herzegovina looked like a land with no tomorrow.

The Rajic home was not easy to find, down a gravel road off the already beaten path of the outlying villages in Capljina. A United Nations compound was at the top of the gravel road. Kerrigan was introduced to Nedja's husband, Marijan, and their four children, Tomislav, sixteen, Marijana, twelve, Petar, six, and the now-pink and chubby Tea, ten months old. The priest sat down to enjoy a splendid lunch that consisted of fish soup and assorted homemade pastries.

The Rajics discussed their life. "Since the war started in 1991," said Nedja, "we have been left without a source of income. Sometimes we receive help from humanitarian organizations." Marijan defended Croatian territory from the Serbians as a member of the Croatian army.

"When I was pregnant and when Tea was born, I had problems with the veins in my right leg," recalled Nedja. "So when she was born, I was afraid and happy at the same time."

Twenty days after Tea's birth Nedja felt well enough to take her newborn daughter for routine inoculations. At the clinic the mother was told that Tea had a serious heart defect and must go immediately to a cardiology center in Mostar for further examination. "I cried and wondered what would happen to her," Nedja said. In Mostar the heart problems were confirmed and Tea was hospitalized for a few days, after which she was referred again to Rebro in Zagreb.

"The weather was very cold in February 1995," said Nedja about her bus trip to Zagreb. "The trip was very hard. We traveled for twelve hours through the night. The bus was so crowded that my husband and I had to hold Tea in our arms."

Tea remained at Rebro for one month; early in her stay Marijan had to return to Capljina to look after the other children. Tea and Nedja traveled back to Capljina, and after three months home she returned to Zagreb for a catheterization. After that she was discharged and sent home until her condition necessitated a third trip to Rebro just before the arrival of the ICHF team in June.

When Tea and Nedja returned the hospital was alive with preparation for the ICHF team. "The week before the Americans came, everybody talked about it," said Bosnjak. "Everybody was so busy. Nurses were shifted from one location to another. People were talking, and children started coming from all around the country. It was lovely."

Nedja didn't think things were lovely; when she learned that other children would receive surgery but not Tea, she cried. "I didn't know what else to do," she said. After the intervention of the American team, however, she felt much better.

Kerrigan left the Rajics' after the luncheon, but he knew there would be further contact between the family and the International Children's Heart Foundation. Tea's heart disease was such that another operation would be necessary. "Tea was born with a single ventricle, and she had tricuspid atresia, pulmonary atresia, transposition," said Novick. "On a scale of one to ten for complexity, she was probably a nine. When we first saw her, her face was cherubic but she was really a waif. She would cry, and then her saturation level would drop to the thirties. That's what attracted my attention. An oxygen saturation of 38 tells me, 'she's going to die soon.' There's very little reserve, very little margin for a child like that. It's a scary situation. Her body was starved for oxygen, and she had no way to increase the blood flow to her lungs."

When the Dayton peace agreement went into place late in 1995, the ICHF was overrun with requests for help for children from Bosnia-Herzegovina with heart disease. An ecumenical coalition of churches in Memphis agreed to raise funds. The women's group of the Church of the Holy Spirit wanted to sponsor a Bosnian child. It seemed like a good time to help Tea. "She wasn't going to get help at Rebro, and we were afraid she would never get on the list again," said Novick.

Kerrigan suggested that the women's group at his parish sponsor Tea, and the girl's picture and biography were quickly produced and sent around the parish as publicity for Casino Night. "I think her story touched a lot of people, especially the young families who had children around Tea's age," said Christine Haines, past-president of the women's group and herself a host of ICHF children from Croatia. "The families realized how fragile life is and did all they could for Tea and her family."

More than fourteen thousand dollars was raised at Casino Night, well above the group's goal of the ten thousand dollars needed to bring Tea to Memphis. Other funding sources picked up the remainder of the roughly twenty-thousand-dollar cost of Tea and Nedja's hospital stay and travel.

Mother and daughter arrived May 3, 1996. Patrick and Cathy Lawton, along with their three children, Erin, thirteen, Brendan, eleven, and Kip, seven, met them at the airport and brought them to their home in Germantown. The Lawtons, parishioners at the Church of the Holy Spirit, sat in the front pew every week, when Erin and Brendan weren't already close to the action on the altar as servers. Sunday Mass was one of the few times the family gathered together during the week without distraction. Patrick Lawton, city administrator of Germantown, worked long hours at his job, with many evening meetings. Cathy, a self-described "soccer mom," drove the requisite minivan and was often found on the sidelines of her children's school and sporting activities.

The Lawtons decided to get involved with the ICHF after Kerrigan made an appeal for more host families. They volunteered with the same spirit of optimism and achievement with which they approached their work, school, and family life. "Before we knew Tea, we sat down as a family and talked to the children about what we were thinking about doing," related Cathy. "We told them that there was a chance that the surgery might not be successful, but that we had to look at it as a way of giving the children a chance."

Much fanfare surrounded the ICHF at the time of Tea's arrival. The local FOX-TV affiliate had just accompanied the surgical team to Zagreb in April and aired a five-part series on the trip during the week that Tea was scheduled for surgery. Kerrigan's welcome of Tea and Nedja at Holy Spirit was inserted into the series. Religion editor David Waters of *The Commercial Appeal* was planning to do a feature story on Tea's surgery for an upcoming Sunday edition. The women's group at Holy Spirit kept close tabs on the girl's progress.

Alisa Zustra, a volunteer translator in the ICHF, met Tea and Nedja on the day of pre-operative testing at the hospital. The six-foot tall native of Sarajevo was finishing up her senior year at Christian Brothers University, where she was an All-American basketball player.

"I spent the whole day with the Rajics," she said. "You could tell that baby was sick. Nedja was scared; she didn't know what was going to happen. Nedja seemed like a very caring mother. You could see in her face that she had gone through a lot of suffering. She had a lot on her mind, maybe thinking of her other children and her husband. And I got close to Tea—she was so cute and she was so sick. I guess it was different because I got scared, too.

"The next morning, the day of surgery, I met Nedja, Cathy Lawton, and John Dominis in the hospital cafeteria. We had coffee and tried to cheer Nedja up, but she had tears in her eyes the whole time. I came again later in that day, after the surgery. Nedja was now relieved, but you could still sense in her a look of 'what now?' "

All of Memphis got to read the happy details of Tea's successful surgery; in a front-page story in the May 19 *Commercial Appeal*—complete with three color pictures of Tea in the hospital—Waters described Tea's surgery day from the time she entered the hospital waiting room at seven in the morning, through the administering of anesthesia and the specifics of the corrective Fontan Procedure itself, to the moment when Novick greeted Nedja following the surgery. "Novick walked to the waiting room," wrote Waters. "Nedja stared hard at his face. The interpreter was at home. Words were useless. Novick smiled and gave her the A-OK sign. Nedja smiled and hugged him. About ninety minutes later she hugged her baby girl."

A few days after Tea's operation, while the girl was still in the intensive-care unit, Novick left for a two-week trip to Kiev, Ukraine. Kerrigan was in

Europe—in Slovenia—attending part of Pope John Paul II's visit to that country. Anela Bosnjak and Dr. Irena Senecic were also in the crowd of an estimated 100,000 people at the papal Mass in Maribor. "It was beautiful—the people, the pope, everything," said Bosnjak. Tea's original caregivers at Rebro were thousands of miles away, but the girl was doing quite well without them in LeBonheur Children's Medical Center.

Tea left the hospital one week after her surgery. The Herzegovinian mother and child settled in easily with the Lawtons as if they were part of the family. "Nedja and Tea went with me every day to pick up the children from school," said Cathy. "They went to church. But we lived around their routine rather than the reverse. Our whole life was focused on them. Supper became, 'What could we fix that they would like?'" As it turned out, Tea liked tea, which she drank in healthy quantities. She also liked pound cake, and to this day the Lawtons still have the two to remind them of the little girl.

Though the words between the two mothers were few and far between—"we never spoke directly, we never said two words to each other without a translator in between," said Cathy—the suburban American mother learned a great deal from her rural Herzegovinian counterpart. "I've never seen someone so strong emotionally," she said. "When I'm down, her example still gives me encouragement. She was incredibly strong for someone so thin. I'll never forget the day that she helped me plant flowers in the garden. She crouched with Tea in one arm on her lap while she worked effortlessly in the garden with the other. It was amazing."

Though Tea's postoperative course was routine, her stay in Memphis passed too quickly for the Lawtons, who had grown deeply attached to the mother and daughter during their five-week stay. The pair left Memphis several days after the hospital discharge. The airport farewell was especially abrupt and chaotic, even by American standards. For one thing, the Lawtons did not have a translator with them as their entire family accompanied Tea and Nedja to Memphis International Airport. They had to wait several hours while the flight was delayed before learning that the flight had been canceled. "By this point I was frantic with all my children, plus Tea and Nedja," recalled Cathy. "We had to race to another terminal so they could make their re-booked flight. People were already boarding the plane, so we had no real chance to say goodbye. At this point tears were in all of our eyes. I gave Tea and Nedja a hug and told them I loved them. It was very intense, very emotional, and very frustrating. We knew the goodbye was coming after all these hours, but we didn't know when. In the airport, we still followed our normal routine, feeding Tea and giving her medicine, but she was upset and throwing up. It was just a very sad, bad day."

The airport chaos passed once the mother and child were in the air, but by the time they landed in Zagreb Tea was in atrial fibrillation. This unstable atrial rhythm is "especially dangerous for a Fontan because they only have one pumping chamber," said Novick. The girl was taken to Rebro, where her rhythm was controlled. She stayed for three weeks and was then discharged. Tea was in Capljina for about three more weeks before being admitted again to Rebro for atrial fibrillation. She stayed in Rebro for another three weeks and was discharged again. Through a translator, Nedja called ten days later and said that Tea had died suddenly.

"Never, ever, did it occur to us, once Tea and Nedja arrived in Memphis— even when we went to the hospital and through the surgery and intensive care—that we would have to think about her dying," said a brokenhearted Cathy. "It was always, how are we going to get her through this?"

But there was nothing more to get Tea through. When the news arrived that Tea had died, what hit as much as the loss and the shock was the realization that the American dream never had been hers to begin with. By average life expectancy Tea arrived too soon at eternal peace, and her entire life had been enveloped by war. Even in her last few weeks, while the rest of the world wanted to believe there was peace in Bosnia, fighting erupted in Capljina. The hatred and violence that divided her land and indirectly prevented her from getting the lifesaving treatment she needed at the beginning of her life was the same hatred and violence that kept medical facilities unavailable to Tea in closer cities such as Mostar and Sarajevo. This may have contributed to her premature end. "The little girl's life ended as it began, impeded by war and geography from the lifesaving medical treatment readily available to American children," wrote David Waters in an article in the *Commercial Appeal* after Tea's death.

"I was devastated, I was angry, I was sad. I didn't know who to blame," said Alisa Zustra. "After Tea died I decided that I would still help [as a translator], but not as much. It was too hard."

"Helena [Šimundza, Mario Bogdan's nurse] was the one who told me that Tea Rajic died," said Anela Bosnjak. "I just couldn't believe it. The best reward of my job is when a child gets well and goes home. The worst is when you get to know a child, when you bind yourself to a baby, and he or she dies. There is nothing more devastating than that."

> One of the scribes, when he came forward and heard them disputing and saw how well he had answered them, asked him, "Which is the first of all the commandments?" Jesus replied, "The first is this: 'Hear, O Israel! The Lord our God is Lord alone! You shall love the Lord your God with all your heart, with all your soul, with all your mind, and with all your strength.' The second is this: 'You shall love your neighbor as yourself.' There is no other commandment greater than these." The scribe said to him, "Well said, teacher. You are right in saying, 'He is One and there is no other than he.' And 'to love him with all your heart, with all your understanding, with all your strength, and to love your neighbor as yourself' is worth more than all burnt offerings and sacrifices.'" And when Jesus saw that (he) answered with understanding, he said to him, "You are not far from the kingdom of God." (Mk 12:28–34)

No one would say that Tea Rajic was far from the kingdom of God either, even though she did not have much of an opportunity to live out that greatest commandment of Jesus. "With all your heart"–it took every bit of effort for her to keep her unsound heart beating during her twenty-month life on earth. "Love your neighbor as yourself"–it was the disregard of this command by those responsible for the violence and destruction in the former Yugoslavia that limited any chance Tea Rajic may have had for a long and happy life.

Kerrigan held a memorial Mass for Tea at the Church of the Holy Spirit on September 14, a week after the girl's passing. A peach tree was planted in her honor on the parish grounds, alongside pear and plum trees planted in memory of five ICHF children from Croatia and one from Jamaica who had come to Memphis, been hosted at Holy Spirit, and died. Small marble blocks mark the child's name, home country, and the year of birth and death:

Ivan Pozaric, 1992–1995, Croatia
Stjepan Goricki, 1993–1995, Croatia
Ivan Ivic, 1992–1995, Croatia
Matei Marinic, 1992–1995, Croatia
Josip Špoljar, 1995–1995, Croatia
Camere C. Clarke, 1992–1994, Jamaica

At the hour of the service voting had just ended in Capljina, Mostar, Sarajevo, and throughout Bosnia. The elections, the first since the Dayton peace agreement, were supposed to show that Bosnia was ready to function as a democratic country, but the elections only showed that the hatred and nationalism had become institutionally ingrained.

No one could be consoled by the mere narrative of Tea's death. Consolation would have to come from elsewhere. As it turned out, the day of the memorial mass for Tea, September 14, was also the date of the Catholic feast of the Triumph of the Cross. "Our theology tells us that Christ died on the cross to provide eternal life for all of us, to redeem our faults, to perfect our needs," said Kerrigan in his homily that day. "Eternal life for Tea, redemption of the faults and sins of Bosnia and the international community, perfection of the needs of all of us gathered here in grief—each in his or her own way is no less subject to the power of the cross than anyone else. Indeed, seen in this victorious light of the cross, Tea did not die in vain. Seen in this light, we can even be grateful for the opportunity to know her, to love her, to serve her, to discover this cross through her." As he spoke, the priest had in mind this passage from St. Paul: "We are afflicted in every way, but not constrained; perplexed, but not driven to despair; persecuted, but not abandoned; struck down, but not destroyed; always carrying about in the body the dying of Jesus, so that the life of Jesus may also be manifested in our body" (2 Cor 4:8–10).

Pope John Paul II once wrote at length on the whole question of suffering. In an apostolic letter entitled *On the Christian Meaning of Human Suffering*, the pope stated:

> The Gospel of suffering is being written unceasingly, and it speaks unceasingly with the words of this strange paradox: the springs of divine power gush forth precisely in the midst of human weakness.... Human suffering evokes compassion; it also evokes respect, and in its own way it intimidates. For in suffering is contained the greatness of a special mystery.... Suffering is present in the world in order to release love, in order to give birth to works of love toward neighbor, in order to transform the whole of human civilization into a "civilization of love."[10]

In their own way the Lawtons witnessed to the truth of this statement as they kept Tea's memory alive in their home. "A day doesn't go by that we don't think about Tea and her family; she'll always be a special part of our family," said Patrick Lawton. "We've felt that way since the minute we first saw her at the airport." Indeed, from the first minute one enters the Lawton house today, reminders of Tea are in abundance, from a photo of her in the foyer to another framed picture atop the mantle in the living room, to an unusual and poignant memorial in the sun room. A hand-painted border runs across the top of the wall. In mauve letters about ten inches in height, intertwined with ivy, a citation from the letter to the Hebrews reads, "Be not forgetful to entertain strangers, for thereby some have entertained angels unawares" (Heb 13:2).

"God opened our eyes to see that the world is a small place, that there's more out there than us," said Cathy. "Angels are messengers, and Tea was the angel who brought us that message. Before she came, there was so much love in our family. We were content and happy to keep it to ourselves. Once we hosted Tea and Nedja, our own concerns seemed inconsequential. Our own little world got bigger."

Tea Rajic

Franciscan seminarian Mišo Sirovina

12
Mišo Sirovina

"Oh, that today you would hear his voice:
Do not harden your hearts"
—Psalm 95:7–8

The downtown Sarajevo Nadbiskupijat Ordinarijat, or archdiocesan center, was abuzz with activity late in the afternoon of April 11, 1997, the day before Pope John Paul II was due to arrive in Sarajevo for a long-awaited pastoral visit. Visiting archbishops, bishops, and other church dignitaries filed in and out of the offices throughout the day. The archdiocesan staff members busily attended to their multiple tasks. Standing over his desk with phones to both ears, hoping the cell phone in his pocket would not ring, Father Ivo Tomašević, secretary for Sarajevo Cardinal Vinko Puljić, epitomized the frantic atmosphere. Other workers were scattered throughout the building, putting the finishing touches on a freshly laid carpet, a newly painted elevator, and the refurbished guest room where the pope would sleep the next evening. Excitement and energy filled the halls and spilled out into the street, where the presence of Bosnian police officers and NATO soldiers created its own aura.

In an unlit room off the main entrance of the archdiocesan center, in a high-ceilinged space that originally may have been a parlor but was now serving as a storage room, two teenage Franciscan seminarians sat at a table with an English-speaking priest from the seminary. Like the rest of Bosnia, they eagerly awaited the pope's coming, but at this moment they were looking forward to the arrival of a priest from the United States who would bring news concerning impending heart surgery for one of the boys.

Kerrigan did not keep the group waiting long. After spending the morning and a good portion of the week at the archdiocesan headquarters, where he assisted with the English translation of Cardinal Puljic's addresses to the pope, he walked to the home of his hosts, Heda and Kemal Causevic, for a delicious Bosnian meal, complete with baklava and Turkish coffee. He could have stayed at the Causevic table all day long, but he excused himself and headed back downtown, for he also was eager to meet Mišo Sirovina and tell him that everything had been cleared for his travel to Memphis for corrective heart surgery.

"So you are Mišo!" said Kerrigan as he grasped the student's cold hand, after having been introduced to Mišo's older brother Stjepan, nineteen, and Father Josip, the Franciscan priest from the high-school seminary. (Although high-school seminaries are virtually extinct in the United States, they are still important sources of priestly vocations in other parts of the world.) "I'm glad to meet you finally, since so many people in Memphis have heard about you already. Your hands are cold—are you nervous or is your circulation not good?"

"I just came in from the outside," the seventeen-year-old said in broken English.

"Don't worry, it's not cold like this in Memphis. Are you ready to go there?"

"Yes, I am."

A matter-of-fact youngster, Mišo didn't hesitate to answer the priest's question. He knew he needed the surgery; he was starting to tire more easily, and he had frequent nosebleeds. Mišo could have passed for an American teenager. He was dressed in a dark jacket with *Motorsports* written across the front of it in English, and he wore jeans and basketball shoes. He was tall and razor-thin, and his fair features—pale skin, thick light-brown hair, blue eyes—appeared more Irish than Bosnian.

Kerrigan briefed the trio on the successful fund-raising that had now made it possible for Mišo to come to Memphis for surgery. The fund-raising was so successful, in fact, that the International Children's Heart Foundation did not have to launch a special campaign to raise the needed twenty-five to thirty thousand dollars for the boy's travel and hospitalization, as was first anticipated. When Kerrigan informally mentioned Sirovina's plight to churchgoers at a daily mass attended mostly by retirees at the Cathedral of the Immaculate Conception, he received several hundred dollars for the boy that very day. Another gentleman stopped by the church with a check for one thousand dollars later in the week. The Episcopal Diocese of West Tennessee had another eight thousand dollars earmarked for the program, and, to top it off, a philanthropic foundation in Memphis sealed the campaign with a grant of twenty-five thousand dollars.

After a discussion about what a surgical trip to Memphis would entail, including the hospital stay and the host-family arrangement, all that was left to settle was when Mišo could leave the seminary and fly to the United States. Kerrigan, Mišo, Stjepan, and Father Josip bounced around several dates before agreeing on late June, just after the end of the school year.

"See you tomorrow at the cathedral!" said Kerrigan to the group when they parted on the street. Nearby, a three-story poster of Pope John Paul II was draped from a building where Tito's visage had once looked down upon pedestrians at the busy downtown intersection.

"See you tomorrow!" rejoined Mišo.

The next evening at Sarajevo's Sacred Heart Cathedral, Sirovina and Kerrigan met again, as they joined hundreds of other priests, seminarians, and women and men religious in packing the church for Pope John Paul II's appearance there. The high-school seminarians, true to their youth, had more energy than they knew what to do with in the cramped cathedral; they climbed the pillars and moved frequently around the church looking for better camera angles. This contrasted markedly with the slow, shuffling, seventy-six-year-old pope, who was said to be battling Parkinson's Disease. In between, Cardinal Vinko Puljic, at fifty-one the world's youngest cardinal, reflected the vigor of his seminarians as he spoke strongly and smiled broadly. At the same time, like a son caring for an aging father, Puljic helped the ailing pope maneuver through the church, taking him by the arm at some points and shepherding him. "It was very interesting to see," said Kerrigan. "Here was the cardinal of Sarajevo, the 'martyr city,' the victim, helping the leader of the Roman Catholic Church get around. The symbolism was fascinating. I've seen a lot of these papal visits, where the archbishop or cardinal from the host city accompanies the pope, and they are usually in the background. But here Cardinal Puljic's presence was inseparable from the pope's.

"The non-Catholics I spoke to on the street picked up on this, too. I heard a lot of comments about how proud and happy people were to see Cardinal Puljic right there with the pope. I think the joy in his face reflected their joy, and the vibrancy in his being reflected theirs. It was a great moment for Sarajevo."

At the cathedral vespers service Pope John Paul II made a special acknowledgment of seminarians like Sirovina who were present. Calling them "the hope of the church in this land," John Paul II exhorted the young men to "let yourselves be captivated by Christ! Discover the beauty of giving your life to him, in order to bring his gospel of salvation to your brothers and sisters. A vocation is an adventure worth living to the full! A generous and persevering response to the Lord's call is the secret to a life that is completely fulfilled."

Mišo was born in 1980 in the small town of Kotor-Varoš in northwestern Bosnia. "When I was growing up, everything was fine until I was twelve years old," he said. He and his older brothers, Petar and Stjepan, had more Serbian friends than Catholic or Muslim friends. Mišo's father, Ante, was a customs officer, and his mother, Ivka, was a housewife and mother for the four males in the simple, one-story home built by Ante shortly after the birth of their first child, Petar. There was a garden in the backyard, with fruits on one side and vegetables on the other.

The worst childhood trauma Mišo can recall happened when he was seven years old. He and Stjepan were playing by the small river that runs through town. Mišo was thirsty, and near the river was a house his uncle was building. The boy went to get a glass of water in the house, but a dog was there. "I said hello to the dog, but he jumped on me," said Mišo. He still bears the scars of the attack on his skull, but it could have been worse had not an electrician, a Serb, intervened and pulled the dog off the boy.

That same year Mišo was accidentally hit in the eye by a missile from a slingshot fired by Petar. In Memphis ICU nurse Blake Jones noticed an anomaly in the eye and referred him to his father, optometrist Larry Jones, who gave the seminarian a free eye exam and his first pair of glasses. Even though he said he never felt sick, Mišo's heart defect was discovered in his seventh year, and he had to travel to Ljubljana in Slovenia every year afterward for checkups.

Everything changed in the summer of 1992.

"One day, I think it was the seventh of July, my father went to work the same as always," said Mišo. "Our house was outside of the city. All of a sudden he came home much earlier than usual because barricades had gone up in the city. When the barricades went up, the townsfolk fled to the mountains where they had weekend houses. We were there for a week or two. Our town surrendered; we didn't fight. Just before all this, we had had all kinds of problems with Serbs who came into town seeking money and looking for things.

"A small river runs through my town. Every day there was shooting, because the river that bordered my town bordered a Serbian town and there was shooting across the river. One day after the shooting began, I was with my father when a big truck with Serbian special forces in it passed us on the road. About ten people from the truck started shooting into a house.

"On the edge of town is the house of my mother's uncle. On the night of July 14, at his restaurant, there was shooting throughout the night and windows were broken. In the morning, we found that one of my uncles was shot in the arm and another uncle was killed on the road.

"When I was in school I studied the First World War and the Second World War. I never thought a war would come to Kotor-Varoš; everybody got along there, whether they were Muslim, Serb, or Croatian."

The Sirovina family's happy rural lifestyle was fractured; they fled as refugees to Germany. Ivka gave birth to her first daughter, Ivana. After several months the oldest son, Petar, returned to school in Zagreb. Stjepan had already decided to become a Franciscan seminarian and was waiting to return to Bosnia. During this time Mišo also decided to reveal his desire to become a priest.

"As a little boy I often met priests. I was fond of going to Mass and catechism and there I learned about the priesthood," he wrote in a letter to Kerrigan. "While I was a little boy I decided to become a priest. I cherished this in my heart and did not want to reveal it to anybody. When asked what I planned to do after leaving primary school, I used to say that I did not know, although I knew well.

"The war that started in my hometown has not discouraged me from my intention to become a priest. On the contrary, it has made me firmer in my decision. During the war, I found that people needed priests very much, and that priests willingly suffered to help people.

"I look at all of life, not just the war, and I still see God is with us."

Mišo's fragmentary impressions of war and vocation, suffering and hope, may be the raw material used someday by God for a powerful priestly vocation that feeds thousands of spiritually hungry people in Bosnia. "I was impressed from the first moment I met him," said Kerrigan. "He's refreshing in his innocence, his maturity, and his humor. I think he can be a leader who attracts others to himself. I hope he perseveres in the seminary, but he will do well no matter what he chooses to do."

Kerrigan likes to ask prospective priests or married couples what their favorite scripture passage is. Their choices give him a clue about the kind of priest or the kind of spouse they see themselves as. Mišo responded without hesitation to this question. "In the Old Testament, I like the story of Abraham and Isaac (Gn 22:1–19), and in the New Testament my favorite is the story of the lost son (Lk 15:11–32)," he said.

"These are interesting selections for someone so young," Kerrigan mused. "On the one hand, you have the well-known testing of Abraham, in which Abraham is cruelly brought to the brink of killing his son in answer to God's command. And then, in the story of the lost son we have a son who finds himself in exile but calls upon his father, who is overjoyed at his return. Both selections are about bad things that happen, or almost happen, to sons. There's also a lot of adversity and suffering in these passages, more than you might expect a seventeen-year-old to relate to, but these choices tell me that Mišo is using his faith to sort out what has happened in his life—with the war and his heart defect. And we can't forget that in these two stories there is also deliverance. If he can continue to respond to stories about deliverance in adversity, he's going to make a terrific priest."

Mišo can aspire to any long-term future only with a repaired heart. He was born with aortic stenosis and regurgitation, which means that the blood has a hard time being ejected from his heart; it tends to slide back in again. "His aortic valve is stuck, and it leaks," said Novick. "It doesn't open all the way, and it doesn't close all the way." The surgical repair Novick selected, the Ross operation, requires the removal of the aortic valve, followed by the removal of the patient's pulmonary valve and surrounding muscle in order to preserve the architecture. The pulmonary valve is then put where the aortic valve was and sewn into place. A human tissue valve is placed where the pulmonary valve was located. "It's a pretty radical operation if you have his kind of stenosis," said Novick. "The issue with the operation is that you have a human tissue valve that is not yours instead of a repaired valve or a mechanical valve. However, if you poll pediatric cardiac surgeons who do a lot of valve work, I think you will find that most would rather replace the human tissue valve in the right ventricle than redo an operation on someone's aortic valve. In my opinion he could not have a mechanical valve because he was going to be an active teenager. He would need an anticoagulant for the rest of his life, and we are talking about Bosnia. How available will the drugs be for him?"

Mišo knew that one day he would have to have surgery, but he didn't know when or where—Italy, Germany, or the United States. Even though he was referred to the International Children's Heart Foundation as early as June 1995, it was not until nearly two years later that his surgery was scheduled. The seminarian was elated as he left the meeting with Kerrigan.

"I felt every kind of lucky feeling," he said. "For years they had been talking about this operation and nothing happened. Finally it's happening."

At the time Mišo met Kerrigan, his symptoms were worsening. The boy couldn't walk up one flight of stairs without becoming breathless. "He was reaching a point where he didn't have much time left," said

Novick. "He probably could have lived a few more years, but he was already in congestive heart failure. In other words, he wasn't making up for his poor cardiac function. We wanted to operate on him before he got to a point where even the valve replacement wouldn't help, which happens to some patients."

Along with his sixty classmates Sirovina took part not only in the papal vespers service at the cathedral but in the April 13 papal Mass attended by fifty thousand people at Koševo Stadium. Mišo was one of the acolytes who helped the priests distribute communion. "I used to tease my brother that I would never be a seminarian, and here I am," he said.

The seminarian heard the pope encourage the assembly through a driving snow squall: "Sarajevo, Bosnia-Herzegovina, arise! You have an advocate with God. His name is Jesus Christ the righteous!... Sarajevo, Bosnia-Herzegovina, your history, your sufferings, the experiences of the years marked by war, which we hope will never return, have an advocate with God: Jesus Christ, who alone is righteous. In him, the many dead, whose tombs have multiplied in this land; those who are mourned by their mothers, their widows, their orphaned children: they have an advocate with God."

After the papal visit Mišo finished the remaining weeks in the school year. He had another visitor in early May—Novick, who was in Sarajevo to perform the first pediatric heart surgery in Bosnia's history. "I met Mišo on a day I did two operations," said Novick. "There was a lot of hustle and bustle associated with my stay in Sarajevo, and I met him when we were between cases. The minute I saw him coming toward me, I knew immediately who he was. Here was this lanky, knobby-kneed, mop-haired kid, grinning from ear to ear. I don't think we even spent four minutes together. I listened to his heart; I told him I looked forward to seeing him in June and that we were delighted to finally provide him with this operation. We talked about his progressive shortness of breath. I told him that it was our hope that the operation would provide complete relief for him, and that was it."

Mišo and his mother, Ivka, flew in late June to Memphis, where they were greeted by Mark and Maureen Martini. A year earlier this couple had welcomed Afan Šabanac, an eight-year-old heart patient from Bihac,

Bosnia-Herzegovina. Many years before, the Martinis had lost a child, Kevin, to sudden-infant-death syndrome when he was six weeks old. Once the Sirovinas and the Martinis got acquainted, Maureen Martini found that Mišo's surgery wasn't the only thing on Ivka's mind.

"I could tell that Ivka was very worried before surgery, but Mišo was pretty relaxed," she recalled. "It was really hot when they arrived, but Ivka went outside in the backyard every day to say the rosary. She and her husband come from big families that are dispersed now. Her husband was in Hamburg with Ivana, her four-year-old, from whom she had never been away for this long. No one knew how long they would be able to stay in Germany as refugees. Petar was at the university in Zagreb, and Stejpan was in Sarajevo. She had an awful lot to deal with.

"One day my daughter Christine came over to copy some recipes. After she left Ivka said to me, 'I have no recipes—they're gone.' She lost all that when she was forced from her home. They had been married for twenty-five years, and they had lived in the same house for most of that time. But in 1992 they were 'cleansed,' forced out of their home. It really hit me how much she had lost."

Mišo kept things on the light side, bonding well with the Martini's two boys, Nick, twenty, and Matthew, seventeen, playing soccer and learning lacrosse in the family yard. Quickly learning Southern culture, he invited the Martinis to his ordination and told them he would set aside a special "redneck" section for them. He displayed a bit of dark humor when he met Novick before surgery, telling the surgeon that if he died, he wanted to be buried at Graceland next to Elvis Presley. "He's an all-right kid with both of his feet on the ground," said Novick. " I liked his dry sense of humor. He was very easy to deal with, mature, but I think a lot of the kids who go through what he went through are extremely mature for their age. You don't face death constantly that young and not mature rapidly.

"What made him different and unusual for me was the weight of the responsibility I felt in treating him. He was a Croatian living in Bosnia who had no desire to leave Bosnia. He wanted to be a seminarian and go back to his diocese and help keep the Catholics spiritually alive in his neighborhood. That's a significantly different outside pressure on me for him to do well. Here he is supported by Cardinal Puljic, who may at some point be nominated for a Nobel Peace Prize for his stance in Sarajevo during the war. How can you have the Cardinal of Sarajevo stand behind this child and not feel the pressure? Mišo represents the future of Catholicism in Bosnia."

If there was pressure on Novick, it didn't show in the operating room. Mišo's surgery was an unqualified success, only the third Ross operation performed in Memphis. (The first two were also on children from the former Yugoslavia.) Mišo was off the ventilator the next morning, out of the ICU the following afternoon, and out of the hospital on the morning of his third day after the operation.

The Martinis had become motivated to become a host family when they went to a talk given by Novick and Kerrigan on the former Yugoslavia at a nearby Catholic parish in the summer of 1994. The two were asked by a church group to comment on the still-raging war, which for many people was incomprehensible. The surgeon and priest did their best to provide background information on the conflict, which they discussed in the context of their work with children with congenital heart disease. "It was like a geography lesson," said Maureen. "With all the awful things going on over there, I wanted to participate somehow. This war seemed so much like World War II, when I was too young to help, and hosting seemed like a natural way to help." An X-ray technician for nearly thirty years, Maureen also saw hosting as an opportunity to get reacquainted with pediatric heart surgery; she had begun her work at Georgetown University Hospital in Washington, D.C., where pioneering work in children's heart surgery occasionally intersected with her duties in the X-ray department. "My job helped because not only could I help the family in my home, but I could also protect them at the hospital and answer some of the scary questions," she said.

The Martinis live in a close-knit, middle-income neighborhood in Bartlett, a suburb just north of Memphis. Their street is heavily peopled with Catholic families from their parish, St. Ann's, the largest in Tennessee. Maureen works at St. Francis Hospital, and Mark is employed as an executive at a company that disposes of paint, floor coverings, and polishes past their shelf lives. "With our children grown, our life was getting very calm, but I still wanted to stay very active and give something back," said Maureen. After Mišo and Ivka left, Maureen concluded, "It's exhausting when you're doing the hosting, but after they're gone there is an empty feeling."

When Mišo left the hospital, Ivka finally revealed to him that a friend with whom he grew up had died suddenly after playing soccer. The boy had had a heart problem similar to Mišo's. "Now I know why my parents always told me not to overexert myself in soccer," he said. "When I play soccer now, I won't be scared of anything. I have an American heart now, so who knows? I get four out of five in my grades; now I will get five out of five."

Eleven days after his surgery, Mišo, Ivka, and Maureen joined Novick at the Cathedral of the Immaculate Conception, where Kerrigan had formed a weekly exercise group called the Cathedral Twilight Steppers. Each Tuesday evening walkers and joggers—up to seventy in number on some occasions—gather on the steps of the church to hear a brief motivational talk, to pray, and then to walk or to run through the scenic, tree-lined neighborhood in midtown Memphis. Afterward the group convenes in the church's reception hall for light refreshments and discussion. Kerrigan asked Novick to speak on "cardiovascular wellness," and the surgeon brought Mišo along as living proof. It was a hot and muggy July evening in Memphis, but it didn't prevent Mišo, with Novick at his side, from walking two miles with the group after the surgeon's presentation.

"It was certainly unusual for me to go on a two-mile walk with one of my patients," said Novick. "I was absolutely delighted to see him, knowing what sort of heart disease he had had and how short of breath he would have been had he not been fixed. It was wonderful to see him respond so positively to the operation.

"On the way we chatted about football and basketball and Bosnia. We talked a lot about how he felt after the operation compared to how he had felt before the operation.

"'How are you doing?' I asked him at one point. 'I am fine,' he said. 'You're not out of breath?' I said. 'No—I will show you,' and he took off running down the street. It was an amazing moment for me, very emotional."

The raw material of Bosnia's future may have been running toward an uncertain destination, but he was running nevertheless, newly healed and with restored hope. We couldn't be more grateful.

Mišo Sirovina feels strong enough to arm wrestle with Dr. Novick after his heart surgery in Memphis during the summer of 1997.

Epilogue

"A clean heart create for me, God"
—Psalm 51:12

In June 1995 Kerrigan left Memphis for Croatia a few days before the rest of the ICHF surgical team. He used the time alone to travel around the country and check on the growing list of ICHF "alumni"—patients and their families who had come to Memphis for treatment. In Dalmatia he met three-year-old Zvonimir Rak and his family. They drove the priest for three hours down the coastal highway to Ploce, where they handed him off to Marija Culjak and her parents. Before parting company the Raks, the Culjaks, and Kerrigan made a day trip through the Neretva River valley to Medjugorje, the Catholic pilgrimage site in Bosnia-Herzegovina.

The two old, white Renault wagons sputtered along the road in the Herzegovinian countryside. The hot afternoon sun and the restlessness of Zvonimir and Marija occasioned more than one stop at roadside *gostionicas*—little cafés where the adults refreshed themselves with coffee while the children enjoyed ice cream and soft drinks. As they pulled over at one café Kerrigan noticed what he thought were the ruins of a mosque atop a hillside along the road. He said he would walk farther to get a good picture of the mosque and join the Raks and Culjaks at the café across the street.

As the families enjoyed their refreshments, Croatian soldiers already seated at a table noticed Kerrigan's interest in the mosque. "Look at that stupid Muslim tourist," one said, pointing in Kerrigan's direction. "We'll show him," said another. They drew their guns.

"What are you doing?" exclaimed someone from the Rak and Culjak table. "That's our friend. He's a priest from America." The soldiers grumbled something and put away their weapons.

The incident occurred the same day that American pilot Scott O'Grady was dramatically rescued farther inland in Bosnia (his plane had been shot down days earlier). Kerrigan would not know of his own deliverance until he returned to Croatia four months later. Safely inside the Raks' home outside Šibenik, Zvonimir's mother, Snjezana, recounted the episode for the priest. A chill went through him as he listened.

"Why didn't you tell me this when it happened?" Kerrigan asked.

"We didn't think you would come back here if we told you," she said.

To represent accurately the heart of Croatia, we must note the partitioned, or "balkanized" Croatian heart. Unquestionably, the Croatian people were terribly victimized by the war and its aftermath. The children and families featured in this book were all at least indirect victims—and some were directly affected—and many Croatians suffered even more severely.

However, some Croatians did not shy away from participating in the nationalistic hatred—along with the Serbians and Bosnian Muslims—that rent the former Yugoslavia asunder and still fuels the region's sinister divisiveness today. Many other books and articles have discussed the political, sociological, psychological, and religious aspects of this hatred at great length; that has not been our aim here. But our efforts to work in Croatia were sometimes hampered by prejudice borne of nationalism, and as a physician and priest who are trained to diagnose and treat physical and spiritual illness, we would be derelict in our professional duties to see something wrong and say nothing. The subtle and not-so-subtle inclinations to hatred are too pervasive within all human hearts—including our own—to pretend such hatred does not exist in postwar Croatia.

"Why do you have Tea Rajic and Mišo Sirovina in the book? They are from Bosnia, not Croatia," exclaimed a student friend of ours from

Sarajevo. She was satisfied with our rationale but added, "If you don't explain why they're in the book, you'll be just like the rest of them, annexing Bosnia as you wish."

She was right. In the thinking of some Croatians, there should be no explanation surrounding the inclusion of Tea Rajic and Mišo Sirovina. Tea was born in Capljina, in the Herzegovinian, or southern, region of Bosnia-Herzegovina. The divided heart of Croatia believes in an ethnically pure "Herzeg-Bosna," indivisible from Croatia proper. As we write, in the fall of 1997, five years after the internationally recognized independence of Bosnia-Herzegovina—and nearly two years after the signing of the Dayton peace agreements—there are still strong elements of Croatian nationalist thinking that do not acknowledge Bosnia's sovereignty. It would be as if the United States annexed part of Mexico and then instituted all forms of American life there. Such is the Croatian mentality, in some quarters, toward Herzegovina. It is more than a mentality: Croatia's currency, flag, and local governing style are all in use there today. This mindset has also helped bring labels like Croat and Muslim to the fore, labeling people, which in turn produced the violent conflict between Croats and Muslims in Herzegovina, including the partitioning of Mostar into eastern and western sections that uneasily divide the Muslim residents from the Croatians.

To place Tea Rajic in *Healing the Heart of Croatia* without explanation would be to fall prey to the same sort of thinking. Tea was from Herzegovina, her parents were Catholic, so therefore, she was from Croatia. We say, "Wait a minute!" The cruel irony in her case was that Tea was passed over for surgery until we found her at Rebro University Hospital because it was assumed that she was Muslim and poor—two unforgivable sins. To be a Muslim is a sin according to Croatian nationalists; to be poor is a sin according to old-time Yugoslav communists, who cannot make money under the table for a child's preferential treatment if the family is poor.

Tea's eventual medical treatment—at Rebro, no less—was testimony to temporary triumph over this discrimination. (We must add that the Croatian physicians at Rebro were committed to maintaining at least the same percentages in their patient population as existed in the general population, 90 percent Croatian, 10 percent non-Croatian). Why is Tea in the

book? Because of the merits of her story, including the way she symbolizes another side of the Croatian heart.

Likewise, the tale of Mišo Sirovina, a Catholic seminarian who was
born near Banja Luka, Bosnia, finds a place in this book without nota-
tion if one accepts the view that all Catholics in Bosnia are Croats first. It
is analogous to writing a book called *Healing the Heart of Ireland* and
including Kerrigan as one of the subjects only because he has Celtic
blood, regardless of the fact that he has never lived in Ireland and thinks
of himself as a Catholic American (if he has to be reduced to one classifi-
cation). Young Sirovina is a Catholic Bosnian. That is how he refers to
himself, and in these tense postwar years we have not submitted to the
volatile temptation of including him in the book simply because he may
be of the Croatian tribe.

Mišo is included in these pages because his story points to an incon-
gruity in the heart of Croatia. As a victim of Serbian "ethnic cleansing"
in his hometown of Kotor-Varoš and as a Catholic seminarian in an
increasingly Muslim country, Mišo is a good example of one who has
harshly experienced a bit of the heart of Serbia and the heart of Bosnia.
During our lengthy attempt to find Mišo and bring him to Memphis for
surgery, an effort that took nearly two years, our endeavor was thwarted
for a time when Croatians in Zagreb claimed that Mišo "could not be
found," even though it was the Croatians who brought Mišo to our attention in the first place. When the Croatians learned that extra funding
might be made available to Mišo from Catholic institutions in Memphis
because he was a seminarian, these same Croatian sources also began to
speculate that Mišo was probably really a Muslim and should not receive
help from the Catholic church under "false pretenses." When we veri-
fied Mišo's status ourselves at his seminary and through the cardinal's
office in Sarajevo, we learned that the claims from Croatia could not be
further from the truth.

If Kerrigan, Rajic, and Sirovina all died from the hatred that briefly
swirled around them, the deaths of these Catholics at the hands of other
Catholics would have been tragically ironic and again would have proved
the point that all hatred is ultimately self-destructive. Many, many others
were not as lucky as Kerrigan, Rajic, and Sirovina. They did lose their

lives because they were deemed the "them" that could never be reconciled with the "us." At the time the gun was pointed at his "Muslim tourist" head, Kerrigan had his back turned. Tea Rajic and Mišo Sirovina also had no clue to the prejudice that threatened their health. Now, however, we do not have that excuse. We have heard and seen in Croatia the gamut of good and evil, and we cannot turn our backs in silence just because a bit of what we have experienced in the heart of Croatia was less than pure.

This book's conclusion finds us at the beginning of initiatives with Serbia and Bosnia-Herzegovina along the same lines as our work in Croatia. By the end of 1998 we hope to have completed our first ICHF trips to both Belgrade and Sarajevo, as we continue our efforts in Zagreb. As the only republic of the former Yugoslavia not based on ethnicity, and as the republic that suffered the most during the war, we are especially eager to attend to the needs in Bosnia-Herzegovina. That is why we include the reflections of Vinko Cardinal Puljic, archbishop of Sarajevo, for our afterword. We asked Cardinal Puljic to comment on the cathedral in Sarajevo and on his own episcopal coat of arms, both of which feature the image of a heart.

But no matter where we go next and no matter whom we serve, our prayer for ourselves and for those we meet is simple: "A clean heart create for me, God, renew in me a steadfast spirit" (Ps 51:12).

Afterword—
Vinko Cardinal Puljic, Archbishop of
Sarajevo, Bosnia-Herzegovina

The Sarajevo Cathedral was dedicated in 1884 to the Sacred Heart of Jesus, according to the wishes of the archbishop of the time, Josip Stadler. As the first archbishop after the Turkish occupation, he realized that only the love of God could revive the faith in these areas and elevate the dignity of each person. He especially dedicated not only the cathedral but the entire archdiocese to the Heart of Jesus. That is why, at the beginning of his pastoral service, he decided that a monthly paper, *Glasnik Srca Isusova* ("The Voice of the Sacred Heart of Jesus") should be published as the official newspaper of the diocese.

Back then, the people needed to recuperate both materially and spiritually. Love is the source of strength and hope, and its center is in the heart of God, which needs to fill each person's heart. That is why the center of the whole diocese is the cathedral as the heart of one living organism.

In the cathedral the stained-glass window that pictures Christ on the cross was damaged in this war. It is symbolic. The hatred of the war wounded God's heart because it wounded humanity. That is why I want to see God's heart in the revival of each person, especially in the healing of each heart to be freed from hatred and ready for love. This cannot be without God's mercy, God's heart. In a special way, I want to experience that in the lives of the children and youth, who should be brought up for a new world and a happier future.

My coat of arms has three symbols, the cross, anchor, and heart, for the three virtues of faith, hope, and love. The cross is a symbol of faith, and in that manner I accept the sacrifices of my calling. In the symbol of the cross Christ defeated evil, and this is the source of victory over evil. The anchor is the symbol of hope, which is the last one to die. In these uncertain times faith is the one I need most in my personal life and for those I was sent to serve. The heart is the symbol of love, and I want the contents of my life and work to be under that sign. Beneath the sign of love is "AM" for "Ave Maria." Those are Mary's symbols. With these words the angel greeted Mary when God decided to become a man in order to create the child of God. Mary is our model and our path to God. In the middle of the coat of arms is the heart of God toward man, the heart of Mary toward God and toward man, and the heart of man for man.

Notes

1. *Heart Disease in Infancy and Childhood*, 3d ed., ed. John D. Keith, Richard D. Rowe, and Peter Vlad (New York: MacMillan, 1978), p. 4.

2. James H. Moller, and William A. Neal, *Heart Disease in Infancy*, (New York: Appleton-Century-Crofts, 1981), pp. 8–11.

3. John of the Cross, "Maxims and Counsels," no. 23, in *The Collected Works of St. John of the Cross*, trans. Kieran Kavanaugh, OCD, and Otilio Rodriguez, OCD (Washington, D.C.: ICS Publications, 1979), p. 675.

4. C. S. Lewis, "Love's as Warm as Tears," *Poems*, ed. Walter Hooper (New York: Harcourt Brace Jovanovich, 1979).

5. Sherwin B. Nuland, *How We Die* (New York: Alfred A. Knopf, 1994), p. 17.

6. William Wordsworth, "We Are Seven" (1798), from the *Norton Anthology of English Literature*, 5th ed., vol. 2, M. H. Abrams, general editor (New York: W. W. Norton and Company, 1986), p. 147.

7. Claudia Wallis, "Faith and Healing," *Time* (June 24, 1996), p. 60.

8. In the United States and most industrialized countries, surgery usually occurs in the first six months of life.

9. Quoted by Tom Gjelten in *Sarajevo Daily* (New York: Harper
Collins, 1995), p. 149.

10. John Paul II, *On the Christian Meaning of Human Suffering*
(Boston: St. Paul Editions, 1984), pp. 7, 47, 54.

Acknowledgments

We are grateful to the many people who have helped bring *Healing the Heart of Croatia* to life. In particular, Jenni Scherer Nieman, Amy Burke, and Joe Kerrigan Sr. walked with us through every page, guiding the book with their persistent encouragement and sage counsel on everything from chapter ideas to punctuation and grammar. When we completed drafts, Jenni, Amy, and Joe responded promptly; when our production lagged, they were gentle in urging us to persevere. Nick Cassella, Judy Gray, Elizabeth Jameson, Isa Johansen, Agnes Kovacs, Anne Laulederkind, Cindy Pease, Alan Schwartz, and Ownie Smolko reviewed chapters and provided helpful suggestions. Aida Causevic, Caroline Lenac, Irena Senecic, Maja Stankovic, and Alisa Zustra formed a very generous and reliable group of translators and transcribers of interviews.

We also want to acknowledge the mentors, pastors, and colleagues who have been instrumental and inspirational for us: Paul Nemir Jr., John Kirklin, Albert Pacifico, James Kirklin, John R. Batson, Fred Sauer, and the late Robert J. Ewing.

At Paulist Press, we wish to thank Lawrence Boadt, CSP, Donna Crilly, Hugh Lally, and John Thomas for their expertise and for their enthusiasm for the project.

At our "day jobs" there are many people to recognize for the gracious and nimble way they absorbed visitors, phone calls, and paperwork from

Croatia into their daily routines, especially the following: Sandy McMahan and Melissa Patterson (cardiovascular surgery department at LeBonheur Children's Medical Center); Cathy Fakult and Cindy Smith (International Children's Heart Foundation); Pat Burke, Rose Grantham, and Chris Lemoine (Church of the Holy Spirit); and Angela Moore (Cathedral of the Immaculate Conception).

Our work has been enriched by unselfish professional assistance at many levels: Division of Cardiology, University of Tennessee-Memphis: Tom DiSessa, Bruce Alpert, Mubadda Salim, John Ring, and Judy Becker; Division of Critical Care, Pediatrics: Greg Stidham, Stephanie Storgion, Mark Bugnitz, Mike Quasney, Rick Barr; Pedriatic Anesthesia, LeBonheur Children's Medical Center: Rao Paidipalli, Susan Watson, Mohan Kakarra, Mike Baron; and Catholic Diocese of Memphis: Albert E. Kirk, Thomas D. Kirk, and Fred Sauer.

We salute our partners in humanitarian aid to Croatia: Steve Rukavina and the National Federation of Croatian-Americans; Leo Majic, Ivan Nogolo, Mary Roberts, and their fraternal organizations in Washington, D.C., Cleveland, and St. Louis, respectively; the Variety International Lifeline Program; in Hamburg, Germany, *Initiativgruppe fur medizinische und humanitare hilte in Krisengebieten Sudost-Europas*; and the Big Hearts for Little Hearts program in Zagreb. Locally our work has been aided greatly by organizations such as the University of Tennessee Department of Surgery, the University of Tennessee Medical Group, LeBonheur Children's Medical Center (especially Jim Shmerling); the Assisi Foundation; the Episcopal Diocese of West Tennessee; numerous churches and synagogues; Rotary Clubs in Memphis, and, in Orlando, Florida, the Arnold Palmer Hospital for Women and Children. The *Commercial Appeal* has championed and chronicled our efforts many times through the years; in particular, religion editor David Waters and photojournalist Robert Cohen have brought their keen journalistic acumen to the fore in creating powerful and truly moving stories. We want to thank especially the newspaper for giving us the use, free of charge, of Cohen's outstanding photographs from Croatia.

Volunteers too numerous to list include the physicians, nurses, and technicians who gave their time, their expertise, and their hearts.

Similarly, dozens of host families in Memphis have opened their homes and hearts to international patient families. At the same time, we want to thank the families who have hosted us overseas; special kudos to Heda and Kemal Causevic, who extended hospitality on three visits to Sarajevo, notwithstanding outages in the heating and water supply on each trip.

Much of the medical work described in *Healing the Heart of Croatia*, as well as the publicity for this book, was made possible through the generous donations of our sponsors: Medtronic, Inc.; Siemens Medical Systems; St. Jude Medical; Nellcor; Cryolife; Ethicon; FedEx; Northwest Airlines; Baxter Healthcare Corporation; Variety Club of Memphis; Assisi Foundation; and W. L. Gore and Associates.

In addition to the corporate sponsors who have greatly enhanced the promotion of the book, we want to thank D. Canale Beverages, Inc.; Susan A. Talocka; C. F. Sauer; Mr. and Mrs. Thomas Scherer; Mr. and Mrs. Ernest Mrozek; Ronald L. Speck; the ICHF's Mardi Gras Committee; and Christian Brothers University.

Finally, special acknowledgments must be made to these three men:

Ivan Malcic: our program in Croatia would not exist if not for the dedication, persistence, and support of this friend and physician. Over the years Ivan has served the children of Croatia with heart as well. He has battled disinterest, destruction, and politics for the well-being of children. We owe him a debt of gratitude.

Billy Hicks: past-president of the local Memphis Variety Club, Billy listened to our story in 1993 and convinced the board of his local club to support the cause. The Variety Club of Memphis provided our first serious financial support and has been our largest benefactor since our inception. We are forever indebted to Billy.

Donald Watson: special thanks to the chief of the division of cardiothoracic surgery at the University of Tennessee-Memphis. Novick says: "Don constantly reminds me of the night of my final interview in Memphis before I was hired. I casually mentioned that I would like to operate on a few international children." The "few" children now number more than four hundred, and Don's support and guidance has allowed the ICHF to grow to what it is today.

The International Children's Heart Foundation would like to thank the following organizations for their support—

ST. JUDE MEDICAL
HEART VALVE DIVISION

CryoLife, Inc.

Medtronic ⚌

Saint Francis Hospital
Tenet HealthSystem

The ServiceMaster Companies SM

ServiceMaster · Terminix · Merry Maids
TruGreen-ChemLawn · American Home Shield
Furniture Medic · AmeriSpec · Rescue Rooter

Canale
Funeral Directors

If you would like to help the International Children's Heart
Foundation continue its work, please send your tax-deductable
donation to:

International Children's Heart Foundation
777 Washington Avenue, Suite P-215
Memphis, TN 38105
Tax Exempt #: 4–791–941–807–000–7
Federal I.D. #: 62–1570622